ART/TALK

THEORY AND PRACTICE
IN ABSTRACT EXPRESSIONISM

ALWYNNE MACKIE

ART/TALK

THEORY AND PRACTICE IN ABSTRACT EXPRESSIONISM

COLUMBIA UNIVERSITY PRESS
New York

Library of Congress Cataloging-in-Publication Data

Mackie, Alwynne.
Art/talk : theory and practice in abstract expressionism/Alwynne Mackie.
p.   cm.
Bibliography: p.
Includes index.
ISBN 0-231-06648-1
1. Abstract expressionism—United States. 2. Art, American.
3. Art. Modern—20th century—United States. 4. Avant-garde
(Aesthetics)—United States—History—20th century. I. Title.
N6512.5.A25M33   1989
759.13—dc19   88-38830
CIP

Columbia University Press
New York   Oxford
Copyright © 1989 Columbia University Press
All rights reserved
Printed in the United States of America

Casebound editions of Columbia University Press books are Smyth-sewn and printed on permanent and durable acid-free paper

Book design by Ken Venezio

For Patrick Maynard

CONTENTS

Illustrations follow page 116.

ACKNOWLEDGMENTS

Many people have assisted me in the writing and production of this book. To all of them, my warm thanks.

A number of individuals and institutions have assisted me in allowing the reproduction of certain of the artists' works. Full credits are provided in the List of Illustrations, but I would like to record my thanks to the following: Albright-Knox Art Gallery, Buffalo; Australian National Gallery, Canberra; Cleveland Museum of Art, Cleveland; Willem de Kooning; Robert Motherwell; Musée National d'Art Moderne, Centre Georges Pompidou, Beaubourg, Paris; Museum of Modern Art, New York; Mr. and Mrs. S. I. Newhouse, Jr; Annalee Newman; Norton Gallery and School of Art, West Palm Beach; Kate Rothko Prizel and Christopher Rothko; San Francisco Museum of Modern Art, San Francisco; Tate Gallery, London. Peter Tomory and the Art History Department of La Trobe University, Melbourne, assisted with photographs. In addition, I am indebted to Harcourt Brace Jovanovich and Faber and Faber for permission to reproduce an excerpt from T. S. Eliot's *Preludes,* and to Peter Pauper Press for permission to reproduce a haiku by Shushiki.

I would like to record my thanks to James Mollison and Warwick Reader, of the Australian National Gallery, Judith Cousins and John Minx, of the Museum of Modern Art, New York, Linda Cathcart, formerly of the Albright-Knox Art Gallery, Buffalo, Charles Silver, of the Film Archives Section, Museum of Modern Art, New York, and Annalee Newman, New York, for their support and assistance in allowing me access to their respective collections. Many people have assisted me by giving their time in discussions and correspondence, including John Elderfield, Robert Goodnough, Philip Guston, the late Thomas B. Hess, Patrick McCaughey, Robert Motherwell, Annalee Newman, Philip Pavia, the late Harold Rosenberg, and Irving Sandler. Ian Donaldson and Ron Robertson-Swann were helpful and encouraging in their comments on the manuscript. I would like to thank the libraries and librarians of the Museum of Modern Art New York, the Solomon R. Guggenhein Museum, the Australian National Gallery, the Australian National University, Canberra Institute of the Arts, La Trobe University, Canberra College of Advanced Education, and Phillip Institute of Technology. Special thanks are due to Joan Whitehouse and Mary O'Kane for assistance with the manuscript, each in their different ways.

The research for this book was carried out with the assistance of grants from the Australian Research Grants Council and the International Federation of University Women, and of a fellowship from the Humanities Research Centre of the Australian National University.

The jacket design is by Hiroshi Kikuchi, a design student at the Phillip Institute of Technology, Melbourne. I am indebted to him, and to Lauren Murray and Max Ripper of the Design Department. I would also like to thank my editors for their assistance and patience in the production of this book.

Finally, I wish to record my special thanks to three people: to Patrick McCaughey of the Wadsworth Atheneum in Hartford, Connecticut, for the many hours of discussion and support at a time when I was changing careers and contemplating this project; to John Elderfield of the Museum of Modern Art, New York, for his generosity in discussion and his expectation of quality in art criticism; and to Patrick Maynard of the University of Western Ontario, for long correspondence on major issues of intellectual life and commitment, and to whom this book is dedicated.

ART/TALK
THEORY AND PRACTICE
IN ABSTRACT EXPRESSIONISM

INTRODUCTION

What do we expect to find out when we read art criticism? What do we hope to achieve when we talk about art? Within these simple and basic questions lurk a thousand difficulties of art history and criticism.

A simple and perhaps obvious answer is that the purpose of art history and criticism is to help us understand art. Some people, however, would respond that art-talk is essentially untranslatable; for, as some artists would put it, "If I could talk about it, why would I bother to paint it?"

There is something to be said for the view that art is essentially ineffable, as those who have tried to write about art they have found to be profound and moving will testify. There is, on such occasions, a sense of the really important things being left unsaid, that the essence and impact of the work can ultimately only be experienced rather than communicated secondhand.

Nonetheless, it is intuitively implausible that nothing interesting or worthwhile is said when artists and critics talk about art. Art historians, of course, place great store on what artists have to say about their work, and a study that ignored the artists' writings would be a very strange work indeed, for this would be to ignore one of the major primary sources. But what does this mean in practical terms? How *does* one apply what artists have said about their art to the work itself, and is everything they say about their art applicable? And how does what they say about it bear on what critics have said about it?

None of these questions can be answered satisfactorily without first being clear about what it is we expect to understand about art. If the questions "why am I studying this art?" and "what do I expect it to reveal about what?" seem to be naive questions, it is remarkable how often they appear to have remained unasked by those who write about art.

There are those, of course, who see the matter as a simple conflict of dichotomy. From time to time it has been fashionable to characterize, in varying degrees of sophistication, both art and its criticism as a choice between "form" and "content." With respect to Abstract Expressionism, it was often said that Clement Greenberg epitomized the former approach, while Harold Rosenberg adopted the latter. As an indication of how complex, and confused, this issue really is, it could also be said that Greenberg was interested in the work, while Rosenberg concentrated on the artist. That these intersecting dichotomies bespeak the confusion rife in critical thought is borne out by the fact that Irving Sandler, a critic who has attempted to place the structural analysis of Abstract Expressionist paintings in the context of the artists' political, social, and aesthetic thought, is criticized as being a formalist and therefore superficial in his analysis of the art.[1]

A much-favored answer to the questions I have been asking is that art is a manifestation of political and social thought and can be properly understood only as such. The 1970s, for example, saw a spate of writing on Abstract Expressionism that interpreted the movement as an expression and instrument of cold war politics. Typically such writers criticize other writers as superficial and failing to address the significant issues in the art. Serge Guilbaut, for example, in writing about Abstract Expressionism, had this to say:

Because of the lack of critical analysis of the ideology that underlies the images and texts produced in this period, the supremacy of the new American art is often regarded as an ineluctable fact, almost a divine ordinance; its causes are not analyzed. . . . These histories of course subscribe to the formalist analysis proposed by Alfred Barr of New York's Museum of Modern Art, an analysis championed by Clement Greenberg throughout his career.

The most popular treatment of the subject, widely regarded authoritative, is Sandler's *Triumph of American Painting.* This work discusses the output of each avant-garde artist in a formal way. . . . Not once in his book, whose title is so revealing, does Sandler attempt to give a critical analysis of the documents at his disposal, of the conceptual systems of the artists he is describing, or of the function of the avant-garde itself. He ignores the ideological content of the signs he is manipulating. . . . All the complexities are swept under the rug.[2]

It is undoubtedly true that art is a political and social phenomenon just as other human activities and institutions are. Criticism that ignores this fact and looks at art in a vacuum is to that extent deficient, for its fails to take account of the fact that art is a product of the mind, and that the mind of the artist is shaped—in however a complex and indirect fashion—by the society in which he or she lives. In understanding *how* the work came to be made, therefore, we will surely learn something about the work.

The interesting thing about writers such as Guilbaut, however, is that they rarely say anything about the works themselves. Guilbaut's book *How New York Stole the Idea of Modern Art: Abstract Expressionism, Freedom, and the Cold War,* for example, does not discuss a single work, and indeed only mentions one or two by way of quoting writers who refer to them.

This might seem odd to one who is interested in the works themselves and expects criticism to tell us something about them. It is not odd, however, if one's interest is in writing about the political and social impulses of society. But if one is truly interested in that subject, rather than the art itself, why choose art as the instrument of revelation? Surely there are much more revealing, powerful, and direct ways for the artist to express those views, and for the historian to describe those forces and mechanisms, if that is their intent. Insofar as art addresses and expresses those issues, it is tangential and complex and not at all the best way of achieving those ends. As Guilbaut himself acknowledges, art does not automatically "reflect" society.

Sometimes, of course, the subterranean purpose of such writing about art is to deny that it has any significance other than sociopolitical. Its character as art, its aestheticness, is denied, and the question of why some works are better than others is not addressed. If works of art are nothing more than manifestations of political-social acts, then there is no reason to preserve them over and above other manifestations of political social acts that are not art. Not only do successive generations preserve works of art, however, but they talk about them as having a distinctive aesthetic character. To deny this character is to miss an important part of what people regard as interesting about art.

The sort of sociopolitical writing I am describing assumes that the motives that led the Abstract Expressionist artists to develop the art they did were not aesthetic motives. But what makes criticism the complex and difficult activity that it is, is the fact that aesthetic motivation and impulses are intertwined with political, social, cultural, physiological, and emotional ones. The relationship between these factors and aesthetic motives is a neglected one in the literature. Needless to say, it is an important one.

A book such as Guilbaut's is interesting for what it does. Certainly it is sophisticated in acknowledging the subtlety of political influence in the shaping of a historical group and movement. As the writer puts it:

From compromise to compromise, refusal to refusal, adjustment to adjustment, the rebellion of the artists, born of frustrations within the left, gradually changed its significance until ultimately it came to represent the values of the majority, but in a way (continuing the modernist tradition) that only a minority was capable of understanding. The ideology of the avant-garde was ironically made to coincide with what was becoming the dominant ideology, that embodied in Arthur Schlesinger Jr.'s, book *The Vital Center.*[3]

It does not, however, tell us anything about the art as art. It does not, for instance, tell us why the artists painted the way they did, and why each artist's work was different from the next—despite shared beliefs. More important, it utterly fails to come to grips with the question of how the artists translated beliefs, thoughts, and feelings into physical, two-dimensional images.

These are issues that engage a great many people who are interested in art. They are certainly issues that interest artists. If we are to understand these issues, it is important to acknowledge not just that political, social, cultural, psychological, emotional, and aesthetic impulses are related, but also the complexity of that relationship. As Meyer Schapiro so eloquently put it:

When we speak . . . of the social bases of art we do not mean to reduce art to economics or sociology or politics. Art has its own conditions which distinguish it from other activities. It operates with its own special materials and according to general psychological laws. But from these physical and psychological factors we could not understand the great diversity of art, why there is one style at one time, another style a generation later, why in certain cultures there is little change for hundreds of years, in other cultures not only a mobility from year to year but various styles of art at the same moment, although physical and psychological factors are the same.[4]

Schapiro goes on to explain that even in a society that has developed the concept of art as an autonomous aesthetic activity, the individual work of each artist in nonetheless shaped in part by this complex of factors. He writes:

The conception of art as purely aesthetic and individual can exist only where culture has been detached from practical and collective interests and is supported by individuals alone. But the mode of life of these individuals, their place in society, determines in many ways this individual art. . . .

The social origins of such forms of modern art do not in themselves permit one to judge this art as good or bad; they simply throw light upon some aspects of their character and enable us to see more clearly that the ideas of modern artists, far from describing eternal and necessary conditions of art, are simply the result of recent history. In recognizing the dependence of his situation and attitudes on the character of modern society, the artist acquires the courage to change things, to act on his society and for himself in an effective manner.[5]

Analysis of the individual works of art, along with an investigation of the conditions that gave rise to their making, is an enormous task even for one artist, if it is done properly. To do it for a whole movement, especially one in which the individual works are very different from artist to artist, is not possible in a single book. Even if considerations of length were not a problem, it is obvious that such a work would collapse under impossible structural problems. Furthermore, individual writers usually have a particular set of factors that interest them and that they are better equipped to write about.

This in itself does not matter provided the writer is aware that what is presented is only a single aspect of the complex whole. Even then there needs to be some acknowledgment of the existence of the missing parts. A history of an art movement or an artist, for example, that gives no idea of what the individual works are like is a very strange history of art. Yet such histories exist.

Abstract Expressionism has been well served by critics and historians concentrating on the aesthetic quality and structure of the works. There have also been writers of quality who have written about the social origins of the art. What has been singularly lacking, however—not just for Abstract Expressionism but in art-writing generally—is history and criticism that investigates the relationship between social and aesthetic factors.

At first glance this might seem untrue, for there are certainly writings that present artistic elements on the one hand and social factors on the other. What they do not do, however, is explain the *relationship* between them, so that we might understand the process by which idea or feeling is translated into image.

That will be the task of this book. In undertaking this task, I shall focus the discussion on one particular set of factors that contributed to the making of Abstract Expressionist art—namely, the theory that the artists articulated as the substructure of their work. There are, of course, a great many other direct and indirect factors that influenced the development of the work. These have, for the most part, been dealt with by other people, and form part of the background against which the present investigation is conducted. They are from time to time referred to, discussed, but not developed. Rather the focus will be the relationship between how the artists talked about their work, and the nature of what they in fact produced—the nexus, in other words, between theory and practice.

As we turn now to the Abstract Expressionist artist, it will be evident to anyone familiar with their work and writings that they had a great deal to say about their work. Although fiercely individualistic in the art they made, they were, nonetheless, a gregarious bunch of artists, and spent a great deal of time talking about art. In the first place, they were a very small group (what they themselves called "advanced" artists), and from the thirties and early forties on, they anxiously shared ideas as a protective device against what they saw as the crassness of the rest of the art world. Most of them had worked on the WPA Federal Arts Project during the Depression and used to gather in Washington Square at the end of pay day and sit talking.

This pattern of socializing continued informally through the forties and became institutionalized on a more ordered basis in the art school called "Subjects of the Artist," set up by Robert Motherwell, David Hare, William Baziotes, Mark Rothko, and Clyfford Still. This gave way to Studio 35, at 35 East Eighth Street, where artists gathered and discussions were organized, and which became a very lively focus of Abstraction Expressionist talk. In April 1950, Studio 35 was disbanded, and the Club (which lasted until 1962) took its place. The "advanced" art world was abuzz with a "farrago of ideas," as Dore Ashton put it, and some of this ferment is evidenced in the transcripts of the three-day Round Table Conference, organized to mark the closing of Studio 35. Heavily edited and reduced, this transcript is bursting with ideas started up, interruptions, arguments running off at tangents, and the vigorous efforts of the moderators to bring order to the discussion.

The talk the artists engaged in was passionate and various. Much of it was concerned with the need to deal with subject matter that reflected the basic experience of human beings: nothing less was worthy of art. "We assert that the subject is crucial and only that subject matter is valid which is tragic and timeless," was how Mark Rothko and Adolf Gottlieb put it, and this attitude is repeated throughout the writing and statements of all the artists. They talked about eschewing images drawn from the visual world (the shopworn images of illustration), and sought instead to "discover" the image in their own unconscious, to fashion a truly abstract image out of the "chaos of nothingness," an image that would strike a chord of primeval reverberations.

The processes of artistic creativity exercised them greatly, and they agonized at length about the demands of being an artist. There were all the problems associated with working in an intuitive manner, where the image was "discovered" rather than planned and executed. There were forays into automatist techniques of working, the *angst* of "voyaging into the unknown," and talk about "risk" and the alienation of the artist. At a practical level, there was much soul-searching about how one knows when a work is "finished." And in less generalized terms, there were many occasions on which the artists offered descriptions of their works, usually (as is so with most criticism) in the form of an interpretative metaphor.

How one deals with this material is not an easy matter to decide. It is one thing to decide that these ideas must be applicable to the work, and quite another thing to apply them so that they quite evidently become the key that opens up our understanding of the character and quality of the work.

There are straightforward, but clumsy, ways of applying ideas to art, but they afford little insight into the aesthetic and conceptual structure of the work. An example in point is the attempt of some art historians to apply the important eighteenth-century idea of the Sublime to the painting of that period simply by looking for some of the hallmarks of Sublime literature—namely, subject matter such as precipitous mountains, storms, grandeur of scale in nature, and so on. Another, more recent and slightly more sophisticated example is the practice of some writers of applying theosophical principles to the art of Kandinsky—to see his work as simply the working out of those principles in a visual form. Sometimes it takes the form of asserting (though never demonstrating) that there are synaesthetic correspondences in the works. More often, and notably in the writer Sixten Ringbom, it consists of an attempt to recognize some of the "thought forms" of theosophists like Annie Besant and C. W. Leadbetter in Kandinsky's paintings.

Such attempts assume that there is a very simple one-to-one correlation between the artists' ideas and the images they make. These endeavors assume, in fact, that the art simply *illustrates* ideas. While some art does this, that sort of critical approach fails to account for the complexity of the art it deals with, and fails to engage with the very complicated creative processes by which an idea is translated into a visual image. For if there were no challenging process of translation involved, why would anyone bother to make art—especially since our verbal language (in which the ideas are first articulated) is so much better equipped to express ideas with precision and subtlety?

That some process of translation from idea to image is always involved can be seen if one takes that most illustrative form of realist painting, Photo Realism. It is astonishing just how much manipulation and translation is involved in copying, in oil or acrylic (each presenting different problems), a photographic image. One cannot safely copy each tiny area of transition of tone and expect that the result will look like the object copied, because the paint does not behave the way a photographic surface does; it sits on the canvas in its own distinctive way, throws lights and shadows and impressions of depth, and generally lacks the appearance of a totally flat image floating in a bed of emulsion.

Accordingly, the artist must alter the details to simulate the photographic image. To render the photographic realism of crisp snow, for example, one must avoid applying the paint in round or oval dots (which is more or less the way it is), and apply it instead in tiny squares. The sharp angles then somehow simulate the glint of light. Perception is a very complex and largely unconscious thing, and most observers do not notice these tiny but important differences any more than they notice that the horse in Gauguin's painting *White Horse,* which *looks* white, is actually green.

If translation is necessary even at this level of visualization, how much more complex it must be when it involves the expression of an idea, belief, or systematic theory. Even if these ideas are depictable in a more or less literal way (as with the Annunciation to the Virgin, for example), or through a more or less straightforward symbol (such as a lily for purity), it is an awkward fact of life for the painter that even very simple objects are capable of being bearers of many different, and often conflicting, connotations which the painter must filter out in order to express the meaning intended. Painting a lily as a heavy, exotic feature of interior decoration, for instance, or as a delicate member of the natural world, is quite different from painting it as a symbol of purity.

When the ideas the artist is dealing with are either general or abstract, a further set of problems occurs. In communicating a general idea, one is forced to depict it not in a general, but in a particular, form; and in the case of abstract ideas, it is impossible to depict them at all. Some other means, therefore, must be found to suggest or evoke these ideas. How else, for instance, could one paint an abstract picture that was "timeless and tragic"; or how could the French Symbolists hope to "externalize an interior idea" so that the idea, or atmosphere, or event, transcends its physical manifestation?

Obviously what the artist is involved in is the discovery and development of a highly complex and sophisticated grammar of translation, not merely from the verbal to the visual medium but also from one mode of thought to another. Just as a novelist or a poet will write a work in one way and talk about it in another, so the painter must convert visual, sensual, and emotional experience, along with conceptual articulations, into marks of paint. Furthermore, these marks, in order to be successful, must combine to trigger a network of responses that, while quite different from the experiences and thoughts that went into the conceptualization and making of the work, nonetheless combine to weave a fabric of perception and thought that produces the intended idea or feeling. The other side of this coin is that good criticism then has to find a language in which to translate the presence and effects of this very complicated and sensitive visual structure into terms that not merely describe its source but capture the look, feeling, and flavor of the work itself.

The single most difficult task of art history and criticism, therefore, is the problem of understanding the process of metamorphosis of an idea or feeling into a physical, two-dimensional image. This is the key to understanding the relationship between what artists say about their work and the nature of the work itself. Not only is it the key to the relationship between theory and practice, but it is also essential to an understanding of how other considerations, direct and indirect, whether political, social, cultural, psychological, or emotional, feed into the work and help make it the sort of work that it is.

Beyond the problem of translation, however, there is a further consideration. One cannot afford to assume that all art-talk serves the same purpose; in particular, one cannot afford to assume that its purpose is to describe the work. Indeed, even when it does describe the work, it may not necessarily describe the *look* of the work, but the work considered in some other way. When Clement Greenberg talked about the "Gothicness, . . . paranoia and resentment" of Jackson Pollock's work, he did not mean that these things are depicted, or even expressed, in the paintings; rather, he meant that if one considers the nature (that is, the pictorial structure) of the paintings, and the development of the whole oeuvre, then one can deduce that certain states of mind and personality traits must have existed for the works to be the way they are.

Sometimes, on the other hand, the talk—whether it comes from the artist or from the critic—may describe conditions for creativity. If one were to take Adolph Gottlieb's statement "It's the pulse, not the look. I'm not involved with the external appearance of the city; it's the vibrations," then one might be inclined to accept this as a description of what is in the work, its subject matter, albeit expressed in abstract terms. An examination of the full context of the remark, however, reveals that Gottlieb is really talking about what he needs to make him paint. In explaining why he could stay no more than a few weeks in Paris, he talked about the rhythm and tempo of New York, something he found exhilarating and that profoundly affected his work. And that casts quite a different light on his statement.

Art-talk is a multifaceted activity, just as art itself is not simply an object *in vacuo*. Art objects grow out of a very complex network of thought and feeling, and in many respects are themselves "incomplete." They need to be perceived and "read" by observers, and that process of perception involves bringing into play certain conceptualizations, connotations, information, and sensual experience in response to certain marks on canvas that are presented as "cues." That being so, it is not clear exactly what the ontological status of the work of art is, for it is not easy to determine to what extent the processes are a part of the work, and to what extent they are external to it (albeit necessary).

One can see, then, how one might fall into error in assuming that art-talk always is (or ought to be) about the *object*. In asking whether or not artists' writings and comments can be "applied" to their work, it would be prudent first to consider the real function of those comments and to determine what aspect of the whole phenomenon of art and art-making they relate to. Similarly, when comparing divergent criticisms of the art, one should first identify what aspect of the whole thing they are addressing. Only then is one in a position to comment upon their relevance.

Identifying what aspect of the whole art phenomenon a particular comment relates to is not a quick and simple task. In the case of the Abstract Expressionists, one cannot afford to take anything for granted, since it has chronically been the case that certain aspects of the artists' endeavor have been ignored by both critics and historians. My task in part 1, "The Theory," will be to examine their writings and statements with a view to unraveling their attitudes to art-making, their theories about their own work, and their interpretations of particular work from their own oeuvres and those of other artists.

All the artists considered had a quite clearly defined theory about what their art should be. It was a revolutionary theory: not new, but certainly overturning the accepted views of the day and harkening back to attitudes of earlier times. That theory is the theory of the abstract mystic symbol, and the first section of this work is devoted to tracing the development and articulation of this idea in the artists' thinking.

The question which naturally arises at that point is, to what extent is the theory reflected in their work? Part 2, "The Theory in Practice," deals with the critical acceptance of their work and their own descriptions and assessments of it. This section is necessarily limited, since one could obviously write a monograph on each artist. Instead, I have chosen a small group of the major artists, each of them mainstream, and each of them painting in quite a different style. The artists dealt within part 2 are restricted, therefore, to Clyfford Still, Jackson Pollock, Barnett Newman, Robert Motherwell, and Mark Rothko, very different artists in the kind of work they produced but remarkably homogeneous in attitudes and aspirations.

What emerges from part 2 is that, even if one adopts a fairly neutral position on various critical stances, there is a clear sense in which the artists' work is a reflection of the theory they held. Part 3, "Modes of Critical Discourse," looks at the ramifications of that conclusion.

One final point needs to be made perhaps, and that is that this work is not intended as a *comprehensive* study of Abstract Expressionism. Certainly anyone reading part 1 will find important historical points missing, and efforts to place the importance and influence of the movement are limited. I do not attempt to trace the development of imagery in individual artists, nor of the very different kinds of imagery from artist to artist. Nor is the discussion of theory of myth, Symbolist ideas, and Surrealism intended as a historical account of those movements. While that history is important and interesting in itself, my purpose here is simply to establish that the artists were influenced by these currents. As often as not, it was the general flavor of theory of myth that they absorbed, rather than the precise thoughts, accurately interpreted, of individual writers.

Evidence is produced, of course, that the artists were influenced by these concepts and shared some of the important ideas, but I do not set out to describe the actual events that led to the development of these ideas. My interest is, rather, in how these ideas led the artists to paint the sort of pictures they did, and how it led them to talk about art in a certain distinctive way.

Put in general terms, this is not so much a history of the ideas of Abstract Expressionism as a study of a particular theoretical question for which the Abstract Expressionists supply the material. Since it is my view that theoretical issues cannot be studied in isolation from the material out of which they grow—a truism perhaps, but one often ignored—this work is as much a demonstration of that conviction as it is a study of a particular theoretical question.

THE THEORY

David Sylvester: European artists of the same time, European artists of your generation, were in rather a mess after all that had been done by Picasso and Matisse, and yet you here seemed to get out of this mess.

Adolph Gottlieb: The only possible explanation I have for it is that the situation was very desperate and everything seemed hopeless and we had nothing to lose, so that in a sense we were like people condemned to life imprisonment who make a dash for freedom. Nothing could have been worse than the situation in which we were, so we tried desperate things. We revolted in a way against everything—all of the standards—we didn't accept any standards. We were like the people who are nothing but chess players, or tennis bums, and who refuse to do anything useful . . . painting that's useful, and we felt that we were willing to go all our lives and do this despised kind of painting without any hope of success. That was the way it was, and we accepted that.[1]

At the end of the thirties, art appeared to be in the doldrums. After the explosion of artistic activity in the first two decades of the century, artists seemed to have run out of things to paint. "Painting is finished," said Barnett Newman; "we should give it up."[2] And like many other artists, he ceased to paint. Fortunately, however, many of them, and Newman among them, persisted in their conviction about art throughout this period of demoralization, and the beginning of the forties saw them, desperate, as Gottlieb says, weighed down by the bankruptcy of the time, but determined that painting was all they wanted to do.

By the end of the decade, many of the traditional sources of inspiration had been destroyed. The experience of the great depression had left a cynicism about capitalist economic systems. All the artists had left-wing sympathies, but events in Russia had left them disillusioned; the idealism of the Spanish Civil War had soured with the victory of Franco, and Hitler and Nazism seemed depressingly ready to take over Europe. Ideology had not served them well.[3]

And yet their conviction that human experience mattered did not leave them. They distrusted any systems that offered easy answers, but they could not yield to the view that things were not worth bothering about. In particular they could not accept the opinion that the structures of art were more important than its subject matter, for the evidence was all around them, in the form of American abstract art, that when an artist took that approach, the result was decoration. On the other hand, they could not abide the Social Realism schools of painting prevalent throughout America at the time. These, they said, lacked real feeling, fell into stereotypes, and were illustration instead of art.

Decoration and illustration were the elements they despised most in contemporary art, and the two things that epitomized its decadence. The challenge was to make great art, and to do this they must find a subject matter worthy of art, a subject matter that could be expressed only in art and that must force changes in the character of art in order to execute that expression. How it was to happen no one knew, but that it had to happen was part of the desperation described by Gottlieb earlier. And so they set themselves to "attempt to paint as if it had never been invented before," as Newman put it[4] and to trust that eventually something of worth would emerge.

As they moved into the forties (when some of them had been painting for twenty years), there occurred an accident of circumstances and influences that enabled them to grope toward the subject matter, and its realization, that they sought. Gradually they articulated the theory they believed was the center and lifeblood of their art—the theory of the abstract mystic symbol.

Chapter One

MYTH: THE IMPETUS FOR ART

In June 1943 Gottlieb and Rothko, in collaboration with Newman, gave voice to the impulse that was to be the basis of Abstract Expressionist thought and the source out of which the mature work of the movement developed. In a letter to the *New York Times,* and in response to an invitation from the *Times* art critic Edward Alden Jewell, they announced that the basis of their art was ancient myth.[1]

They stated unequivocally that myth was their subject matter, and this indeed was the case, it being quite explicit in the two paintings they discussed—namely, Gottlieb's *Rape of Persephone* and Rothko's *Syrian Bull.* But to regard this development as primarily a question of subject matter would be to misunderstand its place in the artist's thinking. What is important is the way in which this choice of subject matter seemed a natural outcome of a base-structure of thought that determined and articulated their fundamental attitudes to art and picture-making.

Myth provided the initial channel through which these attitudes and commitments could find expression, and, perhaps not surprisingly, it dropped out of their scheme of things as their aesthetic became clarified in appropriate pictorial forms. Gottlieb himself made this point later, in 1963, in an interview with David Sylvester. Sylvester put the question "But there must have been several things that you agreed on.

What were they at the time? How did they change later?" Gottlieb replied:

For example, Rothko and I temporarily came to an agreement on the question of subject matter; if we were to do something which could develop in some direction other than the accepted directions of that time, it would be necessary to use different subjects to begin with and, around 1942, we embarked on a series of paintings that attempted to use mythological subject matter, preferably from Greek mythology. I did a series of paintings on the theme of Oedipus and Rothko did a series of paintings on other Greek themes. Now this is not to say that we were very absorbed in mythology, although at that time a great many writers, more than painters, were absorbed in the idea of myth in relation to art. However, it seemed that if one wanted to get away from such things as the American scene or social realism and perhaps cubism, this offered a possibility of a way out, and the hope was that given a subject matter that was different, perhaps some new approach to painting, a technical approach might also develop. As it turned out, such a new approach did develop. At least, it was a different approach than either of us could have arrived at if we hadn't taken a radical departure with respect to subject matter. Well, eventually, of course, we did not remain loyal to the idea of using mythology and ancient fables as subjects. . . .[2]

The interesting question is, however, why *myth*? Obviously it would be to take too simplistic and superficial a view of it to think that any new subject matter would have served equally well. As Gottlieb pointed out, it was a time when myth was very much in the air, especially myth in relation to art, because myth connected with attitudes, priorities, and webs of belief at a more general and fundamental level. This was true of the artists too (though in their own particular way), and the important thing is to unravel and understand these connections so that the full development of Abstract Expressionism might be appreciated. Without it, one is in danger of accepting the view that their creativity was essentially mysterious and that the gap between words and works is a critical inevitability.

Let us turn, as a starting point, to the famous letter to the *New York Times*. The context is this: Gottlieb and Rothko had exhibited two paintings (*The Rape of Persephone* and *The Syrian Bull*) in the Third Annual

Exhibition of the Federation of Modern Painters and Sculptors, and had received hostile criticism, the reactions ranging from "a bedlam of hysteria" to Edward Alden Jewell's confessed "befuddlement."[3] The reason for the hostility and lack of understanding seems to have turned on the subject matter of the paintings: neither work appeared to illustrate its title, and yet clearly claimed to have a meaning beyond the pictorial dynamics of "pure" abstract art. In response to Jewell's invitation, they wrote their letter to the editor, explaining that since their works draw on myth—indeed, are "a poetic expression of the essence of the myth"—they cannot be explained, except at a superficial level. "It is an easy matter," they wrote,

to explain to the befuddled that *The Rape of Persephone* is a poetic expression of the essence of the myth; the presentation of the concept of seed and its earth with all its brutal implications; the impact of elemental truth. Would you have us present this abstract concept with all its complicated feelings by means of a boy and girl lightly tripping?

They were not interested, in other words, in painting a literal depiction of the content of the myth, and their reason for this was that the real meaning of a myth transcends its literal content and is too complicated—and abstract—to be captured in an anecdotal way. There are, however, ways of expressing these complex thoughts and feelings in a simple form or symbol, and it is that expression which cannot be explained:

But these easy program notes can only help the simpleminded. No possible set of notes can explain our paintings. Their explanation must come out of a consummated experience between picture and onlooker.

Frequently the power of the works will disturb, even when they are ill-understood. As the writers remarked to Jewell:

We do not intend to defend our pictures. They make their own defense. We consider them clear statements. Your failure to dismiss or disparage them is prima facie evidence that they carry some communicative power.

The artists saw this as a new art that involves risks for both artist and spectator; it is an art, or mode of artistic apprehension, that is essentially nonrational, and it aims at revolution:

To us art is an adventure into an unknown world, which can be explored only by those willing to take the risks.

This world of the imagination is fancy-free and violently opposed to common sense.

It is our function as artists to make the spectator see the world our way—not his way.

They ended their letter with a statement that indicates just how radically different they took their art to be:

Consequently if our work embodies these beliefs, it must insult anyone who is spiritually attuned to interior decoration; pictures for the home; pictures for over the mantle; pictures of the American scene; social pictures; purity in art; prize-winning pot-boilers; the National Academy, the Whitney Academy, the Corn Belt Academy; buckeyes; trite tripe; etc.

And the basic reason for that fundamental (and spiritual) difference lay in their commitment to a serious subject matter—one that is valid for all time, that deals with the fundamentals of human thought and experience, and that shares these aims with primitive and archaic art through myth. They wrote:

It is a widely accepted notion among painters that it does not matter what one paints as long as it is well painted. This is the essence of academicism. There is no such thing as good painting about nothing. We assert that the subject is crucial and only that subject matter is valid which is tragic and timeless. That is why we profess spiritual kinship with primitive and archaic art.[4]

In summary, then, the essential elements of this doctrine are as follows: art must concern itself with important truths of human experience; because traditional forms of painting are now too familiar and shopworn to communicate that experience, new modes of expression must be found; these truths are contained in myth, but literal depiction obscures their real meaning; and simple, abstract forms or symbols must be devised to adequately express the complexity and depth of meaning of the myth.

Interest in primitive myth among the Abstract Expressionists was not confined to Gottlieb and Rothko. Barnett Newman wrote about it extensively, not only in private, nonpublished typescripts, of which he produced many, but also in articles and catalogue essays for several exhibitions of primitive art.[5] For instance, he wrote about myth and primitive art in the catalogues for the exhibitions *Northwest Coast Indian Painting, The Ideographic Picture, Pre-Columbian Stone Sculpture,* and *Amlash Sculpture from Iran,* all exhibitions held at Wakefield Gallery and at Betty Parsons' Gallery[6] (which was then the gallery of all the artists of the group); he also published an article on South Pacific art ("Las formas artisticas de Pacifico") in *Ambos Mundos* (later translated into English as "Art of the South Seas," in *Studio International*).

Clyfford Still clearly thought that his own work was correctly described in primitive, mythic terms, since he had his friend Rothko write the introduction to the catalogue for his exhibition at Art of This Century Gallery in February 1946. The introduction reads:

It is significant that Still, working out West and alone, has arrived at pictorial conclusions so allied to those of the small band of Myth Makers who have emerged here during the war. The fact that his is a completely new facet of this idea, using unprecedented forms and completely personal methods, attests further to the vitality of this movement. Bypassing the current preoccupation with genre and the nuances of formal arrangements, Still expresses the tragic-religious drama which is generic to all Myths at all times, no matter where they occur. He is creating new counterparts to replace the old mythological hybrids who have lost their pertinence in the intervening centuries. For me, Still's pictorial dramas are an extension of the Greek Persephone Myth. As he himself has expressed it, his paintings are "of the Earth, the Damned and of the Recreated."[7]

Furthermore, Still, Newman, Rothko, Theodore Stamos, Hans Hofmann, and Ad Reinhardt (plus Pietro Lazzari and Boris Margo) exhibited their work at Betty Parsons' Gallery in a special exhibition called, significantly, *The Ideographic Picture*. Newman connects the basis of their work with the primitive, mythic art of the Kwakiutl Indian, and the titles of the paintings alone are evidence of this train of thought in the artists involved; they include *The Fury, Burnt Offering, The Firmament, Astral Figure, The Alchemist, Gea, The Euclidean Abyss, Dark Symbol, Tiresias, Vernal Memory, The Sacrifice,* and *Quicksilver*. That Reinhardt agreed to join the exhibition is itself very telling, for he was always inclined to reject what others accepted and to lampoon it in the manner of a compulsive satirist.[8]

Even Clement Greenberg, who was not known for his interest in talking about subject matter, acknowledged the extensiveness of this interest among the painters. Reviewing Gottlieb's 1947 exhibition he wrote:

Gottlieb is perhaps the leading exponent of a new indigenous school of symbolism which includes among others Mark Rothko, Clyfford Still and Barnett Benedict Newman. The "symbols" Gottlieb puts into his canvases have no explicit meaning but derive, supposedly, from the artist's unconscious and speak to the same faculty in the spectator, calling up, presumably, racial memories, archetypes, archaic but constant responses. Hence the archaeological flavor, which in Gottlieb's painting seems to come from North American Indian art and affects design and color as much as content.[9]

Jackson Pollock, of course, drew on primitive myth extensively in his paintings in the forties, right up to his break into the dripped and poured works that mark his developed style. How early in the thirties this interest began is not clear, but in 1937 Pollock's friendship with John Graham (the mentor of the Abstract Expressionists in many important ways) was initiated by Graham's article "Primitive Art and Picasso," which Pollock read and found so interesting that he wrote to Graham about it.[10] His interest in ethnology and primitive art as relevant to his own work seems to have developed from around that time, and he read extensively on the subject. He subscribed to the Smithsonian volumes on anthropology and was regarded as knowing the art of the American Indian very well. Alfonso Ossorio, for instance, has reported in an interview:

He had an enormously catholic appreciation of the art of the past: Indian sand painting, Eskimo art, or the baroque. . . . He certainly knew the anthropological collection at the Museum of Natural History very well. And he knew the art of the American Indian because he had lived part of his life in the Southwest. He had the fifteen volumes published by the Smithsonian on American anthropology—he once pulled it out from under his bed to show me—I remember being surprised that someone so poor could have such a publication.[11]

And Pollock's brother Charles gave the following information to William Rubin, Director of Painting and Sculpture at the Museum of Modern Art:

I have the Eighth Annual Report of the Bureau of Ethnology (Washington, Government Printing Office, 1891). Among other things, it contains 12 chromolithographic plates. Four of these are sand paintings, the other ritualistic paraphernalia—blankets, feathers, paints, etc. Jack had several volumes of this kind. As I remember, we bought them together in one of the then innumerable secondhand bookstores on 4th Avenue—sometime between 1930 and 1935.[12]

There is also, of course, Pollock's own statement of his interest in the *Arts and Architecture* questionnaire of 1944:

I have always been very impressed with the plastic qualities of American Indian art. The Indians have the true painter's approach in their capacity to get hold of appropriate images, and in their understanding of what constitutes painterly subject-matter. Their color is essentially Western,[13] their vision has the basic universality of all real art.[14]

His paintings of the early forties to around 1947 are full of primitive, mythic, and totemic figures, some of the titles being *She Wolf* (1943), *Parsiphae* (1943), *Male and Female* (1942), *Guardians of the Secret* (1943), *The Totem, Lesson II* (1945), *Search for a Symbol* (1945), and *Moon Woman Cuts the Circle* (1943). While Pollock said these references to primitive art were unintentional, he did admit they came from early memories and associations.[15] Since he quite pointedly gave most of the works of this period primitive or mythic titles, it is probable that what he meant by "unintentional" was simply that he was neither illustrating primitive art nor depicting myth, but was *using* each to express something more personal and, at the same time, universal.

William Baziotes and Stamos were also affected by the general interest in primitive art and myth. In their case it took the form of the creation of biomorphic forms that seem to have a very primitive, mythic, and fundamental existence. The forms and pictures do not refer to particular myths, but the generality and pervasiveness of the mythic is frequently suggested in the titles: *Cyclops, The Flesh Eaters,* and *Dawn,* of Baziotes, and *Ancestral Worship, Altar, Archaic Sentinel,* and *Ancestral Flow,* of Stamos. Stamos, of course, exhibited in *The Ideographic Picture* exhibition, and in the catalogue of his 1947 exhibition at Betty Parsons' Gallery, Newman—in distinguishing between the primitive response to nature, which seeks to understand the essence and inner life of things, and the refined, nonprimitive response, which is more concerned with the personal feelings one's response to nature engenders—described Stamos as truly communicating with nature in the primitive way:

His ideographs capture the moment of totemic affinity with the rock and the mushroom, the crayfish and the seaweed. He re-defines the pastoral experience as one of participation with the inner life of the natural phenomenon. . . . In this Stamos is on the same fundamental ground as the primitive artist who never portrayed the phenomenon as an object of romance and sentiment, but always as an expression of the original noumenistic mystery in which rock and man are equal.[16]

Of Baziotes' involvement with myth, Thomas B. Hess had this to say:

But of all the New York painters who emerged in the 1940's, Baziotes, in a profound way, was closest to the Surrealists. He seized their injunction to seek myth in the subconscious and through myth, identity. By painting dreams, he would renew the form of archetype. . . .

Probably he was also reinforced in this decision by pride in his Pennsylvania-Greek ancestry. . . . He was a card-carrying Hellene, member of a race for whom myth is not exotic, but as domestic and necessary as the love of bread.[17]

All of these artists were to discard myth as a direct source of subject matter and inspiration in their developed work, but there is no doubt that it was myth which pointed them toward the realization of their artistic impulses. But why *myth*? What was it about myth that connected so surely and positively with their own thinking and feeling, and made possible new modes of artistic and pictorial thinking?

Looking back over their writings, and especially those that mention myth, it is possible to reconstruct much of their thinking and to see what elements emerged as important to them. The single most important element, and the point from which all their thinking began, was that of content. All were agreed that the basic premise and motivation for modern art must be a deep commitment to serious subject matter, and it is hard to find statements in which this conviction is not explicitly expressed or implicit in what else is said. Their rejection of the abstract art of the time, and especially that prevailing in America, resulted precisely from its exclusion of subject matter. As Barnett Newman put it:

The insistence of the abstract artists that subject matter must be eliminated, that art be made pure, has served to create a similar result to that of Mohammedan art which insisted on eliminating anthropomorphic shapes. Both fanaticisms which strive towards an abstract purity force the art to become a mere arabesque. Modern abstract painting is only a new form of the decorative arabesque.[18]

And in a whole essay devoted to this question and called "The Problem of Subject Matter" (written around 1944), he examined the history of modern art and put together the two elements that he took to be fundamental:

If we could describe the art of this, the first half of the twentieth century, in a sentence, it would read as the search for something to paint; just as, were we to do the same for modern art as a whole, it must read as the critical preoccupation of artists with solving the technical problems of the painting medium.

When the search for something to paint forsakes serious subject matter and turns to the nature of painting itself for inspiration, what results is decoration:

Abstract art in America has to a large extent been the preoccupation of the dull, who by ignoring subject matter, remove themselves from life to engage in a pastime of decorative art.[19]

So acute was this conviction about the subject matter of art that it became the focus around which the discussions organized by the Subjects of the Artist school revolved, the school having been set up to encourage among young artists the growth of the idea that profound subject matter is intrinsic to good art. According to Robert Goodnough, who was one of its members, it was called Subjects of the Artist "in order to emphasize that abstract art, too, has a subject, and that the 'curriculum' consisted of the subjects that interest advanced artists."[20] At their Friday evening public lectures the topics ranged from Indian sand painting, to Dada, early fantasy films, to the abstract image.[21] All the artists were to retain this commitment to content to the end of their careers and, in the case of living artists, to this day. Robert Motherwell, for instance, said in the 1970s:

In my sixties and not without regard for the popularization and vulgarization of so much abstract art during the last twenty years, I find a certain personal atavism, a growing desire for an almost primeval force (that has always been more or less latent in some of my work) becoming stronger. I now think as often of Stonehenge as of Brancusi, of Lascaux and Altamira as well as of *Guernica,* of the Vikings rather than the Parisians or New Yorkers. At any rate, the winter of 1976 was devoted to more barbaric and megalithic images, more so perhaps than at any time since I first stumbled on the *Spanish Elegy* theme.[22]

Direct statements like these are common enough among all the artists, but more often than not their concern with content is expressed in remarks about the kind of images and paintings they are creating. Arshile Gorky, for example, made the following comments about the importance and meaning of his forms in his *Riveria Cafe* abstract murals:

Of course the outward aspect of my murals seemingly does not relate to the average man's experience. But this is an illusion! What man has not stopped at twilight and on observing the distorted shape of his elongated shadow conjured up strange and moving and often fantastic fancies from it? Certainly we all dream and in this common denominator of everyone's experience I have been able to find a language for all to understand.[23]

In a quite different style of thought, though expressing the same intentions, Clyfford Still wrote:

I held it imperative to evolve an instrument of thought which would aid in cutting through all cultural opiates, past and present, so that a direct, immediate, and truly free vision could be achieved, and an idea be revealed with clarity. . . .

The work itself, whether thought of as image of idea, as revelation, or as a manifest of meaning, could not have existed without a profound concern to achieve a purpose beyond vanity, ambition, or remembrance, for a man's term of life. . . .

Therefore, let no man under-value the implications of this work or its power for life;—or for death, if it is misused.[24]

This force for life or death, which Still attributes to his paintings (and it is a belief that did not diminish over time)[25] may seem a little overdramatic, but it accurately expresses the conviction that all the artists had, that their art, and art in general, had enormous potential for good. Where ideology had failed, and seemed bound to fail, only the arts had the capacity to bring humanity back to the profundities of life, and reconstruction could take place only if these truths about human existence were faced and taken account of. As Rothko said of his and Gottlieb's work:

If our titles recall the known myths of antiquity, we have used them again because they are the eternal symbols upon which we must fall back to express basic psychological ideas. . . .

Those who think that the world of today is more gentle and graceful than the primeval and predatory passions from which these myths spring, are either not aware of reality or do not wish to see it in art. The myth holds us, therefore, not thru its romantic flavor, not thru the remembrance of the beauty of some bygone age, not thru the possibilities of fantasy, but because it expresses to us something real and existing in ourselves, as it was to those who first stumbled upon the symbols to give them life.[26]

The agony about subject matter, however, was not simply an anxiety, or questioning, about what to paint, or what was suitable to paint. It was not a case of *choosing* myth as a suitable subject matter. Rather, it seemed to have worked in reverse. From a deeply felt need to use art to say things that mattered at a fundamental level of life, the artists gradually articulated a position where myth seemed the only vehicle capable of bearing that expression. How and why they arrived at that position is something which needs to be explained. But it must be remembered that subject matter was not something that could be separated from technical means. As they saw very clearly, art in which subject matter and technical style were not conceptually united was bound to be merely illustration or decoration. True artists articulate their subject matter so that it carries with it implications for its realization in paint: the one simply cannot develop without the other, because they are conceptually two sides of the same coin. As Pollock said, "The method of painting is the natural growth out of a need."[27]

Looking at the problem from a different point of view, there was also the important point that familiar and shopworn forms and images are not capable of conveying important subject matter. Rothko explained this transition in the case of archaic artist to present mythmakers particularly well:

Even the archaic artist, who had an uncanny virtuosity, found it necessary to create a group of intermediaries, monsters, hybrids, gods, and demigods. The difference is that, since the archaic artist was living in a more practical society than ours, the urgency for transcendent experience was understood, and given an official status. As a consequence, the human figure and other elements from the familiar world could be combined with, or participate as a whole in the enactment of the excesses which characterize this improbable hierarchy. With us the disguise must be complete. The familiar identity of things has to be pulverized in order to destroy the finite associations with which our society increasingly enshrouds every aspect of our environment.[28]

And in the Gottlieb-Rothko broadcast:

Our presentation of these myths, however, must be in our own terms, which are at once more primitive and more modern than the myths themselves—more primitive because we seek the primeval and atavistic roots of the idea rather than their graceful classical version; more modern than the myths themselves because we must redescribe their implications through our own experience.[29]

Of the forms they must use they assert that

they have no direct association with any particular visible experience, but in them one recognizes the principle and passion of organisms.[30]

In "The Sublime Is Now" (itself a revealing title), Barnett Newman described the new subject matter and commented on its plastic realization:

We are reasserting man's natural desire for the exhalted, for a concern with our relationship to the absolute emotions. We do not need the obsolete props of an outmoded and antiquated legend. We are creating images whose reality is self-evident and which are devoid of the props and crutches that evoke associations with outmoded images, both sublime and beautiful. We are freeing ourselves of the impediments of memory, association, nostalgia, legend, myth, or what have you, that have been the devices of Western European painting.[31]

The new art must therefore discover new forms. But the articulation of new forms is not something for which directions can be given. It is a slow and painful process in which the artist gropes forward in the dark, trusting that the gropings will eventually lead to the desired goal. This is almost always true of some stages of any creative activity, of course, and Newman describes it very well in his essay "The Plasmic Image":

The subject matter of creation is chaos. . . . All artists whether primitive or sophisticated have been involved in the handling of chaos. The painter of the new movement[32] clearly understands the separation between abstraction and the art of the abstract. He is therefore not concerned with geometric forms per se but in creating forms which by their abstract nature carry some abstract intellectual content.

The present painter can be said to work with chaos not only in the sense that he is handling the chaos of the blank picture plane but also in that he is handling the chaos of form. In trying to go beyond the visible and the known world he is working with forms that are unknown even to him. He is therefore engaged in a true act of discovery in the creation of new forms and symbols that will have the living quality of creation.[33]

With this attitude to subject matter and technical means, how did the artists meet the demands of myth? What was it about their view of myth that made it adaptable to their artistic aims? First of all, it should be said that this interest in myth was not something that the artists developed alone, in isolation. Myth was very much in the air at this time, not only among anthropologists, sociologists, and psychiatrists but also among those associated with the arts. As Gottlieb was to say later, "at that time a great many writers, more than painters, were absorbed in the idea of myth in relation to art."[34]

However strange it may seem to us of the later generations, it was a very powerful and positive idea in the thirties and forties, involving a profound belief in the universality of human nature and experience and in the communication of that experience. It was the last expression of idealistic hope before the despair of existentialism, and artists who were affected by it are profoundly different in their thinking from the generations that succeeded them. They are, if you like, the last of the romantics, a thought which Robert Motherwell gave expression to in February 1951:

If I were asked to generalize about this condition as it has been manifest in poets, painters, and composers during the last century and a half, I should say that it is a fundamentally romantic response to modern life—rebellious, individualistic, unconventional, sensitive, irritable. I should say that this attitude arose from a feeling of being ill at ease in the universe, so to speak—the collapse of religion, of the old close-knit community and family may have something to do with the origins of the feeling. I do not know.

But whatever the source of this sense of being unwedded to the universe, I think that one's art is just one's effort to wed oneself to the universe, to unify oneself through union. . . .

What new kind of *mystique* is this, one might ask. For make no mistake, abstract art is a form of mysticism.[35]

In the nineteenth century, and especially in the first half, the term "myth" was used, in general currency, as the opposite of "reality." This usage is interesting because it marks the final stage in a long historical process in which myth has become more and more divorced from reality in the minds of succeeding generations. Presumably there is a stage in the early evolution of a myth in which the surface story is taken as literally true: the story is devised as a plausible, believable, and believed explanation of how a certain state of affairs came about. As time goes by, however, it seems that societies cease to believe in the literal truth of the myth and begin to seek out its "hidden meanings"—its *hyponoiai,* as it was called in sixth-century B.C. Greece.[36] This, of course, is simply a way of preserving the "reality" of the myth, there being a deeply felt reluctance to let myths go as mere fantasies of imagination, having no bearing on humanity and society.

It is interesting to look at the history of Greek myths in this respect, for as one age has given way to the next, it has become no longer possible even to interpret them as allegories—as was common in the

Renaissance, for instance. By the time we reach the twentieth century, we find artists like Gottlieb, Newman, and Rothko searching for a level of meaning that, at its most specific, becomes something like "the concept of seed and its earth with all its brutal implications; the impact of elemental trust" (of the Persephone myth),[37] to abstract forms that resist verbal interpretation. As Newman says: "The new pictures are therefore philosophic. In handling philosophic concepts which per se are of an abstract nature, it was inevitable that the painters' form should be abstract."[38] Rothko's explanation for this was that the pictures were more primitive than the myths "because we seek the primeval and atavistic roots of the idea rather than their graceful classical version:"[39]

As the nineteenth century progressed, a "scientific" interest in myth developed, along with the study of contemporary primitive societies. In 1856, for instance, Max Muller published his *Essays in Comparative Mythology,* and in 1897 his *Contributions to the Science of Mythology*; E. B. Taylor's *Primitive Culture* made its appearance in 1871. In the early twentieth century, J. G. Frazer's monumental work *The Golden Bough* (which Motherwell said was known to all the artists)[40] appeared, a work which was to have a profound effect on the development of theory of myth, especially through the work of Jane Harrison, Gilbert Murray, A. B. Cook, and F. M. Cornford.

All these writers began from the basic premise that a fundamental, common human nature expressed itself, from society to society, in universal, recognizable ways; the task of the anthropologist was to see beyond surface differences of behavior to the more basic patterns of behavior common to all humanity. Myth was a particularly rich expression of these truths of human nature and experience, and contemporary tribal societies provided a wonderful opportunity for the study of myths still in a live form.

Myth was often believed to be poetic and beautiful—presumably at an abstract, "deeper" level of meaning, since in fact a great many myths are quite prosaic, utilitarian, and sometimes even ugly. This idea of the poetry and beauty of myth and symbol was nurtured by the Symbolist poets, and later passed into Abstract Expressionist thought via the Surrealists. Motherwell and Baziotes frequently speak of the "poetry" of symbols, Motherwell when explaining that, as the French see it, the poetry of painting does not imply "literary content,"[41] and Baziotes when he said of the symbols in his paintings: "It is the mysterious that I love in painting. It is the stillness and the silence. I want my pictures to take effect very slowly, to obsess and to haunt."[42]

Not only was myth taken to be the expression of a universal human nature, but it was also thought to possess a powerful, little-understood, and almost magical force. Malinowski, one of the most influential theorists and researchers, put it well, in the following passage from *Myth in Primitive Psychology:*

. . . myth is . . . a narrative resurrection of a primeval reality, told in satisfaction of deep religious wants, moral cravings, social submissions, assertions, even practical requirements. Myth fulfils in primitive culture an indispensable function; it expresses, enhances, and codifies belief; it safeguards and enforces morality; it vouches for the efficiency of ritual and contains practical rules for the guidance of man. Myth is thus a vital ingredient of human civilization; it is not an idle tale, but a hard-worked active force.[43]

Even when the artists were to abandon myth as the direct subject matter of their painting, they still held this view of the function of symbols in their work—indeed, without it, the whole enterprise would have seemed to them pointless. Clyfford Still went so far as to say his paintings had the power of life and death. Philip Guston said:

Painting permits, ultimately, the joys of the possible. . . . The poise, the isolation, of the image containing the memory of its past and promise of change is neither a possession nor is it frustrating. The forms, having known each other differently before, advance yet again, their gravity marked by their escape from inertia.

Painting is a clock that sees each end of the street as the edge of the world.[44]

Newman had this to say of his work:

Almost fifteen years ago Harold Rosenberg challenged me to explain what one of my paintings could possibly mean to the world. My answer was that if he and others could read it properly it would mean the end of all state capitalism and totaliatianism. That answer still goes.[45]

And Robert Motherwell:

Nothing as drastic an innovation as abstract art could have come into existence, save as the consequence of a most profound, relentless, unquenchable need.

   . . . Abstract art . . . grew up . . . from a primary sense of gulf, an abyss, a void between one's lonely self and the world. Abstract art is an effort to close the void that modern men feel.[46]

The mystical and the sacred were also elements basic to myth. As often as not these were ideas loosely—perhaps poetically—tied to it (Motherwell, for instance, emphasized the element of mysticism in abstract art),[47] but it was formalized in a theoretical way in the writings of Mircea Eliade, again, one of the influential thinkers of the time. Summarizing his early writings, he says:

Myth narrates a sacred history; it relates an event that took place in primordial time, the fable time of the "beginnings." In other words, myth tells how, through the deeds of supernatural beings, a reality came into existence, be it the whole of reality, the cosmos, or only a fragment of reality—an island, a species of plant, a particular kind of human behavior, an institution. Myth, then, is always an account of a "creation"; it relates how something was produced, began to be. Myth tells only of that which really happened, which manifested itself completely. The actors in myths are supernatural beings. . . . Hence myths disclose their creative activity and reveal the sacredness (or simply the supernaturalness) of their works. In short, myths describe the various and sometimes dramatic breakthroughs of the sacred (or the supernatural) into the world. It is this sudden breakthrough of the sacred that really establishes the world and makes it what it is today.[48]

Essential to this view of the sacred is the belief that myth contains a truth—a reference to, or an embodiment of, something that really occurred, whether it be an actual event or certain facts about human behavior. This conviction runs all through the statements of the artists on myth, and is carried over to their beliefs about symbols, once myth proper is abandoned by them. Without this conviction, it would be hard to maintain the belief and expectation that their symbols would communicate on the level they supposedly did. Almost every statement they made implies this belief. For example, Gottlieb and Rothko each said in their 1943 broadcast:

If we profess kinship to the art of primitive man, it is because the feelings they expressed have a particular pertinence today. . . . All primitive expression reveals the constant awareness of powerful forces, the immediate presence of terror and fear, a recognition of the brutality of the natural world as well as the eternal insecurities of life. That these feelings are being experienced by many people throughout the world today is an unfortunate fact and to us an art that glosses over or evades these feelings is superficial and meaningless. That is why we insist on subject matter, a subject matter that embraces these feelings and permits them to be expressed.

The myth holds us, therefore, not thru its romantic flavor, not thru the remembrance of the beauty of some bygone age, but thru the possibilities of fantasy, but because it expresses to us something real and existing in ourselves, as it was to those who first stumbled upon the symbols to give them life.[49]

Newman described this conviction in Kwakiutl primitive art thus:

The abstract shapes he used, his entire plastic language, was directed by a ritualistic will towards metaphysical understanding. . . . To him a shape was a living thing, a vehicle for an abstract thought-complex, a carrier of the awesome feelings he felt before the terror of the unknowable. The abstract shape was, therefore, real rather than a formal "abstraction" of a visual fact, with its overtone of an already-known nature.[50]

It is because myth contains this elemental truth that, according to Newman, we can today feel some affinity with primitive art, while feeling none with traditional Western art, which has become refined and overrefined and has lost its contact with things that matter. He wrote:

The artist today has more feeling and consequently more understanding for a Marquesas Island fetish than for the Greek figure. This is a curious paradox when we consider that we, as the products of Western European culture, have been brought up within the framework of Greek esthetic standards—the tradition of the Greek style—and have had no intimate contact with the primitive way of life. All we concretely know of the primitive life are its art objects. Its cultural patterns are not normally experienced, certainly not easily.

Yet these art objects excite us and we feel a bond of understanding with the primitive artist's intentions, problems and sensibility, whereas the Grecian form is so foreign to our present esthetic interests that it virtually has no inspirational use. One might say that it has lost its culture factor.[51]

There were, of course, a number of different, and frequently competing, theories of the origin and interpretation of myth, but it is unlikely that any of the artists (with the possible exception of Newman) were concerned with explicating a coherent position of this issue. What is more likely is that they read, talked, listened, and absorbed the essentials of these theories simply as basic elements of myth. For example, it was very common at the time to look for deep psychological forces in myth, and this emphasis was intensified by the growth of psychology and psychiatry in America in the thirties and forties, especially with the arrival of refugee immigrant psychologists and psychiatrists from Nazi Europe. Clyde Kluckhohn expressed this line of thought when he argued for a common psychological origin for myths and rituals from different societies (a very popular view, especially among the artists), describing it as "a cultural storehouse of adjustive responses for individuals."[52] This explained the power of myths to communicate across enormous cultural gaps (a phenomenon Newman had specifically talked about), since they in fact alleviated anxiety and directed that energy into safer channels. Franz Boas, whose book *Primitive Art* was published in 1927[53] and who taught at Columbia at the time when Motherwell was a student there, argued that myths are at least in part a form of wish fulfillment and therefore have a universal communicability.

But the strongest voice of all in this area was inevitably that of Carl Jung. Both Jung and Freud had lectured in America before World War I, and most of the émigré psychologists and psychiatrists were deeply influenced by them. But, for whatever reason, it was Jung, rather than Freud, whose influence was most felt in America, especially in New York, and many of the artists subscribed to a Jungian-derived account of the psyche, or chose Jungian, rather than Freudian, analysts. Pollock, for instance, underwent Jungian analysis, and Motherwell certainly read the works of Jung.[54]

Jung's position was that human beings dealt with the difficult and important parts of their emotional life by developing symbols, which permitted emotional activity and sometimes resolution, but without any frightening, conscious awareness. These symbols mostly manifested themselves in art—especially in myth and primitive art, where they were accepted as having a live function—and, of course, in dreams. He wrote:

I have made several comparisons . . . between modern and primitive man. Such comparisons . . . are essential to an understanding of the symbol-making propensities of man, and of the part that dreams play in expressing them. For one finds that many dreams present images and associations that are analogous to primitive ideas, myths, and rites. . . . I found that associations and images of this kind are an integral part of the unconscious, and can be observed everywhere—whether the dreamer is educated or illiterate, intelligent or stupid. . . . They form a bridge between the ways in which we consciously express our thoughts and a more primitive, more colorful and pictorial form of expression. It is this form, as well, that appeals directly to feeling and emotion. These "historical" associations are the link between the rational world of consciousness and the world of instinct.[55]

These views must have struck a deep chord with the Abstract Expressionists, for they echo throughout all their statements on myths and symbols. Whether or not they actually read passages similar to this one is neither here nor there, for even the crudest knowledge of Jung would have to contain the rudiments of the passage above; and given their awareness of Jung, and their interest in myth, primitive art, and symbols, it is hard to see how they could not have known his position. Furthermore, it connected so closely with their own thoughts on the matter that one must postulate either that their beliefs were derived from Jung (directly or indirectly) or that they were already disposed to accept him, pleased to know that their beliefs were shared by one of his stature.

If Jung is right, it is easy to see that myths, the primeval stories of creation and human experience, do not need to be *illustrated* in order to be communicated. Rather, it is a case of finding visual counterparts (forms) for the symbols contained in the myth. That done, these visual symbols will then communicate their fundamental meaning across centuries and cultures—explaining what the artists had already observed, that one could understand the art of a primitive society without necessarily being part of, or familiar with, its culture. This may seem speculative and visionary, but it was passionately believed by the artists; and without that conviction, their art would have been impossible. (And it was the lack of this conviction, incidentally, that made the art of their followers—the so-called second generation—necessarily something different, despite its Abstract Expressionist surface appearance.)

Another theorist whose views were very much part of the general pattern of thought on myth was Ernst Cassirer. Cassirer, whose three-volume work *The Philosophy of Symbolic Forms* was sufficiently well known, even in its German text, for him to have received many invitations to America to translate it into English,[56] spent three years at Yale in the early forties, writing another book on the same subject. His views were also known through his *Language and Myth,* a long essay translated into English in America in 1946.[57] Susanne K. Langer, who translated this text, was also responsible for the spreading of his views, both directly, through her teaching (she taught at Harvard and Columbia),[58] and indirectly, through her own writings, which were at the same time original and yet owing a debt to Cassirer.

Like other theorists, Cassirer assumes the existence of a primitive mentality, which expresses itself not in the surface content of the myth but in its subsurface structure. He wrote:

The mythic mind never perceives passively, never merely contemplates things; all its observations spring from some act of participation, some act of emotion and will. Even as mythic imagination materializes in permanent forms, and presents us with definite outlines of an "objective" world of beings, the significance of this world becomes clear to us only if we can still detect underneath it all, that dynamic sense of life from which it originally arose.[59]

As Gottlieb said:

. . . for us it is not enough to illustrate dreams. While modern art got its first impetus through discovering the forms of primitive art, we feel that its true significance lies not merely in formal arrangement, but in the spiritual meaning underlying all archaic works.[60]

And Rothko:

[My shapes] have no direct associations with any particular visible experience, but in them one recognizes the principle and passion of organisms.[61]

Two of the works Rothko chose to accompany this text were *The Source* (1945–1946) and *Birth of the Cephalopods* (1944), both mythic paintings.

One very important contribution of Cassirer's was his examination of the epistemology of mythic thinking, and his assertion that the mind apprehends the mythic symbol not through the intellect but through emotion and will. He says:

To be sure all attempts to intellectualize myth—to explain it as an allegorical expression of a theoretical or moral truth—have completely failed. They ignored the fundamental facts of mythical experience. The real substratum of myth is not a substratum of thought but of feeling.[62]

This was taken up by Susanne Langer and developed further, and it became a very pervasive element in aesthetic thinking in America at the time. A typical statement from Langer reads:

. . . mythic symbols do not give rise to discursive understanding; they do beget a kind of understanding, but not by sorting out concepts and relating them in a distinct pattern; they tend, on the contrary, merely to bring together great complexes of related ideas in which all distinctive features are merged and swallowed.

Mythic symbols, she argues, are

. . . images charged with meaning, but the meaning remain implicit, so that the emotions they command seem to be centered on the image rather than on anything it merely conveys; in the image . . . many meanings may be concentrated, many ideas telescoped and interfused, and incompatible emotions simultaneously expressed.[63]

Her point about the symbols accruing emotions and meanings in themselves, rather than seeming to refer to things, ideas, or events outside themselves, is an important one that will be taken up in the next chapter. But the general point that mythic symbols are essentially ineffable and noninterpretable is a common one, echoed by most of the artists. Gottlieb and Rothko wrote: "This world of the imagination is fancy-free and violently opposed to common sense."[64] And de Kooning said, more allusively (as is usually the case with de Kooning):

Forms ought to have the emotion of a concrete experience. . . . Content is a glimpse of something, an encounter like a flash. The act now is to slip into this glimpse and . . . paint it. And that's the beginning, and I find myself staying with it—not so much with this particular flash or glimpse, but with the emotion of it.[65]

Myth was recognized as sometimes endowing its user with magical power, its symbols frequently having an incantatory power. Cassirer, for instance, discusses the word-magic that the recital of certain myths have in some societies (frequently to expel or avert evil) and many tribal societies, including some American Indians, have taboos on the use of the names of fathers and husbands by the womenfolk, because of the name-magic.[66] Eliade reports that in many tribal societies, knowledge of the origins of something, through the myth, will give power over that thing; for example, knowledge of the origins of fire will give one the power to endure holding red-hot iron, and knowledge of the origins of poisonous snakes will give power against them, according to the Cuña Indians of Panama.[67] With that background of thought, it was not difficult to think of mythic symbols as at least powerful and mystical in their communicative force.

Finally, there was a great deal of writing and talk which looked at the development of myth and language in tandem. Cassirer was the most noted case in point, but there was a general view that myth was itself a form of language, of a primitive and important kind. Naturally this tends to justify, or at least intensify, the view of mythic symbols as pregnant with communication. There was, too, a common view that language developed in the first place not as a prosaic mode but as a poetic expression. Cassirer describes it thus:

The modern science of language, in its efforts to elucidate the "origin" of language, has indeed gone back frequently to Hamman's dictum, that poetry is "the mother-tongue of humanity"; its scholars have emphasized the fact that speech is rooted not in the prosaic, but in the poetic aspect of life, so that its ultimate basis must be sought not in preoccupation with the objective view of things and their classification according to certain attributes, but in the primitive power of subjective feeling.[68]

Can Barnett Newman have been unaware of these theories when he wrote in his incantation "The First Man Was an Artist":

Undoubtedly the first man was an artist.

A science of paleontology that sets forth this proposition can be written if it builds on the postulate that the aesthetic act always precedes the social one. . . .

Man's first expression, like his first dream, was an aesthetic one. Speech was a poetic outcry rather than a demand for communication. Original man, shouting his consonants, did so in yells of awe and anger at his tragic state, at his own self-awareness, and at his own helplessness before the void.

Man's first address to a neighbor was a cry of power and solemn weakness, not a request for a drink of water. . . . The purpose of man's first speech was an address to the unknowable. His behavior had its origin in his artistic nature.[69]

There is no doubt that the Abstract Expressionists were surrounded by, and were aware of, a complex and very rich pattern of thought on myth. They themselves said so, and it is evident in the sophistication of their writings. This is perhaps symbolized by the inclusion of a very interesting, passionate, and unequivocal article on myth, included in the publication that was, in a loose sense, their manifesto—"a magazine of artists and writers who 'practice' in their work their own experience without seeking to transcend it in academic, group, or political formulas."[70] The magazine was *Possibilities* (which appeared only in one issue) and it carried the article "On Mythology," by Andrea Caffi, translated by Lionel Abel. This article contains in a very succinct form all the elements discussed above and, furthermore, makes it very clear that modern man has as urgent a need to engage in mythological experience as primitive man, though not the ready means to do so. When this mythic experience is frustrated, the psyche is stifled; and the plea of the article is for modern society (and who better than its artists?) to resurrect myth as a viable and living force. I quote the following passages at some length, for it is evident that the article must have struck an important chord for it to have been included in the magazine:

By "myths" everybody seems to mean those creations of the collective mind which take the form of tales, dances, ritual representations and symbols of all sorts in societies designated as "primitive." In these societies are found in undifferentiated state all those elements which "later on" appear in autonomous form as religious experience, metaphysical speculation, pure artistic creation, magical and then rational science, and perhaps even as systems of morality, law, politics, and ecclesiastical organization. . . . It seems to me that far from dying, the myth becomes more complex when the different forms of art, religious dogma, philosophy and science offer it diversified masks, so often bewildering by their cunning elaboration or audacious spontaneity. Moreover, the myth is peculiarly at work when the pressures of rigorous rationalism, of strictly revealed or demonstrated "truth," of political, moral and aesthetic conformism come into conflict with the need to communicate with one's fellows. . . .

From the very beginning the myth has been a representation, and, above all, a communication of "things that do not exist but *are*." For by the sole fact that it is put in the form of a story or symbol, the myth excludes from actual existence the beings, the events, the forms of conduct, the fortunes and misfortunes that constitute its content. . . . The realm of myth has rightly been called "sacred." Now the sacred is beyond attainment, incomprehensible (recalling the original sense of the word *comprehendere:* to seize), ineffable. And the whole effect of myth—inseparable from active magic or passive mysticism—is to touch, to make present (by fiat or insinuation), to symbolize . . . the ineffable by means of the word. . . .

[In modern society] . . . the mythological experience has to turn inward, to put on an armor of diffidence and individuality (closely bordering on mental alienation), and while remaining very virulent in the depths of consciousness, is able to communicate itself only rarely and with difficulty, and then more by means of the "interior dialogue" than by the direct sense of the spoken word. . . .

"Dread" may stimulate the creation of certain myths, but it is only *after* the agony of these moments that men can "invent" what has happened to them. "Dread" as a permanent condition of consciousness, implies intellectual experiences, moral commitments, conflicts of "being" with "existence" and "existence" with "being," which disfigure and destroy mythology. . . .

It is hardly stretching the accepted significance of the term to say that "utopias" belong to the realm of myth. This holds not only for the literary and philosophical works falling under this heading, but also for the collective emotions raised by prophesies (often confused) to some passionate hope of redemption or a revolt of the oppressed. However, mythology of itself does not imply "programs" or "techniques" of any sort: programs and techniques . . . subject us to harsh necessities which darken the mythological experience. And let us not forget that when the human being is reduced to the role of a means, the result is most often a system of organized repression aiming at *inhuman* ends.[71]

So, for the Abstract Expressionists, myth embodied all that they seriously thought and felt about their position in the world ("the situation," as they so often referred to it),[72] the need to communicate, and the possibility of communication. Their belief in the seriousness of subject matter in art, and the need for that subject matter to evolve its own new and vital forms of expression, was answered by myth.

It was answered by myth in a number of ways. First, myth contained and expressed fundamental truths of human nature and experience, true of all people at all times. Its symbols were mystical in their communicative power, and therefore could transcend mere illustration via traditional figurative forms of Western art; and being mystical in their communicative power, they therefore enabled the artists to employ abstract forms, but (unlike the "purist" abstract artists they detested) at the service of significant subject matter. Finally, it implied that fundamental truths are best served by simple forms and, in the twentieth century, by abstract ones.

But all this does not, in itself, provide a prescription for painting pictures and creating art. It is one thing to want to express great truths in art and to do so using abstract forms, but it quite another thing to know how to go about doing so. Indeed, on the face of it, many might think it a preposterous proposal. The artists' thinking on myth had yet to be made into an aesthetic and into a pictorial aesthetic, and to do this, the forces of Symbolism, Dada, and Surrealism had to be drawn on. It is this next stage that is unraveled in the next chapter.

Chapter Two

FROM MYTH INTO SYMBOL

The element that the artists needed to enable them to translate their ideas about myth and art into an aesthetic was that of symbol. Like myth, this was a part of general thinking at the time, and it fed into Abstract Expressionist thought from several different sources—from the French Symbolist poets, the Surrealists, from philosophers, and also from anthropologists. Through the accident of historical timing it seemed like the natural direction for the artists to take.

In the last few years, more attention has been paid to the Abstract Expressionists' interest in serious subject matter, and it has been acknowledged by some writers that many of the artists had an interest in Symbolism.[1] This has been observed and documented, and treated just as an art historical fact. It is very curious, however, that nobody has thought to ask why. For artists as serious and committed as these, it was obviously not simply a mild interest or pleasure that they took in these writers. (One would hardly choose French Symbolist poets for that.) In fact, it was their understanding of the Symbolists' theory of poetry and symbol, along with its development through the Surrealists, that enabled the Abstract Expressionists to make over their thoughts about myth into an aesthetic that met their artistic needs.

The influence of the Symbolists was both direct and indirect. Robert Motherwell, William Baziotes, and, later, Philip Guston were all very interested in the Symbolist writers and were well read on the subject.

Baziotes gained his introduction to the literature through Byron Vazakas, a poet from his home town of Reading, Pennsylvania. With him
he read and discussed Baudelaire, Mallarmé, Rimbaud, Valéry, and Ver-
laine, among others, and became very involved with them—with Baudelaire and Valéry especially. Here is Vazakas' account of Baziotes' involvement.

It was "My Heart Laid Bare," those little notes at the end of Baudelaire's
poems—that was Bible for Bill. I think that was a strong guideline, the things
that Baudelaire said about the artist and his life in those little notes. . . .
Baudelaire loosened it up to subject matter of a sinister nature combined
with sensuality.

Valéry, of course, I spoke of to him. Again, in those days there weren't
many translations. I often had to get copies imported from England. But, of
course, there were, among others, Valéry's "Eupalinos," "Greek" dialogies,
and his "Marine Cemetery." Many of these translations were more magical
in tone than current translations.[2]

Echoes of symbolist imagery can be found in many of Baziotes' pictures,
some of which are entitled after the poems; for example, *The Web*
catches something of Baudelaire's webs in *Fleurs du Mal*, and *The Balcony*
is named after Baudelaire's poem of the same name.

Robert Motherwell, too, was deeply interested in the Symbolists and
has said recently that this was a very important element in the development of Abstract Expressionism.[3] Certainly in his own work, it
was a powerful force. He had a close and deep knowledge of the literature, which he discussed regularly with Baziotes after 1941 (when
they first met),[4] and with Philip Guston in the early fifties.[5] Motherwell
edited (along with Harold Rosenberg) the translation of Marcel Raymond's *From Baudelaire to Surrealism* for the Wittenborn Documents of
Modern Art series. As editor of *Possibilities,* he included selections from
Valéry (chosen by Baziotes) and from Poe; and, like Baziotes, he frequently associated his paintings with particular Symbolist poems, *Mallarmé's Swan* (Mallarmé: "La Cygne"), and *The Voyage* (Baudelaire: "Le
Voyage") being two such cases.[6]

As well as the systematic study of Symbolism by these three artists,
there was a general awareness and interest among the other Abstract

Expressionists. In an interview in 1965 with Max Kozloff, Motherwell said of the creativity of the forties: "I would have said that 'theoretically,' that the esthetic that was operating then was much closer to Mallarmé. The effort to express the content of human experience by indirection." And in response to Kozloff's question "I'm interested in the possible relations of American painting of this time with Symbolism as a movement. Do you think any existed?" he replied, "I think they did, via the Surrealists. After all, Surrealism is one chapter in the history of French Symbolism. And so are Cubism and Dadaism."[7]

The Abstract Expressionists, who, in spite of their visionary commitment, were tough, down-to-earth people, were unlikely to tolerate the obscurity and sometimes self-indulgent quality of French Symbolist poetry unless they felt it had serious things to say—truths about life, and especially the functioning of art, relevant to their own situation as artists.[8] What was it, then, about Symbolism that struck them as being of such value?

In brief and simple terms, the basic elements of Symbolist thought are as follows: (1) the rational processes of the mind can only explore the known; (2) creativity, which is the activity of uncovering the unknown, must operate in a different, nonrational way; (3) the true poetic process takes place through the medium of "pure" words, or pure symbols, which do not establish predictable and rational relations between things but which richly "suggest" in unexpected ways through vagueness and ambiguity; (4) pure symbols are located deep in the unconscious mind; and (5) they are, of course, ineffable.[9]

According to Symbolist theory, since the rational mind proceeds according to logical laws that are unchanging, the operations of the mind and the discoveries of reason are in a sense preordained, in that they are dictated by the rules and are essentially predictable. Reason is always concerned to clarify—which means defining, establishing the limits of concepts, in such a way that ambiguity is (ideally) eliminated and the generation of new meaning (as in metaphor) is made impossible. The rules of logic constrict, because they seek to impose order on our conceptual world, and order can be achieved only if the elements are fixed and knowable, if not known. That is the theoretical basis of rationality, though in practice we know that reason can tolerate a certain amount of ambiguity and shifting of meaning (it devises parentheses for dealing with them).

The poetic function, on the other hand, seeks to create, and creation must be permitted to step beyond the constrictions of rules to create what is truly new. After all, the combinations of elements permissible within a stable system of rules is theoretically fixed, and beyond that point nothing further can be discovered.

To artists, so the Symbolists thought, such a possibility is inconceivable; artists expect that discovery of the new can proceed infinitely in time, and they expect it to be not merely the uncovering of what is already contained within a system of thought, but to be *truly* creation—even, perhaps, out of nothing. In practice, this kind of creativity proceeds by choosing words or symbols in such a way that normal, rational expectations are broken down, and obscurity is used to engender ambiguity—a to-ing and fro-ing from possibility to possibility that builds up a richness of association and meaning, with a resultant generation of new meaning, as in metaphor. These elements are summarized by Paul Valéry in a very interesting and clear essay on the process of creativity, called "The Course in Poetics: First Lesson." He wrote:

When the mind is in question, everything is in question; all is disorder, and every reaction against that disorder is of the same kind as itself. For the fact is that disorder is the condition of the mind's fertility: it contains the mind's promise, since its fertility depends on the unexpected rather than the expected, depends rather on what we do not know, and because we do not know it, than what we know. How could it be otherwise?[10]

Mallarmé's principle, reports Arthur Symons, a friend of the poet's who attended the Tuesday evening discussion groups, was "that to name is to destroy, to suggest is to create."[11] Baudelaire was no less equivocal:

Poetry cannot, except at the price of death or decay, assume the mantle of science or mortality; the pursuit of truth is not its aim, it has nothing outside itself. The modes of demonstration of truth are other, and elsewhere. Truth has nothing to do with song. The things that go to make the charm, the grace, the compelling nature of a song would rob the truth of its authority and power. Cold, calm, unmoved, the proving humour rejects the diamonds and the flowers of the muse; it is therefore at the opposite pole from the poetic humour.[12]

It is because the world of reason is essentially understandable, while that of poetry is apprehended through intuitive, inarticulable feeling, that Baudelaire says, "I have a horror of being easily understood," for in that case his poetry has failed, and is no more than the easy, graceful couplets of verse that only aim to please, but never stir. Baziotes chose to quote this remark of Baudelaire's in an article he wrote about his own views of the function of the artist and art. It is an article in which he too says that an easy understanding indicates the death of art and that the demand for easy art represents the threat of destruction to the artist. He writes:

Baudelaire said, "*I have a horror of being easily understood.*"

For the modern artist, an early understanding—an easy acceptance—would be a sensation similar to those great waving movements of the hand on the seismograph as it heralds the coming of death . . . .

And if the artist's guardian angel should ask him "why such desperation, my friend? why such a heaving of the breast?" the artist could very truthfully answer, "I am a strange creature, and strange most of all to myself. . . . My fellow man may prefer heaven after death. But let me, when I die, have the freedom to ramble between paradise and hell."

And if all this seems strange to the practical man—have they ever turned their eyes inward? . . . Have they lit the match in the dark?

No, practical men. Let the poet dream his dreams.

Yet, the poet must look at the world, must enter into other one's lives, must look at the earth and the sky, must examine the dust in the street, must walk through the world and his mirror.

Look back—look now, poet, to your friends. There they stand in the past. The lonely village eccentric—Cézanne. The pathetic mad van Gogh. The arthritic, suffering Renoir, who could say "the pain passes, but the beauty remains." And in our day, is there not something grand in the aged Matisse dreaming his dream of the joy of life?

. . . Or Miró, singing his fantastic songs about the moon, when all men walk with their eyes cast upon the ground? . . .

And when the demagogues of art call on you to make the social art, the intelligible art, the good art—spit down on them, and go back to your dreams—and your mirror.[13]

The Symbolists had much to say about how this poetic process was to be realized, and it was this that exercised such influence on the Abstract Expressionists. The important thing was the development of the idea of the symbol, in which the ordinary, logical, or familiar associations are suppressed so that the "true," "original," meanings, qualities, feelings, or associations might float to the surface. In using a word in that way—as the "pure" word—the poet has created a symbol, and it is only from symbols that art is made. Obviously this doctrine rests on a belief that there are, indeed, "pure" (and therefore absolute, objective) properties or elements of words, and this was something that both Symbolists and Abstract Expressionists passionately believed in. It was this that gave their work its purpose, as well as its objectivity (a reassuring thought), and that gave them the heart and energy to persist when the realization of their own creativity was still unclear, in the face of lack of understanding and hostility.

Mallarmé was the one most responsible for developing this thought, though his writing, obscure and indirect as it is, does not abound in clear, succinct statements made to order for quoting. However, the following provides a glimpse:

[The Symbolist] rejects the "natural" materials, and, as brutal, a direct thought ordering them; to retain no more than suggestion. . . . [Mallarmé says] "I say: a flower! and out of the oblivion to which my voice consigns every contour, . . . musically arises, idea, and exquisite, the one flower absent from all bouquets."

"The pure work implies the elocutionary disappearance of the poet, who yields place to the words, immobilised by the shock of their inequality; they take light from mutual reflection, like an actual trail of fire over previous stones, replacing the lyric afflatus or the enthusiastic personal direction of the phrase.

The verse which out of many vocables remakes an entire word, new, unknown to the language, and as if magical, attains this isolation of speech."[14]

He speaks of the mystery of the nonrational, subsurface associations of the "pure" word, and says:

It is the perfect use of this mystery that constitutes symbol: to evoke an object, little by little, in order to show a mood or, conversely, to select an object and to extricate a mood [état d'âme] from it, by means of a series of decodings.

Where there is symbol, there is creation.[15]

The pure word, says Valéry, "enjoins upon us to come into being much more than it stimulates us to understand."[16]

In 1949 Robert Motherwell edited the English translation of Marcel Raymond's *From Baudelaire to Surrealism,* a wonderfully clear and interesting book. Both Motherwell and Harold Rosenberg wrote a preface for it, and it is probable that the English text circulated among the interested artists even before publication. Writing of Mallarmé's "pure" word, or symbol, Raymond says:

The mystical element in such a conception of language is evident. We have, in short, an attempt to restore it to its full *efficacy* on the presumption that the uttered word has power to create a void around itself, to reject all vision coming from the world of the senses and then to evoke—as music does, according to Schopenhauer—the idea itself, pure as on the first day of the Creation, solitary, divinely useless.

By the "space" around a word, the Symbolists meant that the normal, familiar, and shopworn connections between one word and another are severed, so that each word is turned in on itself, as it were, like a self-referring symbol that stands in its own right striking its own primeval chords of associations, reverberations of which are buried in the unconscious. Again, Raymond puts it particularly well:

Mallarmé's poetics logically implies the continuous disregard of facts and objects, in favor of the allusion, the foam, star, and smoke, that symbolize that astral body which the "pure" poem must be. Such a poem will progress in a discontinuous movement, abandoning oratorical rhythms; the images will slip in obliquely, they will remain undeveloped, implied in one another, they will suddenly flutter by, flashing a bit of color, a spark, vanishing in a rosy cloud. A complex syntax will trace almost invisible relations between the words, and these relations will remain in a sense virtual, up to the moment when the reader perceives them. The poem will stand by a miracle, "sustained by the internal force of its style" (Flaubert), like a house of cards,—in short it will be a gratuitous game, which need not mean anything whatsoever, but must bear witness to its own existence and transfigure Life.[17]

The pure word is buried in the unconscious, and is discovered by tracing images back to their birth, so that utilitarian dross is discarded, revealing the pure elements. Once discovered, the pure word or symbol has an incantatory effect, like a narcotic, as Valéry said, rather like the magical effects of repetition of some myths in tribal societies. It is clear that Rothko thought of his images—one, repeated, unchanging image—in this way. Of their elusiveness he said: "There are some artists who want to tell all, but I feel it is more shrewd to tell little. My paintings are sometimes described as facades, and, indeed, they are facades."[18]

Suggestion, rather than instruction, and the same image, hundreds of times over, year after year; but each image bearing a slightly different—and interesting—face; drawing one in, to become absorbed in its character and meaning.[19] In the words of Raymond:

The poet must avoid imposing a single, indisputably certain meaning at the outset; he needs "elbow room" in his expression, a "blank space" around his words, which will enable them to radiate fully; it is when their meaning is at first uncertain that they assume that strange, unfamiliar and miraculous quality. But it is also important that the poem . . . should be sufficiently attractive to hold all the reader's attention, to fulfill its "narcotic" function . . ., suspending the normal activity of the self, bewitching it like an incantation.[20]

Harold Rosenberg, critic and close friend of the artists from the late twenties on, has this to say about the space around the symbol, in his introduction to Raymond's book:

Any educated Frenchman can make up a poem, just as any American can improve a new "popular" tune. The French language is heavy with old literature, as the American air is loaded with ta ta, ta ta ta.

A word over there, as soon as it enters the mind, begins rolling down into a fine ready-made phrase. No leaf can fall except into an endless series of poetic mirrors of autumn. To get a glimpse of his actual mistress, the Frenchman has to invent ways of singling her out in a bath house full of

suggest colour, that colours could not give the idea of melody, and that both sound and colour together were unsuitable as media for ideas; since all things always have been expressed by reciprocal analogies, ever since the day when God created the world as a complex indivisible totality.[25]

He then quoted part of his own poem *Correspondences*:

> Nature is a temple whose living pillars
> Sometimes give forth indistinct words;
> In it man passes through forests of symbols
> Which watch him with familiar glances.
>
> Like long echoes which from a distance fuse
> In a dark and profound unity,
> Vast as the night and as the radiance of day,
> Perfumes, colors, and sounds respond to one another.
>
> There are perfumes fresh as a child's skin,
> Sweet as oboes, green as meadows,
> And others, corrupt, rich, triumphant,
>
> Having the expansion of infinite things,
> Like amber, musk, balsam, and frankincense,
> Which sing the raptures of the spirit and the senses.[26]

And on another occasion he commented:

Moreover Swedenborg . . . has already taught us . . . that everything, form, motion, number, color, scents, in the *spiritual* as well as in the *natural* realm, is significant, reciprocal, converse, corresponding.[27]

No one has ever succeeded in explaining the logical and mechanical bases of synaesthesia and other correspondences. But there is no doubt that it exists as a phenomenon, and that a belief in it is basic to a good deal of art, whether visual art, performing arts, or whatever. On a broader level, it is common for people to look for "analogues" of thought, feeling, or expression from one area to another, and much intellectual inquiry proceeds on the basis of a particular metaphor as a model.[28] So pervasive has this form of thinking become that we hardly even notice that we use it. But it is a dynamic force for creativity, especially in the arts, and much used, though we are nowadays a little embarrassed to admit it as a theory. As was mentioned earlier, the theory was known long before Baudelaire.[29] But the Symbolists provided a system of thought in which it found a natural home—its conceptual context, as it were—with the result that the theory has now become associated with Baudelaire and the Symbolists.

The Abstract Expressionists were, of course, sympathetic to this line of thought, for how else could the magic of images in great art, and especially in abstract art, be explained? In an article entitled "Beyond the Aesthetic," Robert Motherwell gave expression to just this thought. In it he argues that feelings must be expressed, and that for the painter, the symbols must develop out of the nature of the medium; certain aspects and uses of the medium strike correspondences with other things and feelings in the world:

Feelings must have a medium in order to function at all; in the same way, thought must have symbols. It is the medium, or the specific configuration of the medium that we call a work of art that brings feeling into being, just as do responses to the objects of the external world. The "pure" red of which certain abstractionists speak does not exist, no matter how one shifts its physical contexts. Any red is rooted in blood, glass, wine, hunters' caps, and a thousand other concrete phenomena. Otherwise we should have no feeling towards red or its relations, and it would be useless as an element.[30]

In the Symbolist scheme of things, then, the real essence of poetry (and poetry is the substance of all true art, whether verbal, visual, or aural) is the symbol. The symbol gathers into it, and weaves into a mysterious but eloquent pattern, threads, glimpses, fragments, allusions, which are not related in a logical pattern but in a more primeval and creative way. The symbol speaks because it exists in a void that will not permit the viewer or reader to relate it to the known and absorb it as yet another item of the world of ordinary experience. Seen thus, the poetic symbol is of a different substance or nature from all else in the world. Because it is fundamentally nonrational, it is, therefore, ineffable. Because it crystallizes a myriad of elements into a single symbol, it is simple as an object, though complex in its effect: it distills the essence of a thousand experiences. And because it is what it is, it is nonillustrative, and nonanecdotal. To the artists this meant that it was therefore abstract—though not "abstracted," as Newman pointed out,[31] for an abstracted image is essentially a representation of an object, and therefore a form of illustration.

These were the things about Symbolism that impressed the artists. One can see how such ideas would sit easily with the artists' beliefs about myth, for what else were myths but poetic symbols possible in a tribal society that has not yet succeeded in diverting the energies of mind and language into the mold of rational, noncreative systems of thought? Richard Wagner, idol of the Symbolists, brings myth and the symbol together when talking about the development of his own work:

From this stage I saw that I was inevitably being led to point to the *myth* as the ideal material for the poet. The myth is the primitive and anonymous poetry of the people, and we find it taken up again in every age, remodelled constantly by the great poets of cultivated ages. In the myth, indeed, human relations discard almost completely their conventional form, intelligible only to abstract reason; they show what is really human in life, what can be understood in any age, and show it in that concrete form, exclusive of all imitation, that confers upon all true myths their individual character, which is recognisable at the first glance.[32]

One can imagine that if the Abstract Expressionists had read this remarkable passage, they would have applauded. Baudelaire follows this with a further quoted passage (where "legend" is used to mean the same as "myth") that concludes:

The nature of the scene and the whole tone of the legend combine to transport the mind to a dream state that quickly carried it on to perfect clairvoyance, and the mind then discovers a different concatenation of phenomena, which the eyes could not perceive in the normal state of waking.[36]

This is pure, symbolist language (and in 1850!), and Baudelaire exclaims in admiration, "How could Wagner, who is poet and critic rolled into one, fail to understand perfectly the sacred, the divine character of myth?"[37]

In fact the influence of Wagner upon Baudelaire and the Symbolist poets is extensive and important. What was interesting to Baudelaire about Wagner's music was its power to evoke feeling and images. And since music is an abstract art form, this raised the very interesting point that powerful meaning is capable of communication through the medium of abstract symbols. This explains the Symbolists' insistence on suppression of explicit meaning in words or symbols in order that the unconscious, "pure," and fundamental meaning of a symbol could express itself.

It is not an insignificant point that Symbolist theory had its source in an abstract art form, and indeed Symbolist theory is in reality an attempt to summon the abstract symbol into the poem. It is not surprising then, that this theory appealed to the Abstract Expressionists. Symbolism was essentially a theory about abstract symbols and meaning in abstract art, and was, as it were, ready-made for translation into abstract art. Having its beginnings in another abstract art form, namely music, it acquired, by its passage through literature, an articulation which raised it from mere phenomenon to theory.

Symbolist theory is not an alternative to the theory of myth. Symbolism accepts myth, but goes further than theories of myth in seeking to offer some explanation of myth's poetic function. (All myth is poetic, and all true poetry is mythic.) For those artists interested in myth, it would have been hard to avoid formulating a theory about symbols, for not only was there the influence of the Symbolists, both direct through their writings, and indirectly through the Surrealists, but there was also the influence of Cassirer and Langer, especially in New York and on the East coast.

Probably Cassirer's and Langer's greatest contribution lay not so much in particular positions each adopted on aspects of myth, language and symbol, but in the fact that they opened up these subjects to extensive epistemological enquiry, elaborating the mechanics by which these various processes work. Whether or not their actual views were known and shared by any of the artists is not very important; the artists could not help but benefit from the seriousness, care, and acceptance that Cassirer and Langer brought to the general discussion of these subjects. Myth and symbol were not only very much in the air, but there was a large community of people for whom they were no longer esoteric, fanciful ideas.

Langer, especially, had a knack for expressing the abstruse principles of the French Symbolists in very clear, matter-of-fact terms. For example, in explaining why ordinary language is not suited to poetic uses, she put it this way:

Everybody knows that language is a very poor medium for expressing our emotional nature. It merely names certain vaguely and crudely conceived states, but fails miserably in any attempt to convey the ever-moving patterns, the ambivalances and intricacies of inner experience, the interplay of feelings with thoughts and impressions, memories and echoes of memories, transient fantasy, or its mere runic traces, all turned into nameless, emotional stuff. If we say that we understand someone else's feeling in a certain matter, we mean that we understand why he should be sad or happy, excited or indifferent, in a general way; that we can see due cause for his attitude. We do not mean that we have insight into the actual flow and balance of his feelings, into that "character" which "may be taken as an index of the mind's grasp of its object." Language is quite inadequate to articulate such a conception.[34]

In terms of actual ideas, however, there was one very important element in the theory of symbol that both Cassirer and Langer formulated and stressed which would have been important to the Abstract Expressionists. It was the point that a poetic symbol impresses one as being self-sufficient—as being of interest in itself, for all the meaning that it telescopes into itself. Cassirer writes:

For a person whose apprehension is under the spell of this mythico-religious attitude, it is as though the whole world were simply annihilated; the immediate content, whatever it be, that commands his religious interest so completely fills his consciousness that nothing else can exist beside and apart from it. The ego is spending all its energy on this single object, lives in it, loses itself in it. Instead of a widening of intuitive experience, we find here its extreme limitation; instead of expansion that would lead through greater and greater spheres of being, we have here an impulse toward concentration; instead of extensive distribution, intensive compression. This focusing of all forces on a single point is the prerequisite for all mythical thinking and mythical formulation.[35]

And, as Langer put it:

[Mythic symbols] are charged with feeling, and have a way of absorbing into themselves more and more intensive meanings, sometimes even logically conflicting imports. . . . their meaning seems to dwell in them as life dwells in a body; they are animated by it, it is of their essence, and the naive, awe-struck mind *finds* it, as the quality of "holiness." Therefore mythic symbols do not even appear to by symbols; they appear as holy objects or places or beings, and their import is felt as an inherent *power.*[36]

These, then, were some of the elements that went into the making of a theory of symbol. The attractions of such an aesthetic for the Abstract Expressionists are obvious, for it drew upon all the seriousness and energy that would have been poured into art committed to a social and political ideology had the times permitted that illusion, and re-channeled it into a more deeply effective art. The new abstract art would be effective because it would tap the deep impulses that shape the human psyche and that are usually repressed or distorted both in the individual and in the institutions of society.

Better still, the Symbolist aesthetic expressed and satisfied the social conscience of the artist, but through an aesthetic that came to terms with the nature of art itself, and the characteristics and demands of the medium; and indeed, as the Symbolists had put it, attempted to grasp the very essence of poetry (or art) itself. The next step was to devise a means of realizing the theory in practice.

Chapter Three

CREATING THE SYMBOL

But a theory of symbols is as it stands, just a theory, and whatever the art form, still needs to be translated into a practical method of realization. The Symbolist poets did not have much to say about this; nor did other theorists like Cassirer and Langer, whose interest, as philosophers, was in the theory itself. Perhaps the poets found themselves making good poetry in spite of the absence of an articulated method, or possibly even in spite of the theory. But whatever the case with them, the translation of the theory to both a quite different medium and a different century, necessitated some thought about what all this meant in practice. The Abstract Expressionists insisted, unequivocally, that in the final analysis it was the art itself that mattered: if the images they created lacked the power to speak, and to speak of disturbing, fundamental things, then all effort was pointless. In this sense, they were not idle Symbolist dreamers, but very much people of action. The theory, and the symbol, had to be made to *work,* and this meant thinking it through to the point where the theory dictated its own practical realization.

Help came from the Surrealists, who had moved to New York early in the forties to escape the war in Europe. André Breton, the "Pope of Surrealism," arrived in New York in 1941 with André Masson and a group of followers; Dali, Tanguy, and Nicolas Calas, the poet, had arrived in 1939, and, before long, virtually all the major Dada and

Surrealist artists were there too—Marcel Duchamp, Max Ernst, Matta, Kurt Seligmann, Marc Chagall, as well as other artists in exile, such as Léger, Mondrian, Ozenfant, Zadkine, Lipchitz, and Tchelichew. Breton did not enjoy the experience in exile, refused to speak English, and was considered by the Americans as arrogant.[1] Salvador Dali was unpopular with both foreigners and locals alike for his extreme right-wing views and his preoccupation with making money (he was renamed Avida Dollars, by Breton).[2] But the other artists did have contact with the Americans, partly through the *First Papers of Surrealism* exhibition of October 1942, in which Motherwell, David Hare, and William Baziotes took part,[3] but more especially through their gallery, Peggy Guggenheim's Art of This Century, which also exhibited the Surrealists; Peggy Guggenheim had married Max Ernst, who was frequently at the gallery, as were the American artists.[4] Ernst, and indeed several of the Surrealists, had extensive collections of primitive art, and these works were sometimes exhibited with the active interest and often cooperation of some of the Abstract Expressionists.[5] There appears, therefore, to have been a good deal of contact on matters of mutual interest.

The Surrealists had made two important contributions to the development of a method of Symbolism. The first arose from a conviction, which they shared with the Symbolists, that the unconscious was the primary source of rich and significant imagery. This reservoir of significant symbols could be tapped through the practice of automatism, a process in which the artist assumes a state between sleep and full practical awareness, blocking off rational and utilitarian trains of thought, and permitting the "stream of consciousness" to take over and suggest images. In "The First Surrealist Manifesto" (1924), Breton defined surrealism thus:

SURREALISM. Psychic automatism in its pure state, by which one proposes to express—verbally, by means of the written word, or in any other manner—the actual functioning of thought. Dictated by thought, in the absence of any control exercised by reason, exempt from any aesthetic or moral concern.

ENCYCLOPAEDIA. *Philosophy.* Surrealism is based on the belief in the superior reality of certain forms of previously neglected associations, in the omnipotence of dream, in the disinterested play of thought.

He then goes on to describe the process of automatism in detail:

After you have settled yourself in a place as favorable as possible to the concentration of your mind upon itself, have writing materials brought to you. Put yourself in as passive, or receptive, a state of mind as you can. Forget about your genius, your talents, and the talents of everyone else. . . . Write quickly, without any preconceived subject, fast enough so that you will not remember what you're writing and be tempted to reread what you have written. The first sentence will come spontaneously, so compelling is the truth that with every passing second there is a sentence unknown to our consciousness which is only crying out to be heard. It is somewhat of a problem to form an opinion about the new sentence; it doubtless partakes both of our conscious activity and of the other, if one agrees that the fact of having written the first entails a minimum of perception.[6]

Max Ernst was the artist who took Breton's idea of automatic writing and found a way of applying it to painting. In 1925 he experimented with Leonardo's advice to explore suggestions of images in casual marks such as cracks and stains; (Ernst had long been fascinated by these remarks).[7] Accordingly, when he found his attention riveted by the grain marks in the wooden floor boards, he rubbed their pattern onto a piece of paper with a soft pencil, by a process he came to call "frottage." He reports: "When gazing attentively at these drawings, I was surprised at the sudden intensification of my visionary faculties and at the hallucinatory succession of contraditory images being superimposed on each other with the persistence and rapidity of amorous memories."

In fact, this became the primary source of visual inspiration for Ernst and the other Surrealist artists. He then goes on to say:

The frottage process—based on nothing other than the intensification of the irritability of the mind's faculties by appropriate technical means, excluding all conscious mental guidance (of reason, taste or morals) and reducing to a minimum the active part of what has hitherto been called the "author" of the work—was consequently revealed as the true equivalent of that which was already known as *automatic writing*.[8]

And as he put it on another occasion:

The fairy-tale of the artist's creativity is western culture's last superstition, the sad remains of the myth of creation. One of Surrealist's first revolutionary acts was to attack this myth with impartial means and in the severest form, and to destroy it, probably for once and for all, by insisting vigorously on the purely passive role of the "author" in the mechanism of poetic inspiration, and by unmasking as adverse to inspiration all "active" control through intellect, morality, or aesthetic considerations. . . .

Just as the poet listens to and takes note of his automatic thought-processes, the painter projects on paper or on canvas that to which his optical inspiration inspires him. Banished, of course, is the old notion of "talent"; also banished is hero-worship and the saga of the artist's "fertility." . . . Since it is well known that every normal person (and not only the "artist") carries in his subconscious an inexhaustible supply of buried pictures, it is a matter of courage or of liberating methods (such as "automatic writing") to bring to light from expeditions into the unconscious unforged (uncolored by control) objects (pictures) whose union one can describe as irrational perception or poetic objectivity, after Paul Eluard's definition: "Poetic objectivity consists only in the union of all subjective elements whose slave—and not, so far, master—is the poet." Hence it follows that the "artist" is a forger.[9]

As Ernst makes very clear in this passage, the basic principle behind this sort of automatism is anti-artist: all creative art comes from the images of the unconscious and all normal people are in a position to draw upon that storehouse. Hence everyone is potentially a creative agent, and the assemblage of images drawn from the unconscious is *sufficient* to make something "art." Whether or not Ernst, Breton, and others really believed this consistently may be doubted, but it is a belief obviously originating in Dada in its anti-artist sentiment.

But not all the Surrealists were prepared to go along with that all the way, though they agreed that automatism was a fruitful method for creation. Masson (who, along with Matta, was the most influential Surrealist of the Abstract Expressionists) was one who dissented. In 1946 he said in an interview in New York:

Fundamentally I am more of a sympathizer with surrealism, than a surrealist or a non-surrealist. In the beginning I tried to satisfy myself with the automatist approach. It was I who became the severest critic of automatism. I still cannot agree with the unconscious approach. I do not believe you can arrive by this means at the intensity essential for a picture. I recognize that there are intense expressions to be obtained through the subconscious, but not without selection. And in that I am not orthodox. Only so much as can be reabsorbed esthetically from that which the automatic approach provides should be utilized. For art has an authentic value of its own which is not replaced by psychiatric interest.[10]

The Abstract Expressionists, as Robert Motherwell said, all loved art too much to be influenced by the anti-art elements of Surrealism.[11] Consequently they were more interested in those Surrealists who aligned themselves as abstract Surrealists, and were opposed to what they described as the reactionary, nonexploratory illustration of the other Surrealists. Wolfgang Paalen, friend of Motherwell, wrote that

Salvador Dali has . . . never made paintings which could be qualified as automatic. This point has to be clearly established, because his defenders pretend that his academic style does not matter since he uses it as a means to relate automatically experienced images [or dreams]. But it is precisely for this reason that his painting instead of being automatic is simply an academic copy of a previously terminated psychological experience. . . . The true value of the artistic image does not depend upon its capacity to *represent,* but upon its capacity to *prefigure,* i.e., upon its capacity to express potentially a *new order* of things. In order to distinguish between reactionary and revolutionary painting, it is enough to distinguish between what I shall call the *representative image* and the *prefigurative image.*

Paalen also had reservations about how far automatism could guarantee a work of art:

Automatism . . . can be no more than incantatory *technique,* and not creative expression. . . . The kaleidoscopic flow of the painter, emancipated in automatism, [is] nothing but raw material. . . . In order that there may be a poem or a painting language must become articulate. The everflow multicolored sauce or the verbal inflation finally becomes as boring . . . as the petty algebra of rectangular plastic purism.[12]

Matta was in agreement and argued that the potential of abstract surrealism was yet to be explored, and it would be best done by using automatism to develop a "psychic morphology of images." Like Masson, he thought that these images had to be developed by the artist, though automatism was invaluable as a means of discovering the nascent image. There was still room, in other words, for the artist to create something of artistic value.[13] Masson said:

The childish mistake has been to believe "that to choose a certain number of precious stones and to write down their names on paper was the same, even if well done, as *making* precious stones. Certainly not. As poetry consists of creating, we must take from the human soul moods and lights of such absolute purity that well hung, and well displayed, they really constitute the jewels of man. . . ." This remark of Mallarmé condemning one kind of literature can be applied very well to a certain kind of painting.

In fact, the mistake is to believe that there is anything except the intrisic value of a work: the personal flavour it gives out, the new emotion it displays and the pleasure it gives.[14]

The American artists agreed with this group of the Surrealists in despising the illustrative work of such artists as Dali, Magritte, and Ernst, and the attitudes of Breton that ruled out abstraction as "merely formalist." They respected the art of Masson, Matta, and Miró, and the fact that these artists could find a way to use automatism creatively encouraged them to try automatism for themselves. Perhaps more important, it meant that the group became a bridge providing access to the general pool of Surrealist ideas.

Robert Motherwell was undoubtedly the one who provided the impetus for the others to become involved in automatism. After studying with Kurt Seligmann in 1941, Motherwell traveled with Matta to Mexico, where they talked a great deal with Paalen. Upon returning to New York, Motherwell talked frequently with Baziotes and Pollock and, in the winter of 1941–1942, attended sessions, organized by Matta, along with Baziotes, Pollock, Peter Busa, Kamrowski, and Arshile Gorky, to explore the possibilities of automatism.[15] These sessions lasted for only three or four months, but they were enough to provide a basis for an individual development of the technique in all the artists, Pollock, Gorky, and Baziotes having been aware of automatism in the thirties, before meeting Matta.[16]

Techniques of automatism had, by the forties, become varied and sophisticated, as Motherwell's account reveals:

In standard English [automatism] really means, in the way we ultimately adopted it, a form of "doodling." But you have to think of doodling in Abstract

Expressionism as on the scale Michelangelo would have doodled, or Rubens. . . . To me, the question of the subconscious as uncontrolled abandon never was an issue. I think doodling is one of the alternative ways of drawing. Paul Klée, after his maturity, invariably begins with doodling. I know that all the classic Tanguys began as doodles. . . . Many Max Ernsts did. All Mirós do. All Arps do. According to his son, Jean, Renoir began his pictures with color-spot doodles, and then turned them into girls, still-lifes or landscapes. There are many, many ways of doing it. "Doodling" as a form of "psychic automatism," as the Surrealists called it (what we would call free association) is only one way of treating association, true. The difficulty of establishing the connection between Abstract Expressionism and Surrealism is that Americans in general tend to detest the standard image of Surrealism—of Dali, and Magritte, and Max Ernst, etc. Their kind of psychic automatism has to do with the free association of ideas, or of objects, or of symbols. But there was another kind of automatism, in Klée (of his mature career), of Masson during the late twenties, and throughout the thirties, and Arp and Miró as well— which is to say, a plastic automatism, a kind of "doodling" that fundamentally respected the French tradition, that is, the Impressionist, Cubist, and Fauve traditions, of the picture-plane, of color, etc. . . . To put it another way, if one is interested in abstract art, and starts a priori to make an abstraction, the human mind seems to be monotonous and limited: one makes squares or circles or crosses or triangles. Basic, rudimentary geometric forms. Now, supposing you wanted to make an abstract picture, that's to say, you wanted a picture that didn't carry normal representation in it, but at the same time, you wanted an abstract picture as rich as nature. The only known means of doing it is through the various modes of automatism. The main means we picked up was linear, which, again, can most accurately be described as doodling. And, as Abstract Expressionism progressed, many people didn't understand that this was the core of it. They thought other things were, and the doodles were often added afterward, to "look" Abstract Expressionist.[17]

By 1947, this form of modified automatism—automatism at the service of artistic creativity—had become so much a part of the system of things that Motherwell and Harold Rosenberg found it natural to include in *Possibilities* a very detailed account of automatic drawing (with illustrations) by Stanley Hayter.[18] This article is a far cry from the loose and general statements of the Surrealists, and is symptomatic of the sophistication reached in the formulation and use of the technique by the Abstract Expressionists and associated artists. Pollock, of course, was closely allied with Hayter both as a friend (whom he met through that wonderful social and intellectual catalyst, John Graham) and as a pupil, for he studied engraving, along with André Masson, with Hayter at the Atelier 17, in 1944–45.[19] Like the other Abstract Expressionists, Pollock was more interested in the ideas of the Surrealists than in their art. In his answers to the *Arts and Architecture* questionnaire of 1944, he said:

Thus the fact that good European moderns are now here is very important, for they bring with them an understanding of the problems of modern painting. I am particularly impressed with their concept of the source of art being the unconscious. This idea interests me more than these specific painters do, for the two artists I admire most, Picasso and Miró, are still abroad.[20]

Surrealism's other important contribution was that of collage. So common has this become today that we tend to think of it merely as a different medium—as an alternative, say, to paint. In fact, it was (and still is) fundamentally a conceptual device, and it arose out of the Surrealists' need to put together ideas which simply did not connect in a rational way, and therefore could not be absorbed in a traditional, familiar pattern. Deriving from Lautréamont, whose influence upon the Surrealists was all-pervasive, this principle was by described by Ernst:

"The casual meeting of sewing machine and umbrella on a dissection-table" [Lautréamont] is today a well-known, almost classic example for the phenomenon discovered by the Surrealists, wherein the reconciliation of two (or more) seemingly incompatible elements within a scheme incompatible to them, provokes the strongest poetic ignitions. Innumerable individual and collective experiments (for instance, those termed "cadavre exquis") have proved this method's usefulness.[21]

Ernst rejoiced to have found a method guaranteed to produce the irrational. Under the heading "What is the noblest conquest of collage?" he wrote:

The irrational. It is the magistral eruption of the irrational in all fields of art, poetry, science, fashion, the private life of individuals, the public life of nations. He who says collage, says the irrational. Collage has slyly insinuated itself into our everyday objects. We have hailed its appearance in Surrealist films (I am thinking of *The Golden Age* by Buñuel and Dali: the cow in bed, the bishop and giraffe thrown out the window, the cart crossing the governor's drawing room, the Minister of the Interior stuck to the ceiling after his suicide, etc.). By placing one collage after another, at random, we were surprised by the clarity of the irrational action that resulted.[22]

In 1942 several of the Abstract Expressionists experimented with this principle of irrationality through collage. Robert Motherwell recalls evenings in which some of them composed automatic poems together:

The times I remember with any detail were not devoted to painting but to literature. Baziotes and his wife Ethel, Jackson and Lee, and my wife Maria and myself spent at least two evenings making abstract automatic poems. In the beginning, each of us wrote a line and then they were simply set down in turn, in no logical order. When we decided that this wouldn't work, I arranged the lines in sequence, but we were still not satisfied and finally we decided to choose a common topic. I remember one rainy night one of the subjects was rain, and an extremely beautiful poem resulted from that. . . . During those two years which culminated in Pollock's first exhibition, there were considerable experiments in automatism of various kinds, I think, including the "Exquisite Corpse", as the Surrealists called it.[23]

What this account makes clear (and what one would expect from their attitude to automatism) is that the artists did not believe that total irrationality was sufficient, nor even necessary, for the making of art. As Motherwell points out, the random juxtaposition of ideas was useful, acceptable, and, indeed, valuable, up to a point; it could provide or suggest the beginnings of a poem or painting, but those ideas then had to be taken and shaped in that peculiarly aesthetic way that marks art off from the rest of the world. As the "orthodox" Surrealists such as Breton and Ernst put it, on the other hand, it was the *irrational* element of the juxtapositions that was of value, so that the more bizarre and unexpected, the better. Max Ernst described the mechanism of collage thus:

What Is The Mechanism of Collage?
I am tempted to see it as the exploitation of *the fortuitous encounter of two distant realities on an unfamiliar plane* (to paraphrase and generalize Lautréamont's

celebrated phrase: *"Beautiful, like the chance meeting of a sewing machine and an umbrella on a dissecting table"*) or, in short, the cultivation of the effects of a *systematic displacement,* according to André Breton's thesis: *Surreality will be, moreover, a function of our will to complete displacement of everything (and it is understood that one can go so far as to displace a hand by isolating it from an arm, that the hand gains as much qua hand and also that in speaking of displacement, we do not only think of the possibility of acting in space.* (Note to the Reader, La Femme 100 Têtes.)

A ready made reality, whose naive purpose seems to have been set for once and for all (an umbrella), suddenly found in the presence of another very distinct and no less absurd reality (a sewing machine), in a place where both must *feel out of place* (on a dissecting table), will be robbed of its naive purpose and of its identity; its false absolute will be transformed, by means of a relative, into a new absolute, poetic and true: umbrella and sewing machine will make love. This very simple example seems to me to reveal the mechanisms of the process. Complete transmutation, followed by an act as pure as that of love, will necessarily occur every time the given facts make conditions favorable. *The union of two apparently incompatible realities on an apparently unsuitable scale.*[24]

Breton said that "the strongest [Surrealist image] is that which presents the highest degree of arbitrariness,"[25] and Arp composed some of his collages by simply dropping the torn pieces of paper and fixing them wherever they fell.[26] Chance was immensely valuable because it arbitrarily wrenched things out of their familiar contexts, and *displaced* them, so that they stood alone. Thus the Surrealists took to its extreme the Symbolists' recommendation to "make a space around a word." It is true that a displaced hand, for example, will look different from a normal one, and may even possibly be interesting; but as Masson said later, "The meeting of the umbrella and the sewing machine on the operating table happened only *once.* Traced, repeated over and over again, mechanized, the unusual vulgarizes itself."[27] For the Symbolists, and especially for the Abstract Expressionists, displacement was merely a tool which allowed the "invisible relations between ideas" to reveal themselves: unusual juxtapositions of ideas would permit chance reverberations, and, of course, some juxtapositions were more fruitful than others. The role of the artist was to arrange a complex of such juxtapositions so that it all added up to something interesting, new, and valuable, albeit strictly untranslatable.

This is a basically positive attitude to the making of art, whereas the Surrealist attitude to collage (and to automatism as well) was really nihilistic. The Americans sensed this in the art of the Surrealists (for which they frequently expressed their distaste), but they could also see that the ideas from which this art came were only slightly off-center, and were simply distorted elements of a set of attitudes which they themselves shared. And none of it was clearly black and white; even the principle of displacement for its own sake had its virtues, for it enabled one to focus on a symbol so that it became iconized, and thus capable of producing a "narcotic" effect.

Clearly, to artists interested in myth, this view of symbol was a very attractive one, and while the Surrealists were not interested in exploiting it, their principle of displacement provided the Abstract Expressionists with the means to do so. Surrealism in America came along at the right time. As Motherwell put it: "What seemed to me to be the situation in the beginning of the 1940s was that there was all the talent to create first-rate works of art, but that there wasn't a creative principle, a rationale. An aspect of Surrealism provided it."[28]

In some of its manifestations, Surrealism was anti-art and anti-artist. In its more positive forms, it was an art more interested in psychic processes than in the making of art; and where it was interested in the making of art, it was more interested in the *process* than in the art made. In the Surrealist scheme of things art had no special intrinsic value or character of its own. If it had value, it did so solely because it illustrated the deeper workings of the human mind; and there was no acknowledgment that the medium had its own character, difficulties, and demands which were to be met and respected by the artist.

This view ran deeply counter to the instincts of the Abstract Expressionists, for they were first and foremost artists.[29] To them, art had its own distinctive character and value, and it was something which could demand a lifetime commitment, with occasional rewards and frequent frustrations and disappointments. And because its value was so great, one did not trivialize it with nonserious subject matter.

The Symbolists, on the other hand, were fundamentally serious in their attitude to art. Their radicalism was not iconoclastic but was the expression of a deeply felt wish to clear away the clichés and "grasp the pure essence" of art and poetry. Their interest in the psyche was simply that it could create poetry, and poetry of course was of the greatest intrinsic value. It is not surprising, then, that the Abstract Expressionists felt a basic sympathy with the Symbolists and derived much of their theoretical position from them—or perhaps, more accurately, found that they held views in common, and used what the Symbolists had to say to help articulate their own position. From the Surrealists they borrowed important techniques—the principles of automatism and collage—and put them to their own distinctive use.

Their beliefs about myth led them to think that it must be possible to recover primitive aesthetic ways of thought and feeling, through highly charged symbols in art. If it could be done in the past, it could be done now, though the artist would have to discover or invent new forms with which to do so. Because of their involvement with myth, they went one step further than the Symbolists in setting as their aim not merely access to fundamental, nonrational, "poetic" modes of thought and feeling but, more important, the discovery and expression of certain archetypal thought forms or experiences which were the basis upon which the psyche comes to terms with its environment.

This being so, very special kinds of symbols were required, symbols which could express a complexity of thought and feeling incommunicable in ordinary ways, and which could express that with enormous impact and clarity. It is curious how widespread is the belief that the closer one comes to expressing profound truths, the simpler must be the symbols through which one strives to express them—particularly when the truths are very complex.[30]

On the face of it, it would seem unlikely that complex thoughts could be expressed through simple symbols, but the belief seems to be that it is the profundity, rather than the complexity as such, that demands it. Perhaps what lies at the back of this expectation is an unarticulated desire to perform a special kind of magic and concentrate into a single line, say, all the properties of a dozen lines in a generalized, but condensed and therefore more powerful, way. Thus what one has is a symbol which is built up from a myriad of tiny symbols, as it were; and it is from that fact that the energy and eloquence of the symbol springs, rather than from its simplicity *per se*. The Abstract Expressionists, like other artists before them, were no exception, and they strove for symbols whose simplicity would intensify their power.

For the same reason, an abstract symbol was preferable to a representational one. Representational forms are much more complex in their references and suggestiveness, not all of which will be relevant to their function as a particular symbol. There is, therefore, a relative busy-ness about them which has to be suppressed if the artist requires the symbol to be simple. (Medieval artists achieved this, in part, by eliminating or reducing detail of background, especially in iconic figures.) Abstract forms, being simpler, usually, in both structure and reference, were inherently more suited to the needs of the Abstract Expressionists. The abstract form does not normally have to be excised from a regular, familiar environment, for it has no established references which need to be severed in order that it might speak afresh. (There are odd cases of abstract symbols which have become embedded in traditional references, but they are relatively rare; the Christian cross would be one, and the Nazi swastika is another.) Thus it is easier to establish a "space" around the abstract symbol, and much easier to make it function truly as a symbol, rather than just as a depiction.

The simplicity especially, but also the abstract nature of the symbol, makes it possible to envisage how it might acquire a "narcotic,"[31] incantatory effect, making it something of an icon. Certainly this is an effect many (perhaps, all) of the Abstract Expressionists strove for. The best of their works achieve this, and it is a very strange and quite overwhelming experience to see the great works of the period sympathetically displayed in an exhibition space that gives them room to breathe.

How the artists succeeded in their aim is a complex and very interesting story. It required that their views about the function of art and the structure of symbols be made over into a plastic aesthetic which would do justice to the grandeur of their artistic vision and ambitions. From the Surrealists they took the techniques of automatism and collage, modified them, and used them to create the kind of paintings they wanted. They made over the idea of collage to create arresting, powerful, and beautiful images which spoke of inexpressible, subterranean things. They used the idea to dramatize the fragment and to shatter our normal expectations of pictorial structure and wholeness. And they used their experience of Surrealist techniques to demonstrate what had never been conclusively shown before—that pictures made from abstract forms *could* manage to convey important aspects of human experience.

How they did it is their own peculiar and monumental achievement, but to understand that, a further, and most important, element of their thinking needs to be isolated. In order to transform their aesthetic of myth and symbol into paintings, they needed to rethink their methods—to discover a process of working which led more naturally to the desired end. This they found, and it becomes our next topic of attention.

Chapter Four

THE PROCESS OF PAINTING A PICTURE

In all their talk and writings, the Abstract Expressionists were united and unequivocal in their commitment to the image as the final object of interest and value. They did not see their art as primarily cathartic (as was German Expressionism, they felt), nor as a demonstration of psychic, even creative, processes (which was their criticism of Surrealism). Both these forms of art were essentially autobiographical, and the New Yorkers found it presumptuous to think that their life stories could be of interest and value to others. Art must transcend personal feelings, and create something new, valuable, and illuminating.

This places the full burden, in the final count, on the efficacy of the image, and the artists often said that they were prepared to be judged on how clearly their work spoke—to those prepared to hear. Newman said, "It is full of meaning, but the meaning must come from the seeing, not from the talking."[1] Gottlieb and Rothko said, "[Our pictures] make their own defense. . . . Your failure to dismiss or disparage them is prima facie evidence that they carry some communicative power."[2] Robert Motherwell insisted on "immediacy, . . . sheer presence, beingness as such, objectivity and true invention";[3] and Pollock asserted that "abstract painting . . . confronts you."[4] And, indeed, the best of their work *does* confront one: the image transformed into icon—the final testimony to all their words and efforts.

In their insistance that process is only a means—albeit a fascinating and crucial means—to the realization of an image, and that the final value lies in the object produced, they were very traditional, even perhaps conservative. But set against this is the fact of their extraordinary absorption in the process itself, a phenomenon which came to be formulated, or perhaps misformulated, by Harold Rosenberg as the theory of "action painting."[5] Motherwell put it thus:

They [French painters] have a real "finish" in that the picture is a real object, a beautifully made object. We are involved in "process" and what is a "finished" object is not so certain.[6]

And Newman:

I think the idea of a "finished" picture is a fiction. I think a man spends his whole life-time painting one picture or working on one piece of sculpture. The question of stopping is really a decision of moral considerations. To what extent are you intoxicated by the actual act, so that you are beguiled by it? To what extent are you charmed by its inner life? And to what extent do you then really approach the intention or desire that is really outside of it? The decision is always made when the piece has something in it that you wanted.[7]

And finally, de Kooning:

I refrain from "finishing" it. I paint myself out of the picture, and when I have done that, I either throw it away or keep it. I am always in the picture somewhere. The amount of space I use I am always in, I seem to move around in it, and there seems to be a time when I lose sight of what I wanted to do, and then I am out of it. If the picture has a countenance, I keep it. If it hasn't, I throw it away.[8]

On the face of it, it might seem that there was an ambivalence between these two approaches to painting—between the absorption in the process of making and the attitude that all that matters is the quality of the end product. And the tensions between these two attitudes become very acute if one starts from the point of view of Rosenberg's thesis.

Using language that is usually generalized and metaphorical, Rosenberg frequently describes the canvas as "an arena in which to act" and speaks of art which is "not an object, but an action"—phrases which make one despair of ever making applicable sense of the theory. And yet, behind all the rhetoric about impoverished and collapsed culture, the artist's total alienation, and the carnivorous art world, one feels that Rosenberg does catch echoes of attitudes and beliefs that the artists themselves expressed on numerous occasions. For this reason it is worth trying to unravel what it is he has identified, for it might help to provide a context for understanding those statements by the artists, statements which on the face of it are so much out of step with the artists' proclaimed aims in picture-making.

Whatever else it might be, "action painting" is not a description of a certain physical manner of painting, particularly not of a wild, fast, and frenzied slop-and-drip manner (the baseless myth of the drunken, uncontrolled orgy of paint-throwing that was supposed to have produced Pollock's work).[9] On the contrary, most of these artists worked slowly and meditatively, considering the implications of each possible move, and accepting or rejecting it. And at a filmed discussion in a restaurant, Rosenberg once put the question "Is it possible to paint a slow action painting?" to which de Kooning (supposedly the archetypal "action" painter) replied, "Yes!"[10]

The first step in Rosenberg's argument seems to be a premise that was voiced often enough by the artists themselves—namely, that society cannot provide art with any live and valuable subjects, because the society we live in is culturally dead. Among the artists, as we have seen, this belief manifested itself in the idea that the forms of art, rather than the real subject matter *per se,* were exhausted and no longer capable of carrying real feeling and meaning. And all their talk on this subject is directed toward the need to find, or create, new forms.

In Rosenberg, however, the situation is assessed more radically, for he denies that modern society can any longer supply the subject matter for art. "The social crisis," he writes,

was to have no closing date and had to be accepted as the condition of the era. If it did end, nothing would be left as it was now. Thus art consisted only of the will to paint and the memory of paintings . . ..

There was not in Action Painting as in earlier art movements a stated vanguard concept, yet it carried implicitly the traditional assumptions of a vanguard. Devoid of radical subject matter—except for occasional echoes in the titles of paintings and sculptures of prisons, the Spanish Civil War, Pennsylvania coal towns—Action Painting never doubted the radicalism of its intentions or its substance . . ..

The rejection of society remained unexpressed. This may have deprived Action Painting of a certain moral coherence and reduced its capacity to resist dilution. Its silence on social matters is not, however, decisive either as to its meaning or its public status. Anti-social motifs in art are of doubtful consequence—society calmly takes them in its stride and in time extends its rewards to the rebels who painted them. . . .

Another vanguard assumption taken up by Action Painting with fullest intensity was that which demanded the demolition of existing values in art. The revolutionary phrase "doing away with" was heard with the frequency and authority of a slogan. The total elimination of identifiable subject matter was the first in a series of moves—then came doing away with drawing, with composition, with color, with texture; later, with the flat surface, with art materials. In a fervor of subtraction art was taken apart element by element and parts thrown away. As with diamond cutters, knowing where to make the split was the primary insight.

Each step in the dismantling widened the area in which the artist could set in motion his critical-creative processes, the irreducible human asset in a situation where all superstructures are shaky. It had become appropriate to speak of the canvas as an arena.[11]

Rosenberg seems to approach his position from two different avenues. On the one hand, artists in modern times have no choice if they are to remain truly artists; for since the age they live in is incapable of providing them with subject matter, forms, or procedures for a living art, they are left solely with the "will to paint and the memory of paintings": art must come entirely from their actions. On the other hand, Rosenberg asserts that this is quite proper, since the value of art can never reside in the object *per se,* but only in human action. Art as an object is of no real use to society, because it is only human actions which can disturb; an object can be assimilated, consumed, and rendered impotent (by subjecting it to the demands of formalist criticism, in Rosenberg's view); it becomes just yet another item, admired, analyzed, copied, and so on, in the storehouse of art, fit for the museum, which is the resting place of the dead. "Art has its official pallbearers, charged with removing works as quickly as possible to their place in the cemetery."[12] As soon as we subject the work to the demands of aesthetics, it dies, for taste will never revolutionize.

Taste is a matter of aesthetics, and action is a matter of morality, and, according to Rosenberg, art probably belongs to the arena of morality—but in a way that excludes aesthetics:

An action is not a matter of taste.

You don't let taste decide the firing of a pistol or the building of a maze.

As the Marquis de Sade understood, even experiments in sensation, if deliberately repeated, presuppose a morality.

To see in the explosion of schrapnel over No Man's Land only the opening of a flower of flame, Marinetti had to erase the moral premises of the act of destruction . . ..

Limited to the aesthetic, the taste bureaucracies of Modern Art cannot grasp the human experience involved in the new action paintings. One work is equivalent to another on the basis of resemblances of surface, and the movement as a whole a modish addition to twentieth-century picture making.[13]

So if the ideas and forms inherited by the artist from society carry society's corruption, and if taste and aesthetics are antipathetic to real self-awareness in society, then all the artist is left with is action. Not political action, for then the artist ceases to be an artist, but artistic action in which one's own creativity is exercised.

This obviously holds difficulties for Rosenberg, for it is not easy to see how such activity is to be manifest if it is not in the production of an object that has certain aesthetic characteristics. The answer seems to be that it does result in an object having certain aesthetic characteristics, but its value lies not in those characteristics but in those marks that are the evidence, or symptoms, of certain kinds of actions, and hence valuable only insofar as they reveal those actions. "Art," says Rosenberg,

comes back into painting by way of psychology. As Stevens says of poetry, "it is a process of the personality of the poet." But the psychology is the psychology of creation. Not that of the so-called psychological criticism that wants to "read" a painting for clues to the artist's sexual preferences or debilities. The work, the act, translates the psychologically given into the intentional, into a "world"—and thus transcends it.

With traditional references discarded as irrelevant, what gives the canvas its meaning is not psychological data but *role,* the way the artist organizes his emotional and intellectual energy as if he were in a living situation. The interest lies in the kind of act taking place in the four-sided arena, a dramatic interest.

The question then arises as to how one goes about reading the marks on the canvas in this way, since, in the first place, one is reading them not for their interrelations and pictorial dynamics, and reference to items in the world, but for something quite different, the criteria for which we are unfamiliar with. In the second place, only a small fraction of the marks can be read, since most of them are obliterated by the time the artist reaches the stage of quitting the picture. Recognizing these problems, Rosenberg has this to say:

Criticism must begin by recognizing in the painting the assumptions inherent in its mode of creation. Since the painter has become an actor, the spectator has to think in a vocabulary of action: its inception, duration, direction— psychic state, concentration and relaxation of the will, passivity, alert waiting. He must become a connoisseur of the gradations between the automatic, the spontaneous, the evoked.[14]

The way in which Rosenberg thinks the fundamentals of art criticism must change to meet the new art is illustrated by the way he talks about de Kooning, and especially by the notion of an art work having duration rather than simply existing spatially as a completed object. "In de Kooning's *oeuvre,*" he writes,

there are long paintings and short paintings, in terms not of size but of the time they took to paint. His key works have tended to be the long ones: "Excavation," "finished," in the spring of 1950, "Women I," begun almost immediately thereafter, on which de Kooning worked almost two years. . . . For de Kooning problems of painting . . . do not exist in isolation; they arise inside the moving mixture of the painter's experience. Hence there is no final goal which a painting may reach ("I never was interested in how to make a good painting"), as there is no ultimate fact of which it can be the equivalent.

One event makes another possible, whether or not it itself is perfectly executed. . . . The act of formulating the first conception has given rise to new possibilities, new problems. Any solution is but a point to be passed through on the way to another approximation. Perhaps the next gesture will bring the artist closer to his true self, that is, to something in him which he did not know was there. But "closer" has only a symbolic meaning; for whether closer or less close to some presumed self of the artist, the work has been lived and is therefore the actual substance of his existence.[15]

That is to look at it from the point of view of the artist-as-agent, but the fact remains that there *is* an object to deal with, even if only as a vehicle for indications of the artist's activity. Rosenberg occasionally acknowledges this, as in the following passage:

In emphasizing the creative act rather than the object created, Action painting, or—by the testimony of Allan Kaprow—the *idea* of Action painting, led logically to the Happening. Action painting is ambiguous; it asserts the primacy of the creative act, but it looks to the object, the painting, for confirmation of the worth of the act, and for clues that will lead to beginnings of new paintings. Action painting is subjective, yet it is bound to a *thing,* even though a thing in process. In the end, the action results in an artifact, which, as everyone knows, takes on a life of its own; it enters into the art market, is acquired as a treasure, is displayed in museums as a contribution to twentieth-century culture.[16]

And as an object, the action painting bears witness to the creative act in the following way:

Considering their mode of creation, it seems to me incorrect to treat the "Women" as pictures expressing fixed feelings. Each represents, rather, changing experiences of the artist broken off at an unpredictable point, when the painting was turned to the wall. What makes monsters is the irreconcilability of the forces that produce them, and this ordains that every monster shall also be a cripple. The monstrousness of de Kooning's famous "Woman I" is a product of an irresolvable contradiction in the processes that brought her into being. She is a prodigy born of a heroic mis-mating of immediacy and will. In her de Kooning endeavored to give himself to the flow of memories, associations, present emotions, and changing hypotheses, and at the same time to drive this formless and all-inclusive living toward a foreseen result, a female figure.[17]

Reading Rosenberg is a very stimulating, but also very frustrating, experience. One swings wildly from the conviction that he captures profoundly important things about Abstract Expressionism, to the suspicion (sometimes irrational) that his ideas get one nowhere when it comes to practical criticism. The artists themselves rejected the theory as a description of their work, according to both Tom Hess and Irving Sandler, each of whom knew all the artists and was very much on the scene. Sandler has said that every one of them rejected it,[18] and Hess claimed that Pollock and de Kooning saw the theory as an attack on their work and felt it undermined, or underrated, the discipline in their works. There was also, he reported, an opposition to the title because it was general, and therefore threatened (they felt) their individuality.[19]

On the other hand, Rosenberg said that de Kooning regarded himself as an action painter, and that Pollock thought the "Action Painting" article was all about him but was annoyed that he was not mentioned by name.[20] Robert Goodnough has said they liked the idea of action painting and that everyone wanted to be action painters.[21] Certainly in the television film mentioned earlier, de Kooning concurs to the extent of agreeing with Rosenberg's question that an action painting could take an artist's whole life; however, he does not say it applied to him, and the whole atmosphere of this film is that of a self-conscious public accord among friends who argue and disagree in private. (Hess has said that they were all very grateful to have a critic around who took them seriously, even if he was wrong about their work, and that this was true of their attitude to Clement Greenberg too.[22] Rothko has been quoted as saying: "Rosenberg keeps trying to interpret things he can't understand and which can't be interpreted. A painting doesn't need anybody to explain what it is about. If it is any good, it speaks for itself, and a critic who tries to add to that statement is presumptuous."[23] And Clyfford Still's comments on action painting are curiously opaque:

Action painting? A tricky phrase. Misleading especially to those to whom it is usually applied. By their definitions they really mean "reaction" painting. But that would lose the glamour of the literary *mot,* plus some dialectical footwork. I am not an action painter. Each painting is an act, the result of action and the fulfilment of the action.[24]

One can see why many of the artists, and especially Pollock, might have felt that the theory was an assault upon their work, for it did not do justice to (indeed, might even be said to denigrate) the final image realized. In many cases, and again, especially that of Pollock, the image was frequently beautiful as well as powerful, and this is something Rosenberg never talks about, and presumably would have had difficulty coming to terms with. In fact, he rarely refers to individual works, much less discusses them, in any of his writings.[25] At the same time, his theory was not so obviously wrong as to be ignored, and one wonders whether the argument it raised is an indication that there was sufficient truth in it—perhaps misunderstood or misinterpreted—to make it important. It was discussed formally, at the Club at least once,[26] and was frequently argued about in private discussion. Robert Motherwell has denied its relevance and has given an interesting account of its genesis in an interview with Max Kozloff:

Actually the notion of "action" is gratuitous. A critic's finger in the stew. It was taken by Harold Rosenberg from a piece by Hulsenbeck. In the mid-forties, Wittenborn and Schulz asked me to edit a cultural magazine, dealing mainly with painting, and I felt very strongly that the various arts should be brought together. So I asked John Cage to edit a musical section, and Harold Rosenberg to edit a literary section. (Both Rosenberg's and Paul Goodman's pieces in that magazine are literary masterpieces.) At that time I was editing "Dada" proofs of Hulsenbeck's which ultimately appeared in the Dada anthology as "En Avant Dada." It was a brilliant piece. . . . Harold came across the passage in proofs in which Hulsenbeck violently attacks literary esthetes, and says that literature should be action, should be made with a gun in the hand, etc. Harold fell in love with this section, which we then printed in the single issue of "Possibilities." Harold's notion of "action" derives directly from that piece. Of course this notion of "action" as opposed to estheticism is tailor-made to describe an aspect of de Kooning's pictures; but to use it to characterize Abstract Expressionism is to belie the latter's essential nature, and to diminish, incidentally, the stature of equally great painters such as Rothko and Newman. I honor Rosenberg's devotion to de Kooning; still neither "action" painting nor de Kooning himself are the "center" of Abstract Expressionism, but instead, like the rest of us, one dimension of it.[27]

From reading Huelsenbeck's essay, it is evident that what he has to say is not simply a literary version of the action painting thesis. Rather

Rosenberg's imagination has been caught by Huelsenbeck's anti-aestheticism—by his conviction that art and literature, as aesthetic occupations, cannot change life—and by the exhuberance of his admiration for action:

The Dadaist should be a man who has fully understood that one is entitled to have ideas only if one can transform them into life—the completely active type, who lives only through action, because it holds the possibility of his achieving knowledge. A Dadaist is the man who rents a whole floor in the Hotel Bristol without knowing where the money is coming from to tip the chambermaid.

Of course, the logical extension of this is the elimination, or abandonment, of art and aesthetic value, as Huelsenbeck clearly saw. "In Germany," he wrote, "Dadaism became political, it drew the ultimate consequences of its position and renounced art completely."[28]

Rosenberg, however, wanted to have it both ways; he felt a strong commitment to action (or the idea of action), and the rejection of aestheticism, but he also admired the art of the Abstract Expressionists (some of whom had been his friends since the late twenties).[29] Getting the two together demanded great intellectual ingenuity and a lot of "dialetical footwork" (as Clyfford Still put it), and there is no doubt that this theoretical straining has resulted in a great distortion of what Abstract Expressionism was.[30]

At the same time, however, much as one would like to, one cannot simply dismiss the theory as having nothing important to say about the art. Rosenberg was a highly intelligent man, and it is reasonable—and prudent—to assume that he was not so insensitive as to apply a political theory to the art simply because it was an admirable theory, but rather that Huelsenbeck's argument caught his attention because he had already noticed aspects of Abstract Expressionist painting that seemed to accord with the theory. Perhaps it is a case of a bad theory being illuminating if looked at in the right way.

There is indeed a great deal about Abstract Expressionism which might give support to Rosenberg's thesis. The artists themselves had a great deal to say about the process of creativity. It was not simply that it interested them greatly (which is natural); rather, the tone of their remarks has an urgent, probing edge to it, as though the articulation of what they felt about the creative process was fundamentally important to the development of present and future work. There is the consciousness throughout it all that what they were embarked on was the making of a new and important art, and that they were out there on the frontier, working in the unknown, just trusting their intuition that all this was leading somewhere worthwhile. This feeling of being alone in an uncharted area, with nothing but instinct and faith to tell them it would turn out to be fertile (and this was something each artist had to endure and work out individually), is perhaps symbolized in Pollock's drip method. Not only did Pollock forsake the normal figure-and-ground pictorial structure, refusing even to allow his line to perform its normal function of describing form, but he turned away from the traditional, physical contact with the canvas (through the brush), and instead created a kind of no-man's-land between himself and the canvas, across which his gestures had to pass and perform their alchemy at a distance.

The awareness of the newness and radical nature of their art naturally led the artists to focus attention on the only aspect of the situation that was not new and unknown to them—namely, their own creativity and the processes of creativity. But that only accounts for this preoccupation in a general way. In fact, their talk took quite specific lines of thought consistently throughout, and the important question is, "Why those?"

Among the elements of the creative process they discussed were the following: (1) the idea of the work of art as "duration" rather than as object; (2) the idea of letting the nonpreconceived image "emerge" from the process; (3) the "directness" of their art; (4) the painting process as a process of elimination; (5) the idea of the artist "at risk" in the creative process; and (6) the alienation of the artist from society. Not all of these issues were equally important to every artist, of course; on most of the topics, there appeared to be unanimity, but on one or two others there were dissenters: Newman and Rothko, for example, did plan their images beforehand, though they agreed that the images had their origins in the unconscious. But considering how individual their work was (there was no distinctive Abstract Expressionist "style" for instance),[31] there was remarkable coincidence of thinking.

Why did the artists hold these opinions, and how do they relate to their other views about the nature and functions of art? Is their interest in process to be interpreted as an existentialist element in their thinking? And, if so, is this something which simply existed alongside their other beliefs, or were they integrally related? These are important questions, for although the formal developments in Abstract Expressionism have greatly influenced later art, its attitude to the creative process has probably been even more influential. Let us proceed then by examining each one of the elements mentioned above and seeing what emerges from them.

One of the largest sources of information is the transcript of a three-day discussion at Studio 35 in April 1950.[32] It is evident from this material that one of the problems which exercised the artists greatly was the difficulty of knowing when to stop working on a picture. To some extent this problem is always with an artist—"I think it might need a little highlighting here. Shall I leave it, or will it look better if I bring this up a little more?" But when one looks at what the Abstract Expressionists had to say, one sees that not only is their language quite different in tone but that the concepts involved are different. Richard Lippold, the sculptor, acting as a moderator, set up the problem thus:

I would like to suggest that the question of method might be broken down into this: first—is it possible to say why we begin to create a work? Second—how do we begin the work; from an idea, an emotional point of view based on experience, or form? Where does the suggestion come from? Third—when is the work finished? How do we know that?

What emerges from the discussion that follows is that uncertainty about when a work was finished was often a practical problem. Gottlieb, for instance, said, only semifacetiously, "I usually ask my wife,"[33] and Harold Rosenberg reported that Philip Guston would ask his wife, Musa, to look at the work, and if she could not see what it was about, he would paint some more until the work was "finished."[34]

Part of the difficulty arose for the artists because they believed that, in some very important sense, a work of art was never "finished." The following are some excerpts from the Studio 35 discussion, all making the same point in different ways. James Brooks:

I think quite often I don't know when a work is "finished," because I often carry it a little too far. There is some peculiar balance which it is necessary to preserve all through a painting which keeps it fluid and moving. It can't be brought to a stop. I think you have to abandon it while it is still alive and moving, and so I can't consider a painting "finished."[35]

Herbert Ferber:

I would say that I don't think any piece of sculpture I make is really "finished." Nor do I think it possible to call a piece a realization of any particular idea evolving from a specific emotion or event. There is a stream of consciousness out of which these things pop like waves, and fall back. Therefore works aren't really complete in themselves. I think the day of the "masterpiece" is over. When we look at our own work, in ten or fifteen examples, we really understand what we are doing. The sense of "finishing" a particular work is meaningless.[36]

Barnett Newman:

I think the idea of a "finished" picture is a fiction. I think a man spends his whole life-time painting one picture or working on one piece of sculpture. The question of stopping is really a decision of moral considerations.[37]

David Hare:

A work is never finished, the energies involved in a particular work are merely transferred at a certain moment to the next work.

And finally, Ad Reinhardt:

It has always been a problem for me—about "finishing" paintings. I am very conscious of ways of "finishing" a painting. Among modern artists there is a value placed upon "unfinished" work. Disturbances arise when you have to treat the work as a finished and complete object, so that the only time I think I "finish" a painting is when I have a deadline. If you are going to present it as an "unfinished" object, how do you "finish" it?[38]

It is extraordinary to find a group of artists so much in agreement about something, and especially about something so basic to their work. There are many more artists whom I have not quoted, and among the twenty-five artist-participants, not one dissented, nor even raised the smallest query. They all had difficulty in determining when to stop, and the reason for that uncertainty lay in the fact that they thought the work of art is not a completed, independent object, but simply a moment in a whole chain of creative activities.

The work of art, then, has "duration," because in one sense it is not really an object but an occasion for exercising creativity; and since the creativity continues on beyond the work, into another work and so on, it becomes natural to see the art work as simply an object bearing the signs of that activity.

This phenomenon is partly to be explained, at least among that group sometimes described as the "gesture painters,"[39] by their view of the evolution of the image. As one would expect from their interest in automatism, they did not start with a clear idea of how it was going to look, but rather teased the image out, from an intense interaction between the unconscious, professional skill, and the demands and activity of the medium. They worked from darkness to light. James Brooks had this to say about it: "I can't think of working with a clear intent on a painting, because it often develops as I go. It quite often changes in the middle of a painting."[40] Pollock, too, emphasized this element, in his statement in *Possibilities*:

When I am *in* my painting, I'm not aware of what I'm doing. It is only after a sort of "get acquainted" period that I see what I have been about. I have no fears about making changes, destroying the image, etc., because the painting has a life of its own. I try to let it come through. It is only when I lose contact with the painting that the result is a mess. Otherwise, it is pure harmony, an easy give and take, and the painting comes out well.[41]

Clearly, Pollock thought of the act of creating as a kind of conversation between artist and materials—a communion—and it is perhaps not surprising that when asked, "But, Mr. Pollock, how do you know when you're finished?" his reply was, "How do you know when you're finished making love?"[42] It is the sureness, the trueness, the "directness" of the artist's response to the medium and its changes that allow the image to emerge.

There was, in fact, a great deal of talk about the "directness," or "spontaneity," of the artists' work, because they thought of the image as not being tentatively mapped out in preliminary sketches but as emerging through this direct, "primeval" contact with the canvas. For instance, drawings for Pollock were quite separate, independent works in a different medium. In response to the question "That does away, entirely, with all preliminary sketches?" he replied:

Yes, I approach painting in the same sense as one approaches drawing; that is, it's direct. I don't work from drawings, I don't make sketches and drawings and color sketches into a final painting. Painting, I think today—the more immediate, the more direct—the greater the possibilities of making a direct—of making a statement.

And to the next question, "Well, actually every one of your paintings, your finished canvases, is an absolute original," "Well—yes—they're all direct painting. There is only one."[43]

One can see, then, why the process is crucially important in this kind of painting, for unless it is handled properly, nothing will emerge, except, in Pollock's words, "a mess." While this is true for all painting, the important difference is that with Abstract Expressionist "direct" painting, the opportunity is lost, and one can only go on to create a new, and necessarily different, painting; in conventional painting, where one starts out with a more or less clear image of what one is striving for, one can always try again.

Frequently, with "direct" painting, the artist needed time to recognize what had emerged—another reason why it was sometimes difficult to know when to stop. Lassaw, for instance, puts it this way:

I would consider a work finished when I sense a "togetherness," a participation of all parts as in an organism. This does not mean that I entirely understand what I have created. To me, a work is at first, quite unknown. In time, more and more enters into consciousness.

It would be better to consider a work of art as a process that is started by the artist. In that way of thinking, a sculpture or painting is never finished, but only begun. If successful, the work starts to live a life of its own, a work of art begins to work.[44]

And Baziotes summed it up in a way which probably caught the feelings of all the artists, whether "gesture" painters or not:

Mr. Lippold's position, as I understand it, is that the beginning of a work now has something different about it that would not have seemed quite logical to artists of the past. We apparently begin in a different way . . . .

I think the reason we begin in a differeent way is that this particular time has gotten to a point where the artist feels like a gambler. He does something on the canvas and takes a chance in the hope that something important will be revealed.[45]

For de Kooning, who was not committed to symbol-making in the way that the others were,[46] the situation was more straightforward. He really did believe that for the modern artist, a painting was no longer an object—the end product of a process—but was the accumulation of a succession of acts which could be stopped at will at any point, there being no logical end to which all the activity was directed. Work on *Woman I* covered two years, and the evidence of photographs at its different stages indicates that it underwent quite radical changes and was "better" in some of its earlier stages; de Kooning simply stopped working on it (as he does with many works), and it took a good deal of persuasion, on the part of many people, for him to release it.[47] The other artists thought of art as duration rather than object, too, but at a more theoretical, metaphysical level, whereas de Kooning thought so in practice. He did not share their ambivalence between absorption in the process and commitment to the work as image, for he did not share their Messianic approach to art. He cared passionately about painting as an activity, but he did not expect, or hope, that it would change the world. This is not to say, of course, that he was indifferent to what emerged, for, as he said, he wanted his paintings to have a "countenance," but he apparently had less feeling than the others of being involved in a journey with a terminus; for whereas the others felt some agony about recognizing the finish, he said it did not come from the nature of painting itself, but was simply a personal decision about when to stop; and he followed these remarks with the comment, "I am not really very much interested in the question."[48]

Another element which probably intensified the anxiety about, and absorption in, the process was that of elimination. Apart from the need to dispense with representational forms, which was discussed earlier, all the artists were concerned to eliminate from their work any reliance on earlier historical styles. This is not to say that they turned their backs on tradition, of course, for they knew very well that art cannot take place in a vacuum, and that without their experience of earlier art and, especially in the twentieth century, of Cubism, Matisse, Kandinsky, and Miró, they could not have functioned as artists. Nor did it mean that all evidence of earlier styles had to be eliminated, for, as we know, a Cubist (or a Cubist-derived) conception of space is to be found in its various ways in Gorky through to Newman. Though the question of their relation to past art was much discussed, the artists were wise enough to see tradition as a rich storehouse of experience from which they could learn. What was crucial to them, however, was that in accepting the influence of any previous art, they did not incorporate any of its assumptions into their own work without full awareness. And since this was very easy to do unwittingly, they set about consciously eliminating everything they had learned and proceeding into the unknown, supported solely by their vision or what might be achieved.

It is not so surprising then, that psychologically, so much of their attention was focused on the processes before the realization of the image, for that was the moment when they felt truly tested and exposed before the wonder—or poverty—of their vision. This, according to Robert Motherwell, is how the term "gesture" arose:

Certain artists here constantly used to talk about painting as a form of "gesture." (But I don't think they meant it in the sense that Harold Rosenberg talks about "action" painting at all.) I think they must have meant that painting was, in some way, a ritualistic act. The "gesture" was, so to speak, that of an artist standing alone before the Absolute. In the early forties, I used as an epigraph to an artist (I forget where), a line from Baudelaire, "Art is a duel in which the artist cries out in anguish before he is defeated." But perhaps those who spoke of "gesture" meant the opposite, that one is not defeated in one's manhood. You should ask them![49]

Elimination of "the ancient paraphernalia" (as Newman described it) made the "gesture" possible and necessary. This process was described particularly well by Philip Guston in a statement in *It Is*, a statement which reveals the relations between several of the elements already discussed above. It reads:

The pressing thing for me in painting is "When are you through?" I would like to think a picture is finished when it feels not new, but old. As if its forms had lived a long time in you, even though until it appears you did not know what it would look like. It is the looker, not the maker, who is hungry for the new. The new can take care of itself.

Every idea that I have now or get about painting seems to follow from the daily work: from an infighting in painting itself—in the confusion of painting. What can be talked about? It seems that the possible subject is in fact impossible to discuss. As you paint, changing and destroying, nothing can be assumed. You remove continually what you cannot vouch for or are not yet ready to accept. Until a certain moment.

I feel like insisting on this one point. The only morality in painting revolves around the moment when you are permitted to "see" and the painting takes over. You can't jump the gun. You can't put yourself into that state by merely wanting to see; but the painter knows when that time comes. Which is why there is only realism in painting. And unless you keep going through up to that time, no matter what in particular the picture looks like—as a matter of fact, you don't know what it's looking like—but unless you work up until that point—when you don't even know what you're "seeing" but suddenly make a vault and "see"—you are not finished, no matter how great and reasonable your ideas or intentions are. This sounds nagging and tedious, but that's the way it is. . . .

I believe it was John Cage who once told me, "When you start working, everybody is in your studio—the past, your friends, enemies, the art world, and above all, your own ideas—all are there. But as you continue painting, they start leaving, one by one, and you are left completely alone. Then, if you're lucky, even you leave."[50]

There was, it seems, a great deal of talk about risk, though none of this seems to be documented. It is understandable that such apprehension might have resulted from their view of painting as a journey into the unknown, with the end outside conscious control; it involved greater risk of failure, and it also left one alone and exposed. The absence of any written statements referring to risk suggests, however, that it was not a big preoccupation with them. Indeed, it seems that it was much more a topic of conversation among the so-called second generation, for whom many of these elements, along with a hefty dose of Rosenberg's "action painting," had become exaggerated and formularized.[51]

The artists did, however, talk about their loneliness and alienation from society. On the one hand, it was their preoccupation with process that led them to feel the loneliness, and their commitment to the power of the image, on the other hand, which necessitated the alienation. On the second of these concerns, David Hare offered this explanation:

An artist is always lonely. An artist is a man who functions beyond or ahead of his society. In any case seldom within it. I think your problem would seem to be fundamentally psychological. Some feel badly because they are not accepted by the public. We shouldn't be accepted by the public. As soon as we are accepted, we are no longer artists but decorators. Sometimes we think if we would only explain to the public, they would agree with us. They may agree in the course of years. They won't agree now. . . . They should not agree now.[52]

Of the loneliness of the struggle to produce art free from cliché, Clyfford Still had this to say:

It was a journey that one must make, walking straight and alone. No respite or short-cuts were permitted. And one's will had to hold against every challenge of triumph, or failure, or the praise of Vanity Fair. Until one had crossed the darkened and wasted valleys and come at last into clear air and could stand on a high and limitless plain. Imagination, no longer fettered by the laws of fear, became as one with Vision. And the Act, intrinsic and absolute, was its meaning, and the bearer of its passion.[53]

And Motherwell quoted Baudelaire as saying, "Art is a duel in which the artist cries out in anguish before he is defeated."[54] Of the joys and pain of painting, Motherwell had this to say:

I find that I ask of the painting process one of two separate experiences. I call one the "mode of discovery and invention," the other the "mode of joy and variation." The former represents my deepest painting problem, the bitterest struggle I have ever undertaken: to reject everything I do not feel and believe. The other experience is when I want to paint for the sheer joy of painting. These moments are few. The strain of dealing with the unknown, the absolute, is gone. When I need joy, I find it only in making free variations on what I have already discovered, what I know to be mine. We modern artists have no generally accepted subject matter; no inherited iconography. But to re-invent painting, its subject matter and its means, is a task so difficult that one must reduce it to a very simple concept in order to paint for the sheer joy of painting, as simple as the Madonna was to many generations of painters in the past. An existing subject matter for me—even though I had to invent it to begin with—variations gives me moments of joy. . . . The other mode is a voyaging into the night, one knows not where, on an unknown vessel, an absolute struggle with the elements of the real.[55]

What then, should one make of all this? Does this absorption in the process conflict with the artists' commitment to the primacy of the image? Did the artists simply switch from one emphasis to another, according to the demands of each situation, maintaining a tension between the two, a tension that exerted a positive pressure on their creativity?

Certainly, we should not assume that this could not be the case, for intelligent people may be inconsistent in their views. In the present case, however, all the indications are that it is unlikely. It is important to remember that their approach to art was a revolutionary one, involving the rejection of everything inherited from the tradition of art until the assumptions underlying its elements had been examined. This involves a thorough program of carefully thinking everything through, so that what is finally accepted is accepted knowingly and willingly and is, as Motherwell put it, "what they knew to be theirs."

In this situation, then, it is very unlikely that the artists would hold two such clearly articulated positions as those on the process of painting and on the primacy of the image, and fail to notice their incompatibility (if they are incompatible); certainly there is not the slightest sign of an unease in any one of them. Furthermore, it is probable that they analyzed how the two views were related, for in the light of the developed coherency of the rest of their aesthetic, it would be remarkable if there had been a universal neglect of such a fundamental area of concern. What then is the relation between these two views?

It has been argued by Dore Ashton, and mentioned more briefly by Irving Sandler, that the Abstract Expressionists were influenced by existentialism, and Ashton has said that their interest in process arises from this.[56] Apart from the fact that Sartre wrote the catalogue introduction for David Hare's exhibition in 1949,[57] all the evidence that Ashton cites is indirect. She points to a burst of existentialist writing in *Partisan Review* in 1947 and to other items of information which indicate that it was in the air:

By casting the artist in a role of openness, of restlessness, of spiritual independence, de Kooning announced an attitude that was to sustain the artists in New York for some years to come. It freed them from the insoluble conflicts posed during the thirties, and aligned them with the prevailing current of thought in the intellectual community. Those years immediately following World War II were dominated with ideas that could be called "existentialist" in a broad sense. There could be no "situation of comfort" as de Kooning had said, and the artist could no longer "sit in style." Anxiety—another way of referring to such inspiring discomfort as de Kooning described—was to be a key phrase.[58]

The "anxiety" that Ashton characterizes as "broadly existentialist"[59] had been with the artists, however, at least from the mid- to late thirties. If existentialist thought had any influence on them at all, it was perhaps in articulating publicly what they already felt privately. But there is no evidence that any of them had any specifically existentialist views; the general themes of alienation, dependence upon the self, and the idea of an unknown future and nonspecifiable ends they shared with the thinking community generally, and it gave further explanation to their journey into the unknown to formulate new art. James Brooks is interesting on this question, for he acknowledges the general pervasiveness of existentialism but denies any specific influence. In an interview with Gladys Kashdin, the conversation runs as follows:

Q.: Are you familiar with existentialist philosophies?
BROOKS: In a very vague way. But I haven't really gone into it much or read much of them in straight text. But I think all of us know something about it now [1965] because it has permeated our lives pretty well, and actually

guided our paintings a little, or maybe the painting guided it a little, I don't know. But it was in the air certainly.

Q.: Does the coincidence of time have any meaning—existential philosophy was the philosophy during the same period that you were working and experimenting with ambiguity and the unknown.

BROOKS: Yes. I don't understand what you mean by "time." It seems to me that the coincidence of the writings on existentialism and the painting that occurred around that time such as Pollock's were almost coincidental. That it was a need that was generally felt by both the painters and the writers, and so I don't think that Pollock—I'm sure he wasn't directly influenced by the writing of Sartre and various other existentialists, but that he felt the need for them very strongly at the time. And many other people did also. I think that was actually the birth of the abstract-expressionist movement. I think it was the writers who got the credit for the birth of existialist thought, but I think that's because they write and so were in a verbal situation that spreads more easily but I think it's obviously a movement that was brought through many media and used simultaneously.

Q.: Do you think then the elements of gesture in the large size of abstract expressionist paintings are a manifestation of this?

BROOKS: I really don't know.

Q.: The full-size gesture?

BROOKS: I don't know. I can't bring it down to definiteness that way, because the artist felt that as he didn't place it—the reasons for it all, he didn't know the reasons—but he did it. And it was the only thing that satisfied his psyche at the time. As a matter of fact, the placing—the categorizing of it as a system I think, in speaking of writers is bound to happen after the act. Generally, I think it will occur in the arts first and then in philosophical systems always afterwards.[60]

Even if it could be shown that the artists were greatly influenced by existentialism, it would still leave our question unanswered, for what we need to know is not how they came to think what they did, but *why*. We must, therefore, look for a more specific explanation that allows us to understand how the artists' views on the symbolic image relate to their views about the process.

That explanation is to be found in their attitude toward the image. In traditional art, the source of the image in painting has always been the visual; that is to say, artists have always shaped a visual form taken from the world, to their particular artistic needs. Artists begin with an item in the world—a tree, a person, a piece of silk—which they respond to in a certain way, and paint or depict its form in such a way that it carries the marks of that response.

For instance, they may draw attention to certain physical properties the item has—the ruggedness or delicacy of the tree, the distinctive pear shape of the person, or the tactile quality of the silk; on the other hand, they may choose to draw out, or project upon it, certain non-physical properties, such as the majesty of the tree or its threatening element; fear within a person (as in Munch's *The Scream*) or controlled containment (Leonardo's *Ginevre di Benci*); the luxury and waste of the silk (in a certain context).

And, of course, this account is true not only of so-called representational images but also of abstracted ones (the difference being one of degree). Kandinsky, for example, began (in creative terms) with something in the world, the "inner essence" of which he wanted to paint. This involved allowing the form to shake loose those charcteristics which served to focus one's attention on *what* is was (its identification), in order that other characteristics, normally obliterated, could be perceived. His forms, then, while abstracted, are nonetheless depictive of things observed in the world, even though what they depict are those aspects we do not normally notice. We may not recognize them as such, of course, but that is the account of their genesis for Kandinsky.[61] But whether the image is representational or abstracted, in traditional art (that is, pre-Abstract Expressionist art) the artists start with what is *known*—with a form through observation—and shape it to their purpose, to focus on the object's own qualities, to make it a vehicle of feelings or even a bearer of their own attitudes and beliefs.

To the Abstract Expressionists, this was impossible. Although they greatly admired much of traditional art, its assumptions, aims, and methods of procedure were no longer sufficiently fertile, they felt, to generate new and great works. In particular, forms which basically *illustrated* notions about society and the world were no longer a source of inspiration for the artist who aspired to paint about fundamental truths of human experience; for the modern Western eye, they felt, is so conditioned by the depictive symbol that we have become impervious to its power to disturb. Kandinsky forsook the representational image because it triggered associations which got in the way of our seeing the "essentials"; so deep is our conditioning by now, he argued, that only the abstract (or, more accurately, the "abstracted") image can succeed in pointing us to these other, more important elements.

The Abstract Expressionists, too, were insistent that representational forms were depleted as a source of significant art. "The familiar identity of things has to be pulverized in order to destroy the finite associations with which our society increasingly enshrouds every aspect of our environment," wrote Rothko.[62] But more important, they went further than this in recognizing that *any* depictive form, whether representational or abstracted, will inevitably enable us only to see what is already known. (A depictive form is one which pictures an object, or event, or some aspect of the item, and can of course be highly abstracted and cryptic and could range from, say, the finely painted fur in Van Eyck's *Giovanni Arnolfini and his Bride,* to the Christian cross, or a road sign indicating curves ahead, thus: ▣ .) Ultimately, we will encounter in a depictive visual symbol only what is already known to perception, though, of course, we may come across items in different, and sometimes interesting, arrangements.

To artists with so radical a vision as the Abstract Expressionists, depictive forms and the depictive mode generally were also depleted as sources of significant information. So deeply conditioned are we, they argued, by the visual, and especially by thousands of years of visual art—billions and billions of images bombarding our sensibility—that we no longer see past the form to its real meaning, but, at an unconscious level, simply accept the "story-telling" function of the depictive form as story-telling. So even expressionist art such as that of Munch or the German Expressionists is "illustrative" or "anecdotal" (muchused words with them) because those artists sought to illustrate emotions rather than actually express them.

And of course a work which expresses a certain emotion might in fact not contain any depiction of that emotion whatever. That is why

Pollock's reply to the question "Would it be possible to say that the classical [that is, traditional] artist expressed his world by representing the objects, whereas the modern artist expresses his world by representing the *effects* the objects have upon him?" was "Yes, the modern artist is *working with space and time,* and expressing his feelings rather than illustrating"[63] [my italics]. And in an interview in *Art in America,* Newman expresses his distaste for "anecdotal" art, making it clear that even abstract, and expressive, forms can be anecdotal.[64]

Rather, the modern artist must discover forms which express profound truths rather than depict them. As Robert Motherwell said of his *Spanish Elegies,* he was not illustrating anything about the experiences of the Spanish Civil War but was creating visual *analogues* of that experience. "They are absolutely metaphors, not descriptions,"[65] and since those forms cannot be provided by the visual world (since it is not for their *visual* properties that the artist selects them as appropriate), the artist must discover the forms within himself—and truly create them. "The subject matter of creation is chaos," wrote Barnett Newman:

The painter of the new movement clearly understands the separation between abstraction and the art of the abstract. He is therefore not concerned with geometric forms per se but in creating forms which by their abstract nature carry some abstract intellectual content . . . .

In trying to go beyond the visible and the known world he is working with forms that are unknown even to him. He is therefore engaged in a true act of discovery in the creation of new forms and symbols that will have the living quality of creation.[66]

To draw forms from the visual world (known forms) is to create an art which lacks the mystery of the unknown, and there has always been a strange assumption, says Philip Guston, "that art should be made clear":

For whom? Someone once said, speaking about the public, that if a violinist came on the concert stage and played his violin as if to imitate the sound of a train coming into the station, everyone would applaud. But if he played a sonata, only the initiated would applaud. What a miserable alternative. The implication is that in the first case the medium is used to imitate something else and in the latter, as they say, is pure or abstract. *But isn't it so that the sonata is above all an image? An image of what? We don't know, which is why we continue listening to it.* [My italics][67]

Depictive forms, then, or any forms taken from the visual world, lack the potential for education into the unknown. And it is because of this component of the unknown that the forms of Abstract Expressionist painting were held to be ineffable. In a long debate about whether or not their paintings should be given titles, Robert Motherwell remarked, "The question is how to name what as yet has been unnamed."[68] And Barnett Newman expressed the whole philosophy of the mystic symbol, which is nonvisually derived, with customary acuity when he wrote of the Kwakiutl Indian, as well as of the modern artist:

The abstract shape he used, his entire plastic language, was directed by a ritualistic will towards metaphysical understanding. . . . To him a shape was a living thing, a vehicle for an abstract thought-complex, a carrier of the awesome feelings he felt before the terror of the unknowable. The abstract shape was, therefore, real rather than a formal "abstraction" of a visual fact, with its overtone of an already-known nature.

And, significantly, Newman began this introduction for the exhibition *The Ideographic Picture* with dictionary and encyclopedia entries:

Ideograph—A character, symbol, or figure which suggests the idea without expressing its name.
Ideographic—Representing ideas directly and not through the medium of their names; applied specifically to that mode of writing which by means of symbols, figures or hieroglyphics suggests the idea of an object without expressing its name.[69]

"My painting is direct," said Pollock.[70]

If the image was to be nonvisually derived, it obviously had to come from within—truly a creation of the artist, as they said. Naturally this conviction led the artists to place enormous emphasis on the creative process, for it was out of this that the image did or did not arise. But there was another element that reinforced this belief, and it had to do with the notion of "finish." In the extended discussion on "finish" at the Studio 35 three-day session, it was frequently said that the Abstract Expressionists did not need French "finish" because they were concerned with a different kind of picture-making: According to Motherwell:

[The French] assume traditional criteria to a much greater degree than we do. They have a real "finish" in that the picture is a real object, a beautifully made object. We are involved in "process" and what is a "finished" object is not so certain.[71]

The reason for this doubt about what constituted a "finished" object was that, since the purpose of their work was not the pursuit of beauty or the traditional aesthetics of a "good picture," the artists could no longer use the picture's "looks," in the visual, aesthetic sense, as an indication of whether or not they had succeeded. Rather it was a question of whether or not the image "spoke," and they frequently needed the indication of others that it did. "I need time to see what I have done," said Lassaw.[72]

Therefore traditional beauty and sensuousness as ends were out. "[It is] the ethical character of art, which I think moves us even more than art's delight in sensuality or its beauty of formal structure," said Motherwell; and in listing all the things he wanted to avoid in his painting, he added: "I allow no nostalgia, no sentimentalism, . . . no clichés, no illusionism, no description, no seduction, no charm, no relaxation, no mere taste."[73] And in a very interesting article, with the pointed title "Beyond the Aesthetic," he said:

The aesthetic is the sine qua non for art: if a work is not aesthetic, it is not art by definition. But in this stage of the creative process, the strictly aesthetic—which is the sensuous aspect of the world—ceases to be the chief end in view. The function of the aesthetic instead becomes that of a medium, a *means* for getting at the infinite background of feeling in order to condense it into an object of perception.[74]

Clyfford Still, too, saw the need for art to bypass beauty and sensuous appeal if it was to communicate serious subject matter:

I fight in myself any tendency to accept a fixed, sensuously appealing, recognizable style. . . . I am always trying to paint my way out of and beyond a facile, doctrinaire idiom.[75] That pigment on canvas has a way of initiating conventional reactions for most people needs no reminder. Behind these reactions is a body of history matured into dogma, authority, tradition. The totalitarian hegemony of this tradition I despise, its presumptions I reject. Its security is an illusion, banal, and without courage. Its substance is but dust and filing cabinets. The homage paid to it is a celebration of death. We all bear the burden of this tradition on our backs but I cannot hold it a privilege to be a pallbearer of my spirit in its name.[76]

Barnett Newman gave a very perceptive account of the history of Western art's weakening grasp on the metaphysical dimension of meaning:

It was the Greeks who invented the idea of beauty. Before their time a work of art was concerned with the problem of meaning and was a visible symbol of hieratic thought. Art was an attempt to evoke the metaphysical experience. The Greeks had the romantic will to create such an art which they hoped would function on this level, but they demanded in addition that their art be object too. Their gods had to be not only the serious forces but also ideal sensations. Whenever they strove to achieve the majesty of the Egyptian form, they insisted that their gods be objects of beauty too, and they succeeded in secularizing their divinities, making them things to admire, rather than worship. . . . Greek fanaticism . . . became a fanaticism of refinement. And that is why we have rejected it, for an art of refinement must in the end lead to an art of self-conscious sensibility, to the love of ideal sensations, to an economy of beauty. We now know because of our wider knowledge of comparative art forms that the notion of beauty is a fiction. But what is more serious, beauty, that is, the love of ideal sensations, creates in us today sheer physical embarrassment.

In addition, the Greek idea of beauty instead of being understood as a specific art form, so captured the imagination of men that it has become for many, particularly for the professional esthetes, the art historian, the esthetician, those practicing the science of art, a categorical imperative.[77]

In the light of this analysis, it is not surprising that Newman and his friends should have been enthusiastic about primitive art, which does not set these aesthetic goals as its primary aim. Just how much of a revolutionary he and his colleagues were can be gauged from his statement of the aims of the (truly) modern artist:

[The modern painter] desires to transcend the plastic elements in art. He is declaring that the art of Western Europe is a voluptuous art first, an intellectual art by accident. He is reversing the situation by declaring that art is an expression of the mind first and whatever sensuous elements are involved are incidental to that expression. The new painter is therefore the true revolutionary, the real leader who is placing the artist's function on its rightful plane of the philosopher and the pure scientist who is exploring the world of ideas, not the world of the sense. Just as we get a vision of the cosmos through the symbols of a mathematical equation, just as we get a vision of truth in terms of abstract metaphysical concepts, so the artist is today giving us a vision of the world of truth in terms of visual symbols.[78]

Not all the artists eschewed the sensuous to the extent that Newman did, of course, but there was general agreement that their art was one of meaning rather than of beauty or of sensuous appeal. Their aim was not to paint a picture with a certain kind of look—an aesthetic look— and this being so, they no longer had that standard to tell them when the picture was finished. Because the purpose of their image was not to "look" a certain way but to speak of certain things, it was almost impossible to gauge, in process, whether or not the picture was going to work, until it did.

The process therefore was both bewildering and crucially important, with no help coming from the outside world; the image being non-visually derived but made from the stuff of the artist's experience and creativity, it only rose to consciousness upon its realization. Hence all the artist's anxiety and hopes were focused with intensity upon the creative process. But being, as it was, an art committed to communication of the fundamental experiences of human existence, ultimately everything rested with the power of the image. It was not an auto-biographical art (one reason why they detested Surrealism), and any emphasis on the creative process would have been seen as mere self-indulgence. But absorption in the creative process was necessary for the emergence of the image.

Rather than any paradox existing then as may first appear, the two elements of the primacy of the image and an absorption with the process fit together as necessary, interlocking pieces of a whole view. And this being so, an existentialist "explanation" is beside the point. This is not to say, of course, that the artists did not have these interests, and it may well be that existentialist attitudes enabled them, or perhaps made it easier for them, to give themselves to the process in the way they did. The rationale, however, was clearly thought out, and was designed, as was everything else in their aesthetic, to serve the ends of their art.

Their formulation of the process of making art was distinctive, radical, and important. Some of the elements were practiced by artists of the past: indeed, it would be very odd if the process engaged in by the Abstract Expressionists bore no relation to the art-making processes of previous generations of artists. But the particular concatenation of elements were distinctively their own. More important, their conscious articulation of the process as a theory of creativity, and as a necessary part of their own creativity, is something not seen before and has profoundly affected artists' attitudes ever since. (Whether or not it has equally affected the *kind* of art produced is another question, but certainly artists' talk and attitudes toward the art enterprise have never been the same since.)

And so, in the early years of the forties we see the coming together of several elements of aesthetic thinking. There was the artists' engagement with myth; the development of the idea of a symbol, influenced by French Symbolist poetry and the Surrealists; and finally their anxiety about, and absorption in, the creative process. These elements all came together in an overall view and expectation of their art, a view which can be described as the theory of the abstract mystic symbol. Just how this theory developed out of those elements is the subject of the next chapter.

Chapter Five

THE ABSTRACT MYSTIC SYMBOL

At the beginning of the forties, the Abstract Expressionists found themselves at the end of the line of traditional attitudes and procedures in painting. Traditional styles, traditional forms and imagery, and, indeed, all traditional assumptions about art seemed to them to be depleted as sources of creativity for tomorrow's painting. It was as if, after several thousand years of visual art, not only had the purposes, styles, and manifestations of the medium become threadbare through continual usage—all avenues explored and exploited—but worse, the visual medium itself had become so much a part of our daily world that it passed unnoticed, taken for granted, like a vital metaphor seized upon, enjoyed, experienced often, and gradually made over into a part of ordinary language to become a dead metaphor: so important as to be appropriated into everyday use, and destroyed in the attempt.

At the same time they were artists, and felt a deep need to say something profound about the world and human experience; but they were also painters, and there was no question of deserting the medium and turning to, say, writing instead. For them, being an artist meant being a painter, and being a painter meant being an artist. Since giving up art would mean an unthinkable emptiness of life, they were faced with the bare, inescapable fact of simply having to breathe life into painting, to survive.

A modernist exploration and pursuit of the structures themselves of art seemed quite without point unless they were put to the service of a vision, and yet the artists had reached a point in their experience when any ideology or program—for art, or for anything else fundamental in society—seemed incapable of supporting the depth and complexity of truths and ideals, or was only too easily formularized and emasculated. Such was human nature, that ideology served more to deflect people away from the truth and to offer comfortable illusions of positive activity and remedies.

It is hard now to imagine how those artists must have felt. There they were, standing at the edge of an abyss, absolutely clear-sighted about the poverty of the forms of modern art, seized with a primeval need to speak the denial of which was impossible to them, and yet quite unable to accept any of the known ways of articulating their need conceptually and of rendering it visual stylistically. Their only impulse was to reach out and speak, and the reaching out necessarily had to be into the unknown.

That situation makes for desperation, and in that state artists either are destroyed or they open themselves to all kinds of suggestions and possibilities that, in a more stable situation, might seem esoteric and away from the mainstream of feeling and appearance, or even unrefined, or plain embarrassing.

Those artists who survived to become the Abstract Expressionists of the forties and fifties were receptive to a number of influences and experiences which slowly began to cohere and move them toward a gradual understanding and articulation of what their art might become. What was most important for them was that, since they were starting from the ground up, nothing could be unthinkingly borrowed or inherited; everything that came into their work had to be there because that was what was required—because it was the raw material needed to produce the desired result. In being open to the suggestiveness of other periods, art forms, and experiences, then, they needed a keen sensibility and eye to determine what needed to be rejected as secondhand, and what they might make over as their own.

In fact, the piece of grit around which their aesthetic developed was the idea of the mystic symbol. This is expressed or implied in very specific ways in almost everything they said about art, and, on occasion, it was even acknowledged explicitly in general, theoretical terms. Robert Motherwell, for instance, when speaking at the Museum of Modern Art symposium "What Abstract Art Means to Me" of the rejections involved in art and of its need to stand alone, stripped to its essence, said:

What new kind of mystique is this, one might ask. For make no mistake, art is a form of mysticism. . . .

The need is for felt experience—intense, immediate, direct, subtle, unified, warm, vivid, rhythmic.

Everything that might dilute the experience is stripped away. This is the origin of abstraction in art, as in any mode of thought. Abstract art is a true mysticism—I dislike the word—or rather a series of mysticisms that grew up in the historical circumstance that all mysticisms do, from a primary sense of gulf, an abyss, a void between one's lonely self and the world. Modern art is an effort to close the void that modern men feel. Its abstraction is its emphasis.[1]

From their sympathy with myth and theory of myth, they were able to appreciate and explore several elements of mythical thinking which gradually built up into their own idea of mystic symbol. In the first place, they associated myth with a mysticism because it operated in a realm beyond the rational. Not all theorists, of course, held that the workings of myth were a-rational, for Freud certainly believed that they were susceptible to critical examination and explanation. But the mainstream of theoretical thought (and certainly that in America, heavily influenced, as it was, by Jung) did assert and, indeed, emphasized its mystical base. It was this stream which influenced the artists.

Unfortunately, terms such as "mystical," "nonrational," "irrational," and "magical" are frequently used in an imprecise and often confused way, especially in this area. Nevertheless, it is possible to distinguish a number of different elements (however they might be named) as contributing to the mysticism in myth.

In general terms, mystical thought is a non-rational, special mode of thinking which taps the source of great truths of human experience. This view usually has its genesis in the assumption that language was originally of two radically different kinds, one a poetic, invocatory mode used by primitive peoples to control or harness the mysterious forces of their universe, and the other, a parasitic semantic mode, devised to order what was known. As Cassirer explained it in his *An Essay on Man*:

To the primitive mind the social power of the word, experienced in innumerable cases, becomes a natural and even supernatural force. Primitive man feels himself surrounded by all sorts of visible and invisible dangers. He cannot hope to overcome these dangers by merely physical means. To him the world is not a dead or mute thing; it can hear and understand. Hence if the powers of nature are called upon in the right way they cannot refuse their aid. Nothing resists the magic word, *carmina vel coelo possunt deducere lunam.*

When man first began to realize that this confidence was vain—that nature was inexorable not because it was reluctant to fulfil his demands but because it did not understand his language—the discovery must have come to him as a shock. At this point he had to face a new problem which marked a turning point and a crisis in his intellectual and moral life. . . . All hope of subduing nature by the magic word had been frustrated. But as a result man began to see the relation between language and reality in a different light. The magic function of the word was eclipsed and replaced by its semantic function.[2]

Among the artists, Barnett Newman endorsed this view quite explicitly in his article "The First Man was a Artist."[3] Language having developed in this way, its character and function change so that it becomes a tool whereby humans can impose a comforting structure upon the world and their experience—a mode of apprehension we call the "rational" because it orders what is known. More than that, it is regarded as a mode of thinking which obscures the realities of life because they are too difficult and disturbing to confront directly. Thus rational thought is designed to impede access to the truth, and the poet or artist who wishes to extend our experience by revealing what is unknown must devise a new language which permits that kind of exploration and at the same time makes it communicable to others.

Ironically—and, perhaps, painfully—the development of that language is itself a venture into the unknown, which can be guessed at only by avoiding some of the more obviously structural characteristics of rational thought. Thus mythical thought tends to be nondiscursive, and since discursiveness is quintessentially an element of the rational mode, the familiar patterns of syntactical thinking—the rules about what kind of thought structures can rationally follow such concepts as "and," "but," "if," and "because," for instance—function in such a way that one can liken them to a network of roads which can lead one from A to B, so that one is able to explore a given locale but incapable of creating a new one.

The important thing about nondiscursive thinking in mythical thought is that it allows the mind to focus upon particular phenomena or ideas so that different dimensions of thought and feeling within them are explored, rather than thoughts of what relations they have to other objects in the world. This is an ancient distinction, and one which has found expression in more recent times from Kant through to present-day philosophers in the form of the theory of disinterestedness in art and of aesthetic vision—the view that art invites a special kind of vision of apprehension in which the object is considered not in terms of *what* it is and how it is related to other objects and possible functions, but in terms of *how* it is, what it is like. Whether or not this distinction can be sustained philosophically is beside the point, for it is nonetheless a distinction fundamental to mythical, and much religious, thought, the recitation of mantras being an obvious and well-known example.

This line of thought has been most eloquently put by Cassirer, and it is worth quoting him at some length to get the full flavor of thinking:

The aim of theoretical thinking . . . is primarily to deliver the contents of sensory or intuitive experience from the isolation in which they originally occur. It causes these contents to transcend their narrow limits, combines them with others, compares them, and concatenates them in a definite order, in an all-inclusive context. It proceeds "discursively," in that it treats the immediate content only as a point of departure, from which it can run the whole gamut of impressions in various directions, until these impressions are fitted together into one unified conception, one closed system. In this system there are no more isolated points; all its members are reciprocally related, refer to one another, illumine and explain each other. Thus every separate event is ensnared, as it were, by invisible threads of thought, that bind it to the whole. The theoretical significance which it receives lies in the fact that it is stamped with the character of this totality.

Mythical thinking, when viewed in its most elementary forms, bears no such stamp; in fact, the character of intellectual unity is directly hostile to its spirit. For in this mode, thought does not dispose freely over the data of intuition, in order to relate and compare them to each other, but it is captivated and enthralled by the intuition which suddenly confronts it. It comes to rest in the immediate experience; the sensible present is so great that everything else dwindles before it. For a person whose apprehension is under the spell of this mythico-religious attitude, it is as though the whole world were simply annihilated; the immediate content, whatever it be, that commands his religious interest so completely fills his consciousness that nothing else can exist beside and apart from it. The ego is spending all its energy on this single object, lives in it, loses itself in it. Instead of a widening of intuitive experience, we find here its extreme limitation; instead of expansion that would lead through greater and greater spheres of being, we have here an impulse toward concentration; instead of extensive distribution, intensive compression. This focusing of all forces on a single point is the prerequisite for all mythical thinking and mythical formulation. When, on the other hand, the entire self is given up to a single impression, is "possessed" by it and, on the other hand, there is the utmost tension between the subject and its subject, the outer world; when external reality is not merely viewed and contemplated, but overcomes a man in sheer immediacy, with emotions of fear or hope, terror or wish fulfillment: then the spark jumps somehow across, the tension finds release, as the subjective excitement becomes objectified, and confronts the mind as a god or a daemon.[4]

This intensity of focus and rejection of systematic thought not surprisingly sits very uncomfortably with any kind of anecdotal or illustrative talk or art, for where the former focuses on ideas individually and conceived of as discrete, the latter suppresses that tendency to carry the mind through sequences of events or ideas. Hence, in their early involvement with myth, when they sought to communicate particular myths, the Abstract Expressionists avoided any depiction of the actual "story" by using abstract symbols which would convey the "feeling" of the myth.

In ancient and primitive myths there was, of course, a discursive story which was the vehicle of the myth. But in the views of theorists of myth, this did serve to keep the "true" meaning of the myth from conscious awareness; as soon as one becomes aware of the true nature and function of myth and desirous of expressing it, then one seeks to do away with the discursive outer layer that acts as a curtain between person and myth. As Barnett Newman observed of the Surrealists, they failed to do away with the illusionistic dress of discursive thought, and failed to penetrate the magic of the primitive myths they were stirred by. "For realism, even of the imagination, is in the last analysis a deception. Realistic fantasy inevitably must become phantasmagoria so that instead of creating a magic world, the Surrealists succeeded only in illustrating it."[5]

For the Abstract Expressionists and the Surrealists before them, one way of breaking the patterns and expectations of discursive thought was to seek irrational or random sequences or juxtapositions of things. The mind inevitably seeks to make connections between things, and with an "irrational" or even random assemblage of ideas, the normal expectations will be disrupted, so that similarities and connections will be felt which have always existed but which are normally filtered out by the demands of different criteria and the alignment of the two ideas into more functional categories.

Intellectually, this can be a rather violent phenomenon and experience (as was so often evidenced in Dada and Surrealist practice), but one that creates cracks in the surface of thought through which glimpses of the deep truths of myth may emerge, released by the unconscious activity of mind. (Indeed, the violent rents in the surface of Clyfford Still's images can be seen as visual metaphors of just this kind of experience.)

This element in mystical thinking and in the thinking of the Abstract Expressionists was intensified by their immersion in the Symbolist poets; and, like the poets, they believed that these invisible and very potent relations between ideas could be expressed only in a new and different kind of language. More important, it must be a language without a familiarity or charm that might seduce. Beauty, as Newman said often, will ultimately lead both artist and viewer away from what really matters:

Beauty . . . is nothing more than a manifest of taste, for the manipulation of good color, pure shapes, good composition can only affect the sensuous nature of man. It is a type of virtuoso painting, and the logical outcome of such an esthetic must be a virtuoso act where men of skill and taste, like skillful violinists play with color, line and shape. . . . They have reduced painting to an interpretative [and, for Newman, an anecdotal] art.[6]

In this new tragedy that is playing itself out on a Greek-like stage under a new sense of fate that we have ourselves created, shall we artists make the same error as the Greek sculptors and play with an art of over-refinement, an art of quality, of sensibility, of beauty? Let us rather, like the Greek writers, tear the tragedy to shreds.[7]

The same point was made by Motherwell[8] and also by Clyfford Still in an interview at the Albright-Know Gallery, Buffalo, in which he is reported as saying that he consciously avoided using color in a sensuous or beautiful way."[9]

The new language needed to be an abstract one, so that its forms or terms could be severed from familiar and obstructive associations. Even abstracted images were dangerous in this respect unless one was able to neutralize those associations by generating other, more powerful ones. Again, the disruption of normal juxtapositions might be sufficient to do that, as Gottlieb hints in his remarks about his use of pictographs:

Knowledge of science, of history, of history of art—the significance we attach to them—is a complex of all knowledge about things. Vision gives us little understanding of them. When I say I am reaching for a totality of vision, I mean that I take the things I know—hand, nose, arm—and use them in my paintings after separating them from their associations as anatomy. I use them as a totality of what they mean to me. It's a primitive method, and a primitive necessity of expressing, without learning how to do so by conventional ways. . . . It puts us at the beginning of seeing.[10]

Of course, many of the Abstract Expressionists, most notably Pollock, Still, Newman, and to a lesser extent Rothko, sought to dispense with forms altogether, a move which would obviously lessen the danger of unwanted associations, and they tended to resist interpretations which saw their work in terms of associative abstractions. Newman said, "These paintings are not 'abstractions,' nor do they depict some 'pure' idea. . . . They contain no depictive allusions."[11] and Motherwell said, "They are absolutely metaphors, not descriptions."[12]

We shall return to this eagerness to avoid depictive symbols later, but it is obvious that one of the reasons, at least, for avoiding them was that it was some insurance against slipping into a language that operated through familiar, associative relations. In theoretical terms, the most favored way of developing a nondiscursive language was through conceptual collage and nondepictive symbols. But there was another belief about the nature of mystical thinking which made the need for a nonrational language even more acute, and that was the ineffable nature of the fundamental truths that mysticism sought to attain.

Essentially, these were untranslatable, not simply because of their profundity (and how to explain something important in everyday language and still retain its sense of importance?) but also because of their complexity: not, however, a complexity which, with patience, could be explicitly and discursively described, but one which was immediate and multidimensional and which was grasped in this fashion, or not at all. Ordinary language was regarded as not sufficiently sophisticated to articulate the nuances, tensions, and seriousness of the feeling and experiences myth and mysticism dealt with (one reason, no doubt, for the invention of poetry). As Gottlieb and Rothko said, "Would you have us present this abstract concept with all its complicated feelings by means of a boy and girl lightly tripping?"[13] Such fundamentals could not be described—merely expressed; and this was likely to happen only through the (perhaps chance) ignition of two disparates, which might create objective correlatives, or metaphors of feeling.

And finally, mysticism explained and concentrated the power of myth into magical symbols. In primitive societies and some contemporary non-Western societies myth usually has quite a strong component of (supposed) magic. In myth and ritual this most often manifests itself in the form of images, symbols, dances, songs, or pronouncements, which are thought to have the power to ward off evil spirits, retribution, and natural disasters, or to invoke certain states or events. For example, the image of an upheld hand, palm facing outward, is still today, frequently seen painted on the walls of houses in some Arab communities, where it is believed to hold back evil and disaster. Sometimes such signs, rituals, and utterances are performed to elicit an event normally outside human control (or at least thought to be), and sometimes they are engaged in to induce a certain (beneficial) state in the performer, or to place the performer in communication with a higher power or being; recited mantras are an obvious example of the former, while the pronouncement of the god name "Om" in Hindu mysticism is a case of the latter. In Bali, communication with the Barong beast is symbolized and actualized by touching the forehead against the tongue of the huge Barong maskhead (worn by a villager), and this contact brings each of the trace dancers in the famous Kris dance-drama back to normal consciousness.

The assertion of magic in such events is, of course, a description of, or an explanation for, a certain kind of causality which bypasses the natural laws of physics and behavior in ways not understood; by definition, as soon as these "abnormal," or alternative, chains of causality are understood, they cease to be regarded as magic. Similarly, it is not known why some people and some objects come to have these powers. In some societies and among some people, this "alternative" causality is simply attributed to some supernatural "magic" force, whether a being or not, in which case it is conceived of as an overriding causal agent which simply sets aside, or perhaps short-circuits, normal causal sequences. In Western societies the explanation for unexpected causal reactions, and the peculiar potency of certain images, is more often explained in terms of subterranean psychological and psychic principles the full operations of which are likewise not known.

But whatever might be the explanation offered in different societies for the power of a mythic symbol, when it comes to the making and understanding of art, a much more interesting question concerns the process of operation of such symbols. In terms of philosophy of mind, Cassirer's description of the process has a great deal of intuitive plausibility and certainly seems to sum up how the artists thought about it. On Cassirer's account, the most striking and important characteristic of the primitive mind was its ability and inclination to suspend discursive, relational, sequential thinking, and to fix the attention in time on a single idea:

[In] mythic ideation . . . the mental view is . . . compressed; it is, so to speak, distilled into a single point. Only by this process of distillation is the particular essence found and extracted which is to bear the special accent of "significance." All light is concentrated in one focal point of "meaning," while everything that lies outside these focal points of verbal or mythic conception remains practically invisible.[14]

Cassirer goes on to point out that in logical thinking, when one thing is linked to another, the two things or ideas retain the separate and different identities even though they are subsumed, for some purpose, under a more extensive, third category. Thus, for example, a ship's hold and an ashtray can both be correctly described as containers, though in exploring the concepts to discover this truth, one must be aware of both the similarities *and* the differences—the differences, if you like, which entitle one object to be called an ash tray and the other a ship's hold. The mind hovers from one set of information to another. But in mythic thinking, an entirely different thought process occurs in which one thing is thought of as actually becoming the other; the differences are ignored, the distinction between categories is obliterated, and the one becomes a *part* of the other.[15]

Hence the very powerful principle in mythic thinking of *pars pro toto,* in which the part takes on all the characteristics and powers of the whole:

Whoever has brought any part of a whole into his power has thereby acquired power, in the magical sense, over the whole itself. What significance the part in question may have in the structure and coherence of the whole, what function it fulfills, is relatively unimportant—the mere fact that it is or has been a part, that it has been connected with the whole, no matter how casually, is enough to lend it the full significance and power of that greater unity. For instance, to hold magical dominion over another person's body one need only attain possession of his pared nails or cut-off hair, his spittle or his excrement. . . . Most of what is known as "magic of analogy" springs from the same fundamental attitude; and the very nature of this magic shows that the concept in question is not one of mere analogy, but of a real identification. If, for instance, a rain-making ceremony consists of sprinkling water on the ground to attract the rain, or rain-stopping magic is made by pouring water on red hot stones where it is consumed amid hissing noise, both ceremonies owe their true magical sense to the fact that the rain is not just represented, but is felt to be really present in each drop of water. The rain as a mythic "power"; the "daemon" of the rain is actually there, whole and undivided, in the sprinkled or evaporated water, and is thus amenable to magical control.[16]

In ancient Hebraic society, as well as in many others, punishment of the whole community, or of one part of it, for the sins of another part, obviously derives from this principle of *pars pro toto*; it is also clearly the foundation for the belief in the long Byzantine tradition of icon-making that, in a very important sense, the copy of the image of the saints or of Christ becomes the image itself: thus the icons have the real presence of the saints themselves.

The Abstract Expressionists were well aware of this element in primitive and mythic thinking, and not surprisingly it affected their own attitudes to symbols in art. Over and over again one comes upon the artists insisting that their symbols do not *represent* certain feelings and thoughts but express them *directly,* and this is frequently contrasted with symbols which in some sense illustrate. Barnett Newman, for example, in explaining his series of paintings *Stations of the Cross,* points out that the subject matter is the terrible feeling of alienation in Christ's cry "My God, why hast though forsaken me?" "The cry of Jesus," he said, "was not a complaint but a declaration of the human condition. What comes through is the voice of Jesus rather than the anecdotes."[17] And in case one should be misled by the term "anecdotes" into thinking of a nonabstract, figurative symbol, it should be noted that Newman regarded Kandinsky's use of color correspondences as basically representational in attitude: a particular color "stood for" a particular feeling but did not embody that feeling itself—it did not directly communicate it.[18]

This idea of direct expression rather than "illustration" is echoed by the other artists. Pollock insisted on this in his work: "They're all direct painting"; "Yes, the modern artist is expressing his feelings rather than illustrating"; "I paint it, I don't illustrate it."[19] And, from the film

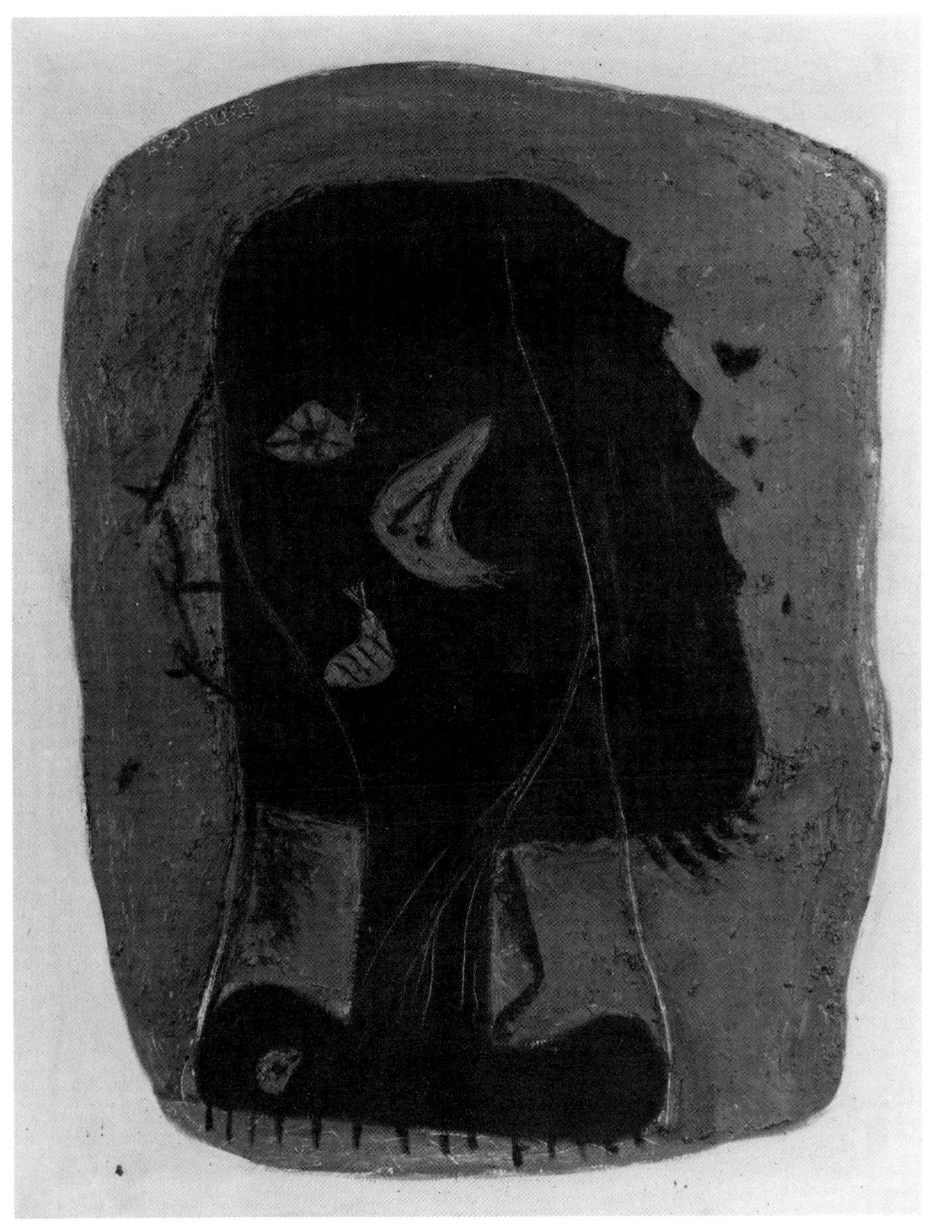

ADOLPH GOTTLIEB, Rape of Persephone (1943).
MEDIUM: Oil   SIZE: 33 1/2″ × 20 1/2″   CREDIT: Collection,
Annalee Newman.

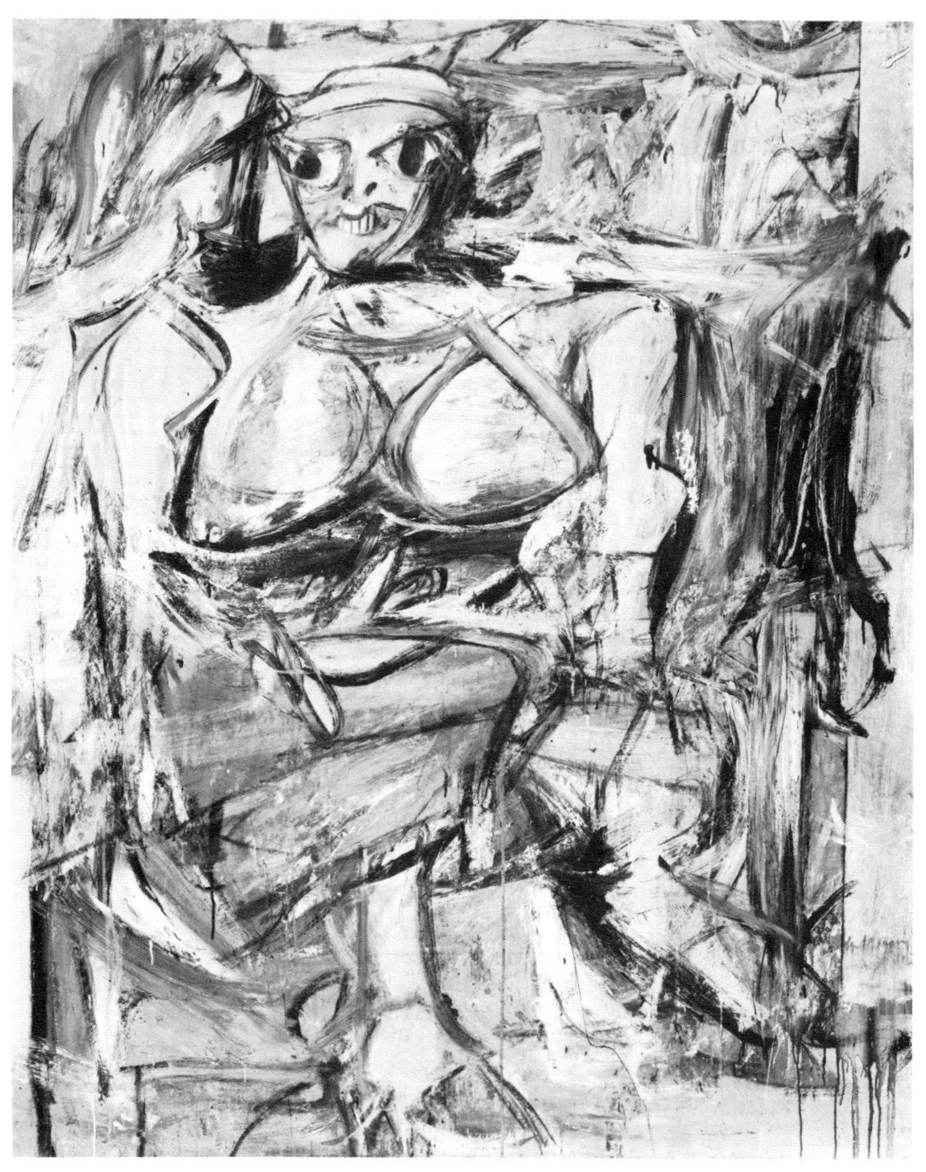

WILLEM DE KOONING, Woman, I (1950–52).
MEDIUM: Oil on canvas   SIZE: 6'3 7/8" × 58" (192.7 cm. × 147.3 cm.)
CREDIT: Collection, Museum of Modern Art, New York. Purchase.

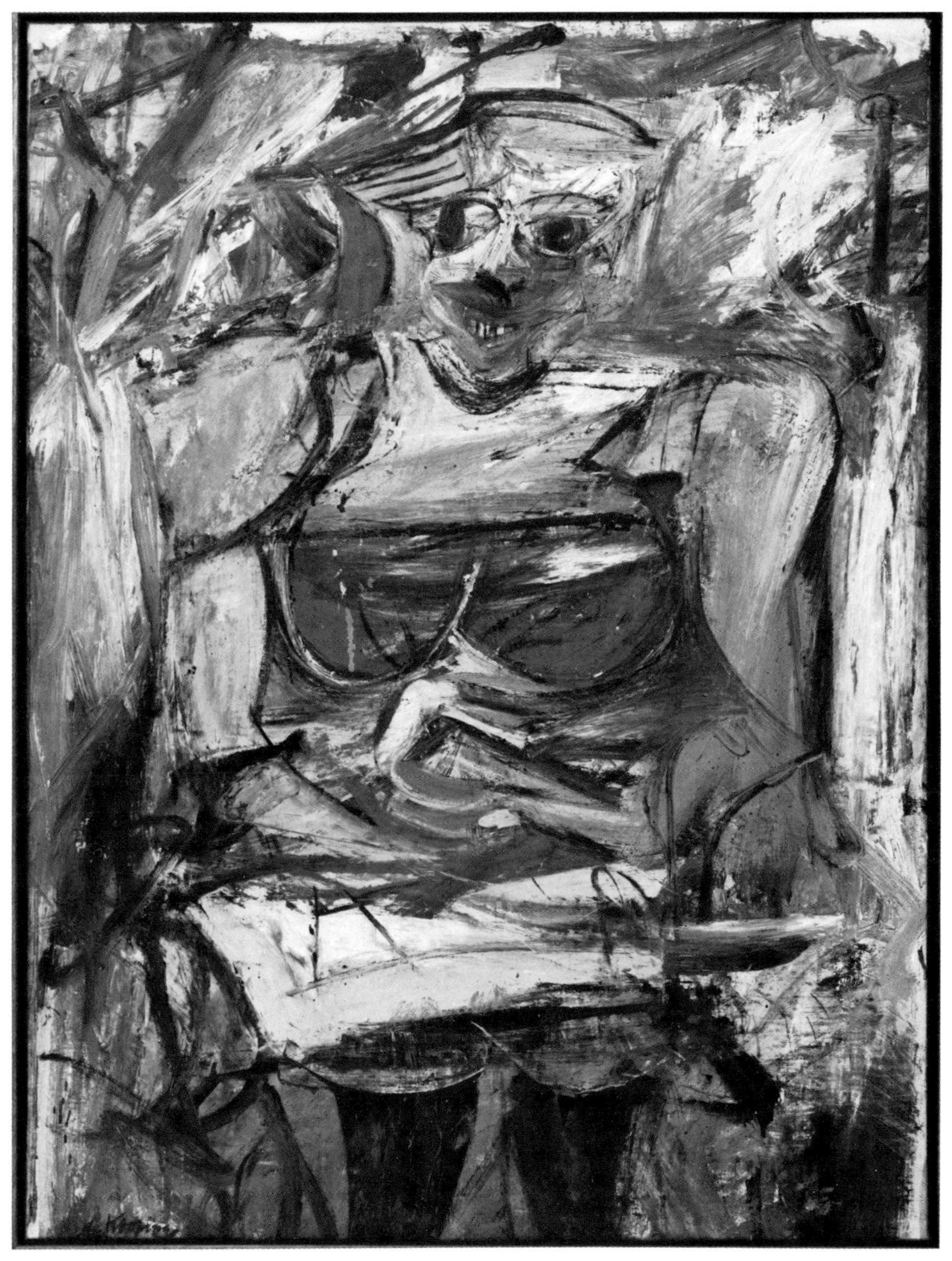

WILLEM DE KOONING, Woman, V (1952–53).

MEDIUM: Oil and charcoal on canvas   SIZE: 155 cm. × 114 cm.
CREDIT: Australian National Gallery, Canberra.

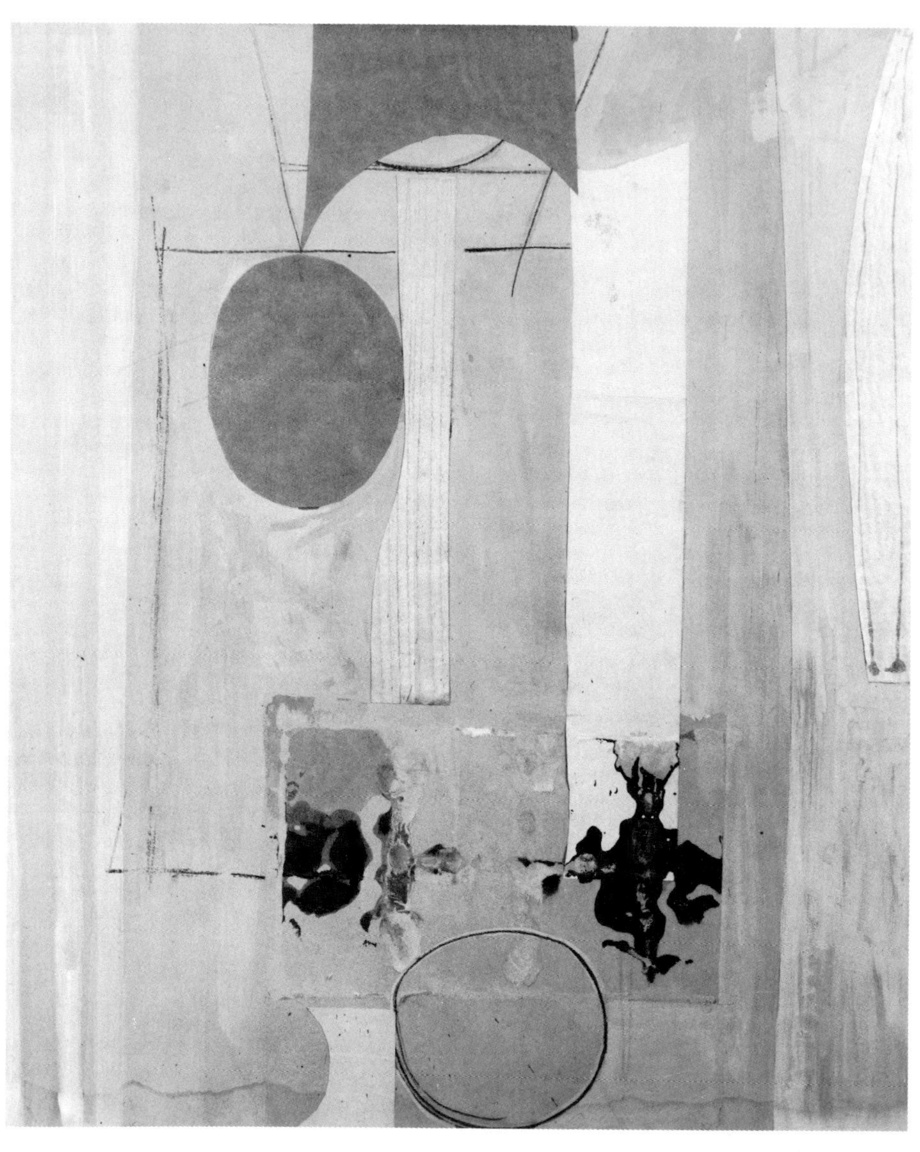

ROBERT MOTHERWELL, Mallarmé's Swan (1944).

MEDIUM: Collage using gouache, crayon, and paper on cardboard
SIZE: 43 1/2″ × 35 1/2″   CREDIT: Contemporary Collection, Cleveland
Museum of Art.

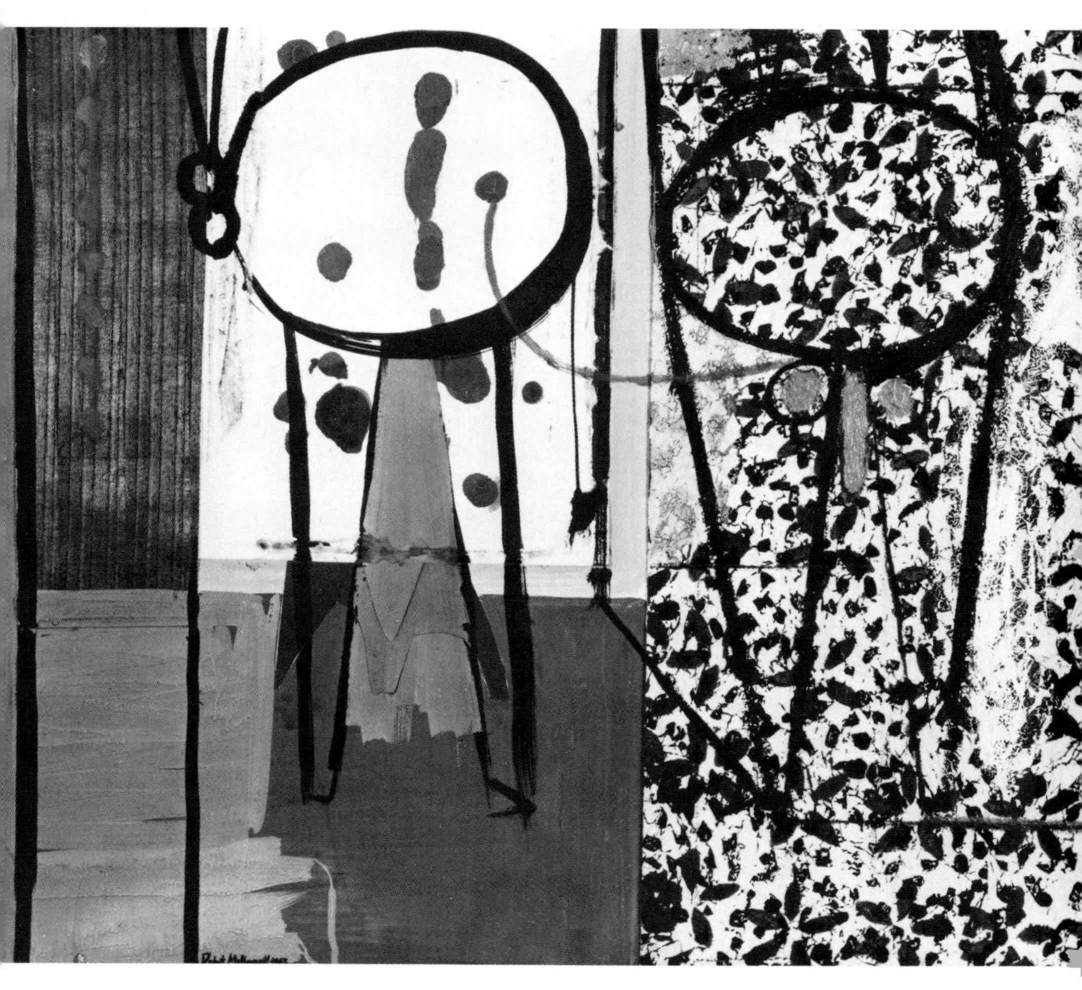

ROBERT MOTHERWELL, Pancho Villa, Dead and Alive (1943).
MEDIUM: Gouache and oil with collage on cardboard   SIZE: 28″ × 35 7/8″
(71.1 cm. × 91.1 cm.)   CREDIT: Collection, Museum of Modern Art, New York.
Purchase.

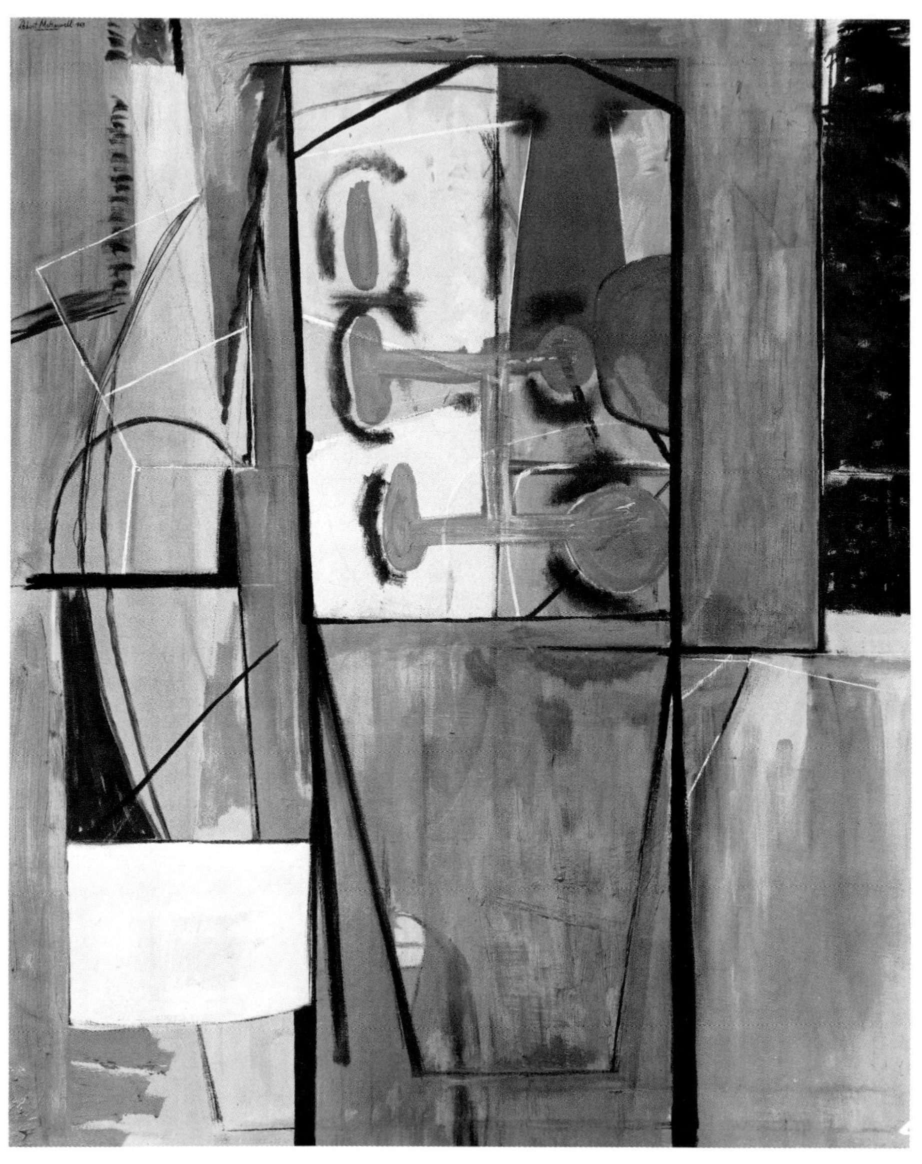

ROBERT MOTHERWELL, Personage (Dead Personage) (1943).
MEDIUM: Oil on canvas   SIZE: 48″ × 38″   CREDIT: Collection, Norton Gallery
and School of Art, West Palm Beach, Florida.

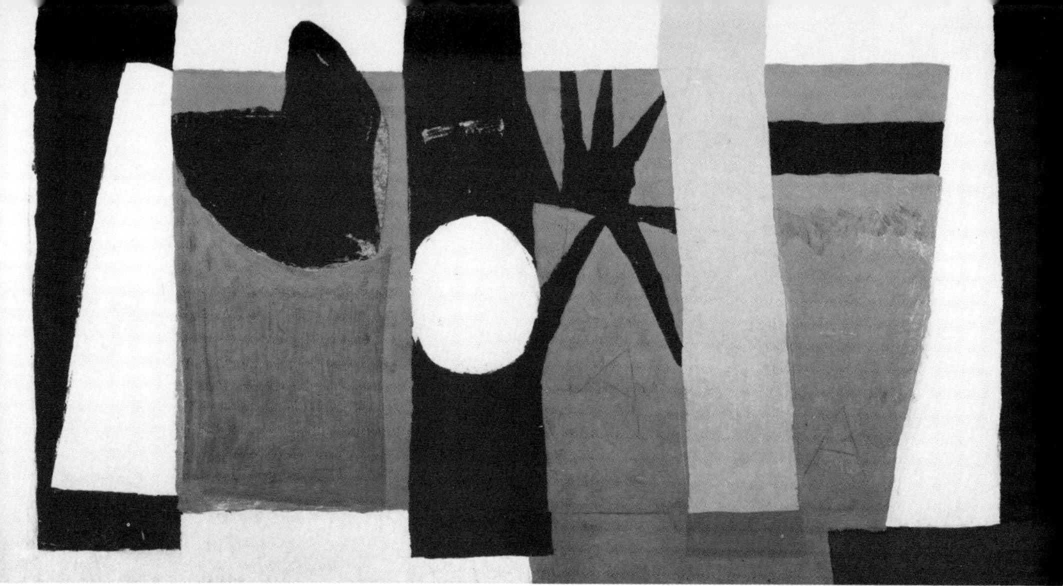

ROBERT MOTHERWELL, The Voyage (1949).

MEDIUM: Oil and tempera on paper mounted on composition board   SIZE: 48″ × 7′10″ (122 cm. × 238.8 cm.)   CREDIT: Collection, Museum of Modern Art, New York. Gift of Mrs. John D. Rockefeller 3d.

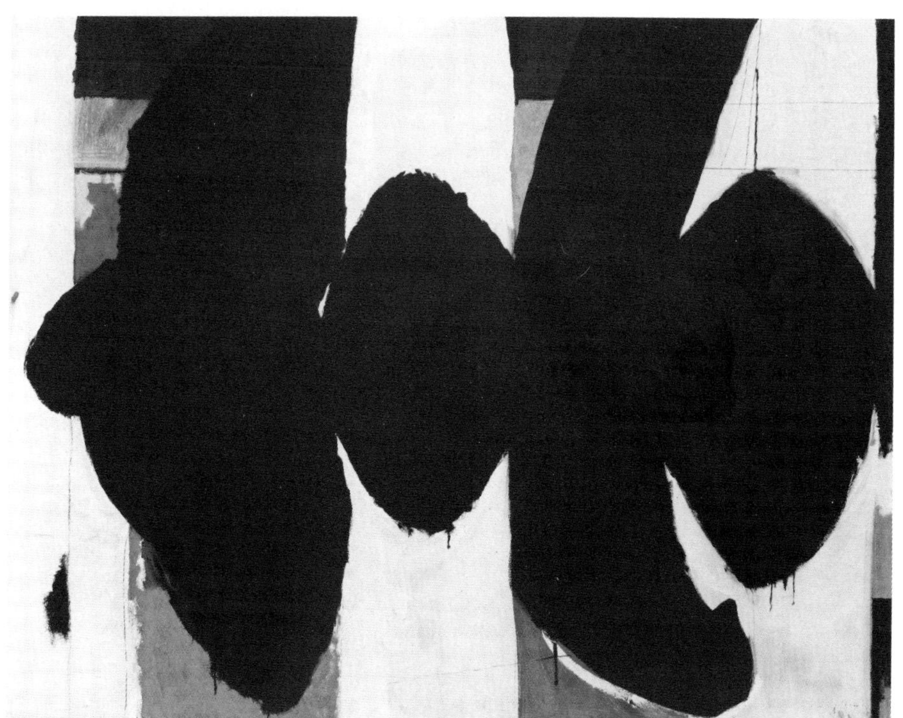

ROBERT MOTHERWELL, Elegy to the Spanish Republic XXXIV (1953–54).

MEDIUM: Oil on canvas   SIZE: 80″ × 100″   CREDIT: Albright-Knox Art Gallery, Buffalo, New York. Gift of Seymour H. Knox, 1957.

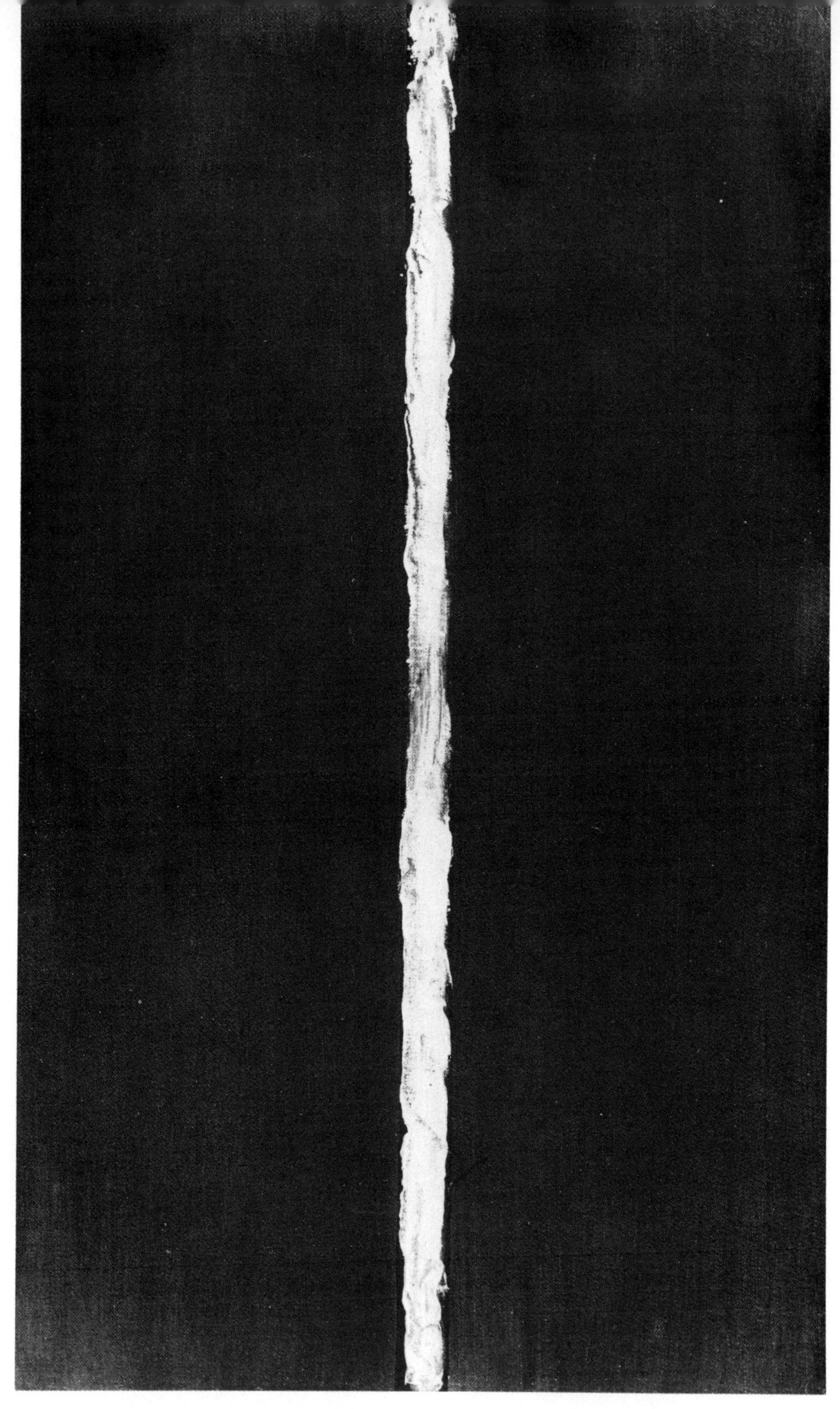

BARNETT NEWMAN, Onement I (1948).
MEDIUM: Oil SIZE: 27″ × 16″ CREDIT: Collection, Annalee Newman.

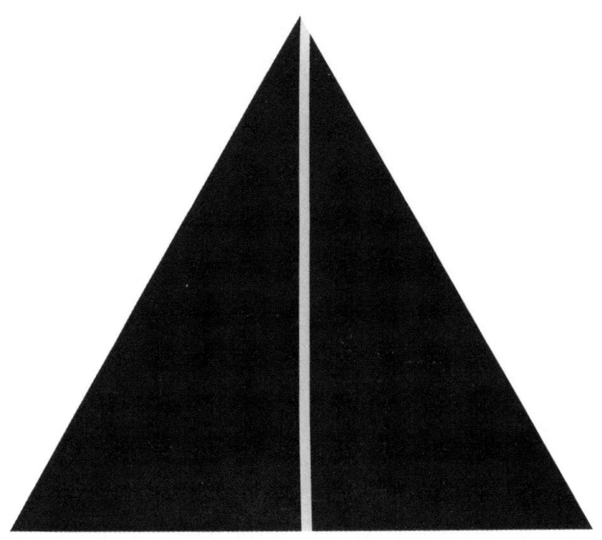

BARNETT NEWMAN, Jericho (1968–69).
MEDIUM: Acrylic   SIZE: 114″ × 106″   CREDIT: Museé National d'Art Moderne, Centre Georges Pompidou, Paris.

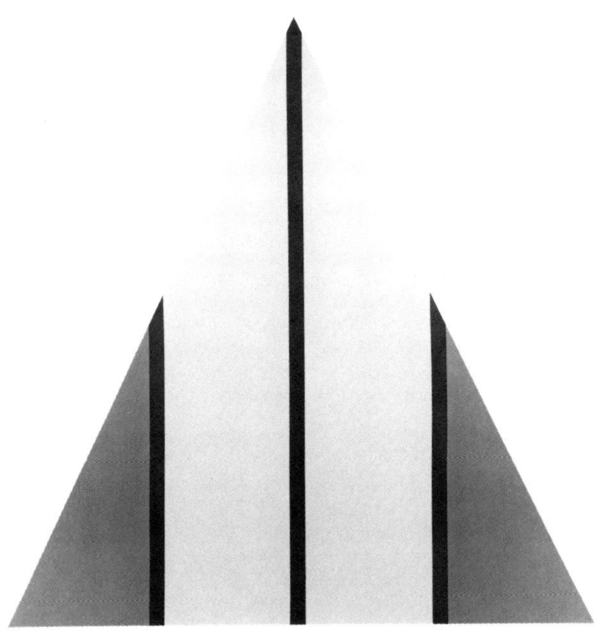

BARNETT NEWMAN, Chartres (1969).
MEDIUM: Acrylic   SIZE: 120″ × 102″   CREDIT: Collection, Mr. and Mrs. S. I. Newhouse, Jr.

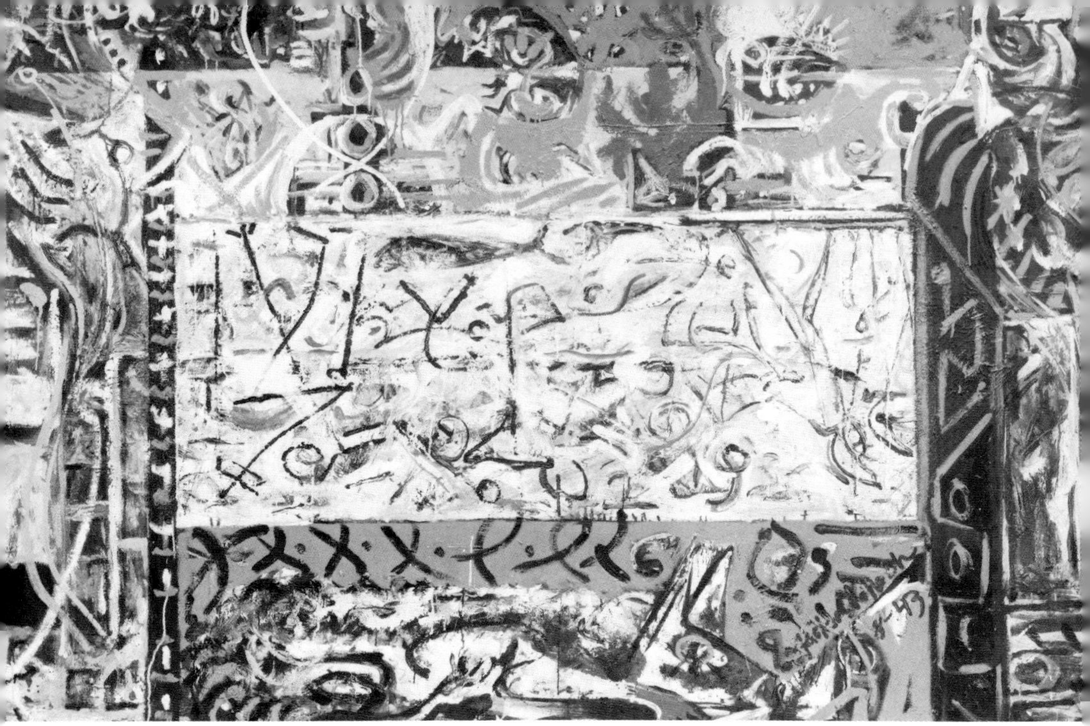

JACKSON POLLOCK, Guardians of the Secret (1943).
MEDIUM: Oil on canvas   SIZE: 48 3/8″ × 75 3/8″ (122.9 cm. × 191.4 cm.)
CREDIT: San Francisco Museum of Modern Art, Albert M. Bender Collection, Albert M. Bender Bequest Fund Purchase.

JACKSON POLLOCK, The She-Wolf (1943).
MEDIUM: Oil, gouache, and plaster on canvas   SIZE: 41 7/8″ × 67″ (106.4 cm. × 170.2 cm).   CREDIT: Collection, Museum of Modern Art, New York. Purchase.

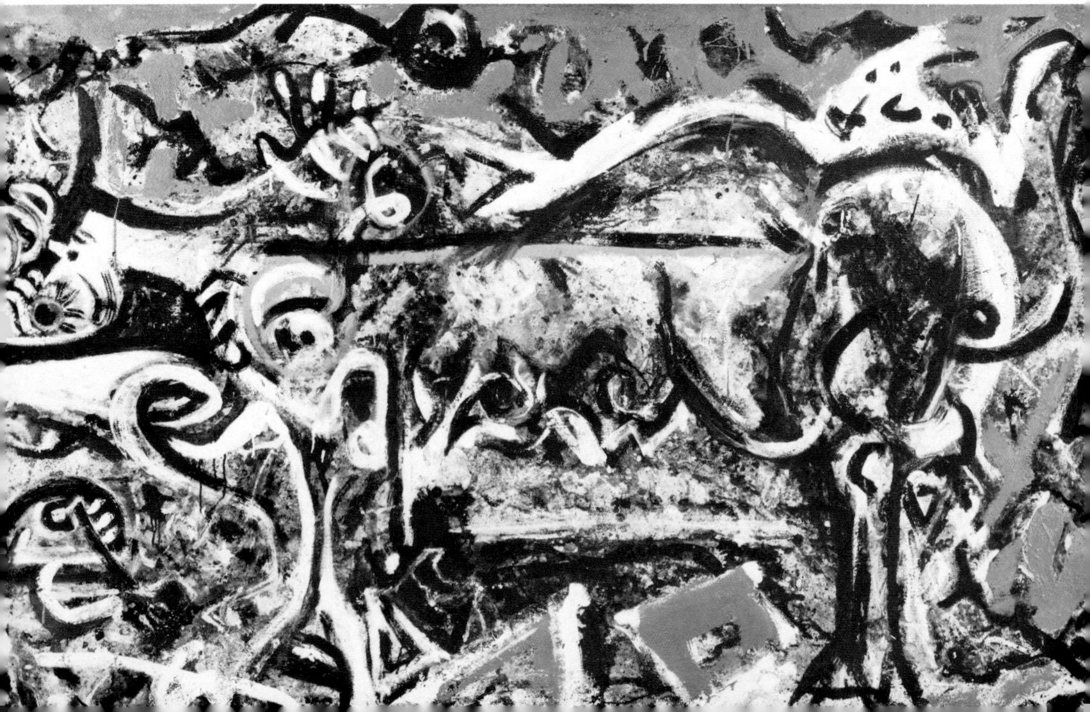

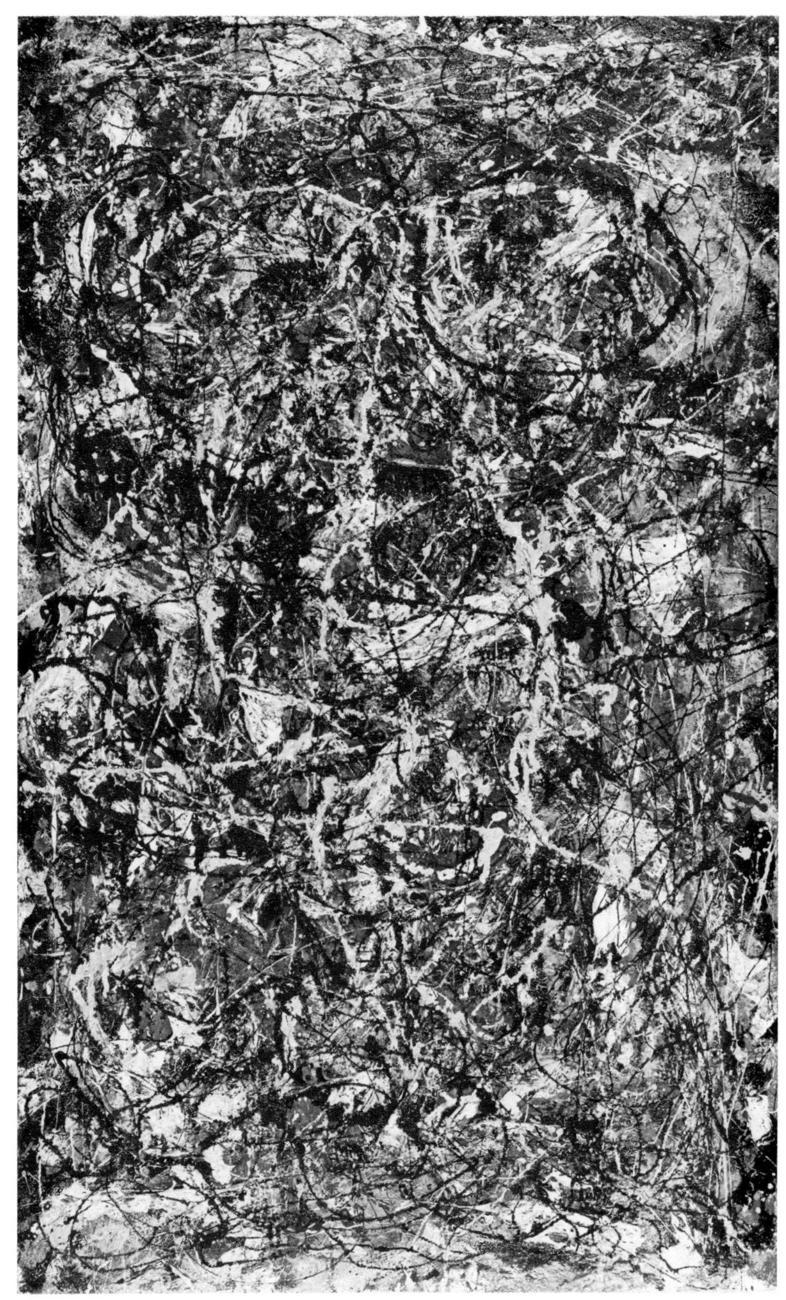

JACKSON POLLOCK, Full Fathom Five (1947).
MEDIUM: Oil on canvas with nails, tacks, buttons, key, coins, cigarettes, matches, etc.   SIZE: 50 7/8″ × 30 1/8″ (129.2 cm. × 76.5 cm).   CREDIT: Collection, Museum of Modern Art, New York. Gift of Peggy Guggenheim.

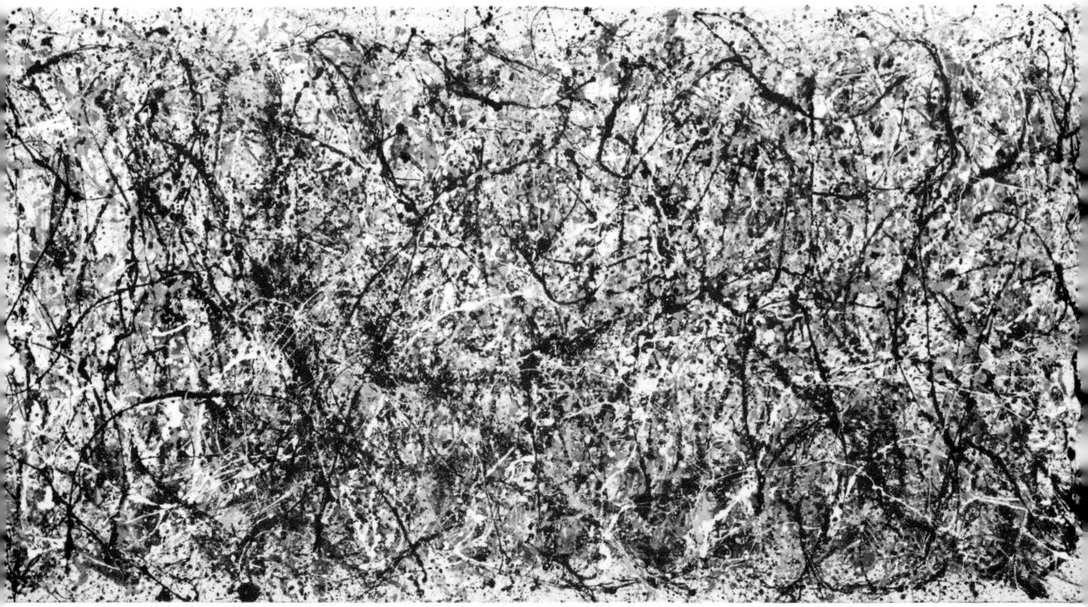

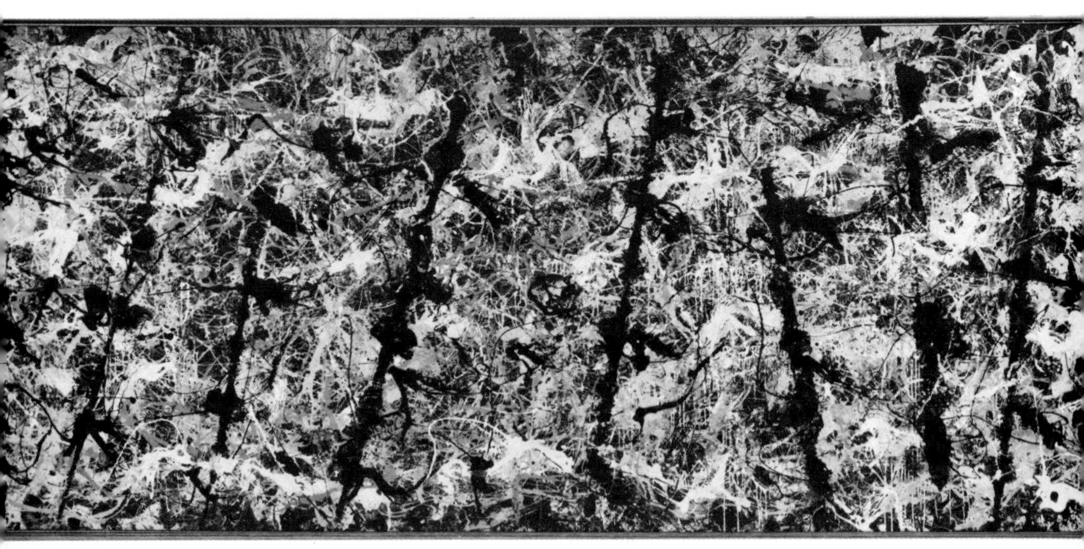

JACKSON POLLOCK, One (Number 31, 1950) (1950).
MEDIUM: Oil and enamel paint on canvas   SIZE: 8'10" × 17'5 5/8" (269.5 cm. × 530.8 cm).   CREDIT: Collection, Museum of Modern Art, New York. Sidney Janis Collection Fund (by exchange).

JACKSON POLLOCK, Blue Poles (1952).
MEDIUM: Oil, synthetic polymer paint, and aluminium paint on canvas
SIZE: 211 cm. × 487.5 cm.   CREDIT: Australian National Gallery, Canberra.

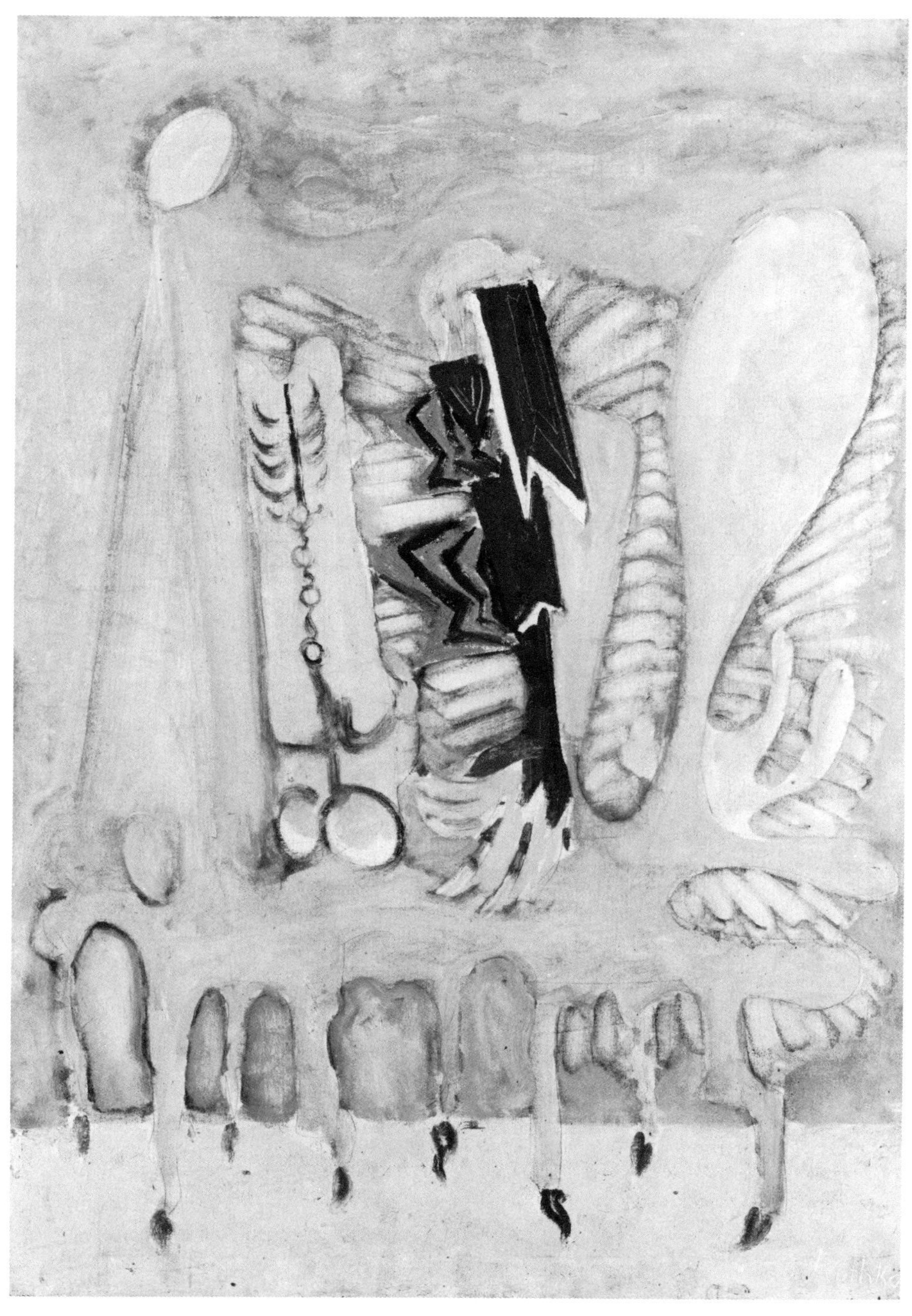

MARK ROTHKO, The Syrian Bull (1943).
MEDIUM: Oil on canvas   SIZE: 39 1/2″ × 27 1/2″
CREDIT: Collection, Annalee Newman.

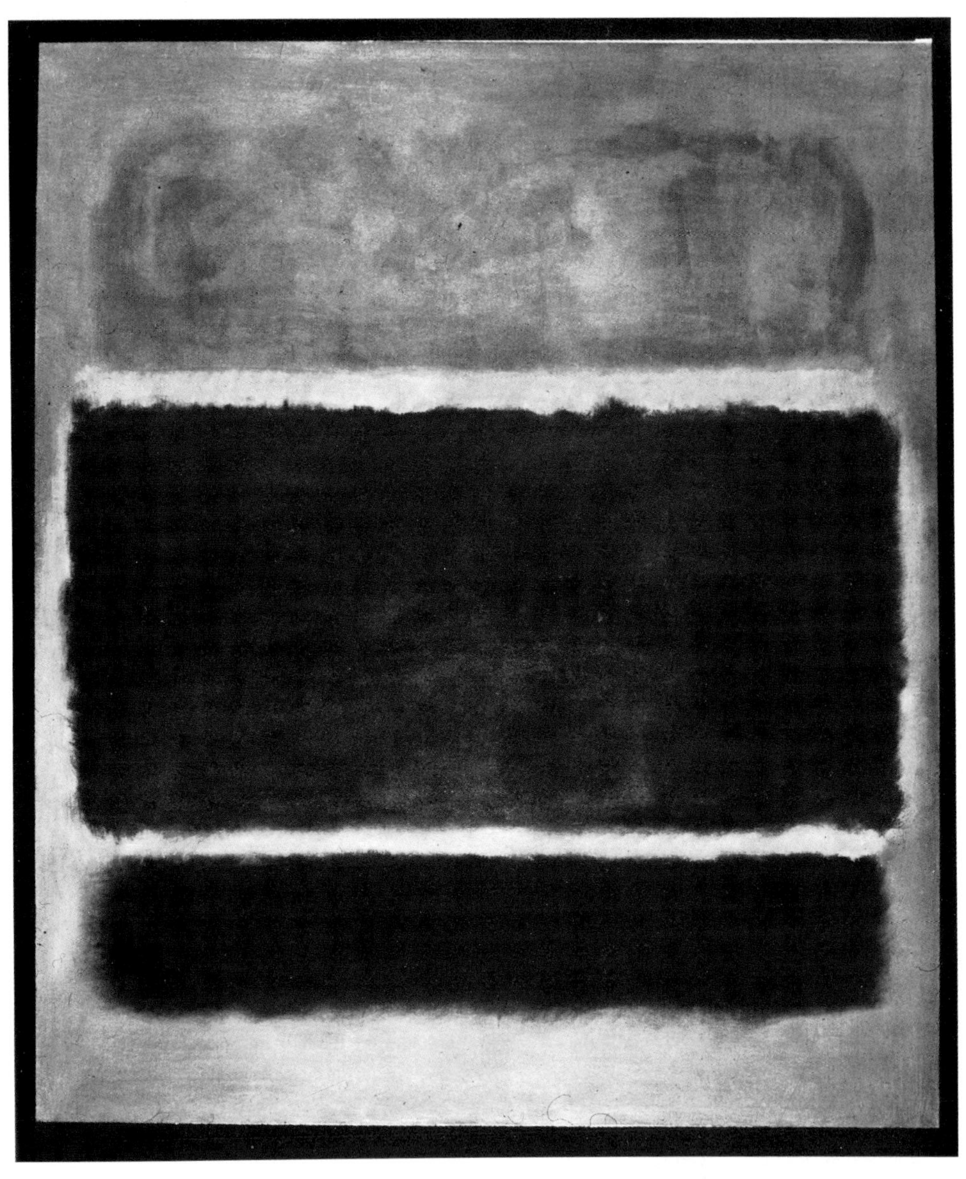

MARK ROTHKO, Brown Black on Maroon (1957).
MEDIUM: Oil on canvas   SIZE: 91 1/2″ × 76″
CREDIT: Australian National Gallery, Canberra.

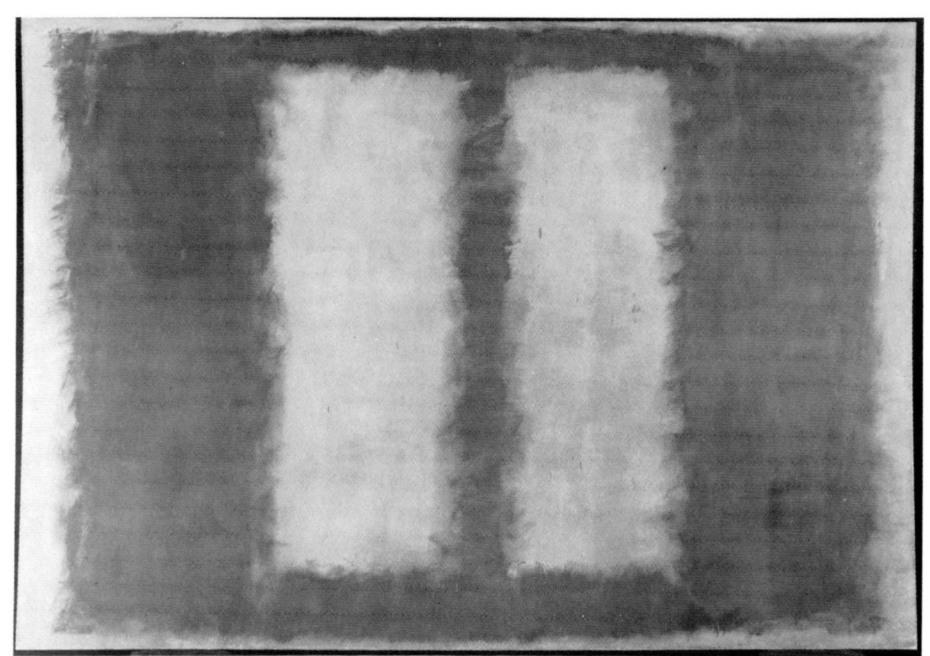

MARK ROTHKO, Black on Maroon (1958).
MEDIUM: Oil on canvas   SIZE: 105″ × 144″   CREDIT: Tate Gallery, London.

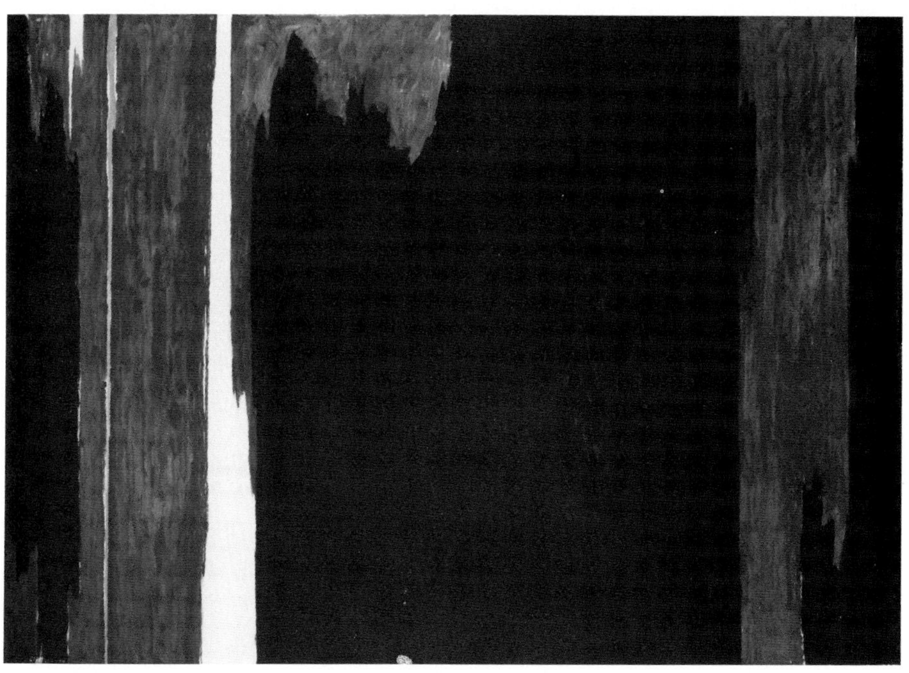

CLYFFORD STILL, 1954 (1954).
MEDIUM: Oil on canvas   SIZE: 113 1/2″ × 156″
CREDIT: Albright-Knox Art Gallery, Buffalo, New York.

CLYFFORD STILL, 1957-D, No. 1 (1957).
MEDIUM: Oil on canvas   CREDIT: Albright-Knox Art Gallery, Buffalo, New York.

of the artist working: . . . "I want to express my feelings rather than illustrate them." "My painting is direct."[20] Philip Guston wrote, of his *White Painting No 1,* "The desire for direct expression finally became so strong that even the interval necessary to reach back to the palette beside me became too long."[21] The need for direct expression becomes so strong because what it aims to produce is the real thing, rather than its mimesis-symbol. As de Kooning put it: "I paint this way because I keep putting more and more things in it—drama, anger, pain, love, a figure, a horse, my ideas about space. Through your eyes it again *becomes* an emotion or an idea."[22] [my italics]

The symbol is, then, not merely a denotative sign which in some way refers to, or points one toward, that which it stands for; rather, in the manner of *pars pro toto,* it takes on all the characteristics of its referent, and, in a fundamental sense, becomes what it is a sign for. This, of course, is an ancient tradition even in Western art: it was a belief that provoked a response of iconoclasm in early Christian times and that survived in the form of Byzantine icons. Different artists had different ways of pointing out the iconic function of symbols, but Newman, perhaps, was the one who expressed it most often. As mentioned earlier, he made the point eloquently in his account of American Indian art: "Ideographic—Representing ideas directly and not through the medium of their names, To [the Kwakiutl Indian] a shape was a living thing, a vehicle for an abstract thought-complex, a carrier of the awesome feelings he felt before the terror of the unknowable. The abstract shape was, therefore, real rather than a formal 'abstraction' of a visual fact."[23] One finds exactly this thought expressed when he said of his own works:

These paintings are not "abstractions," nor do they depict some "pure" idea. They are specific, and separate embodiments of feeling, to be experienced, each picture for itself. They contain no depictive allusions.

Full of restrained passion, their poignancy is revealed in each concentrated image.[24]

It is because the symbol directly partakes of and expresses the thing it refers to, that it is both nondescriptive and essentially nondescribable. It is nondescriptive because in order to describe something (or be an illustration of it, to put it another way), it must obviously be separate and different from the thing it describes. Since the sort of symbol we are dealing with is held to be *of the same substance as* the thing it symbolizes, and just *one part* of it, then obviously it cannot be a description or illustration of itself. In the same way, while a portrait is a description of a saint, an icon is not a portrait of the saint, because it actually *embodies* the saint.

As far as being essentially nondescribable is concerned, at a certain level the symbol is, of course, describable—to the extent that any one thing can be described in a medium other than its own. But this is precisely the point about "direct expression," that it rejected a "translation" or "approximation" as unacceptable *because* it is always lacking—one step behind the real thing—and insisted on the presence of the real thing itself.

These might seem like esoteric and highly theoretical points, but they were in fact important elements in the Abstract Expressionist attitude to symbol. Hence we have the dual insistence so often, on both the nondescriptive nature of the symbol and on its ineffability. On this, Gottlieb wrote:

Now in 1955, as in the early forties and before, I am still concerned with the problem of projecting intangible and elusive images that seem to me to have meaning in terms of feeling. The important thing is to transfer the image to the canvas as it appears to me, without distortion. To modify the image would be to falsify it, therefore I must accept it as it is. My criterion is the integrity of the projection.[25]

These ideas were echoed by Philip Guston, when, using the analogy of a violin sonata, he said that one listened because one *kept on* grasping for an articulation of what it was an image *of.*[26] Catching at a similar thought from a different direction, Bradley Walker Tomlin wrote that the miracle that an artist has wrought slips out of his grasp as soon as he feels that he has understood its heart, its "inner logic":

Moved deeply by a painting, the spectator may say, the artist has convinced me. . . . One can believe in paintings, as one can believe in miracles, for paintings, like miracles, possess an inner logic which is inescapable. But this again is to believe after the fact, which is merely to believe in the concrete.

What does the artist himself believe in, having produced his miracle? Does he feel that he is not in the clear, that in the future the canvases will be solved without pain? . . . Does the artist find that the seemingly effortless structure, which he has evolved with total clarity, tends on repetition to escape him? That in spite of the production of masterpieces, art itself remains infinitely mysterious and that the work in progress is merely a kind of hall rack on which he has hung various nicely woven articles of clothing.[27]

For Clyfford Still, ineffability was a fundamental part of his art. In 1944, he wrote, of his work: "Ultimately, there will be no explanation, logically, whatever the psychologists or psychoanalysts may pretend. Their tools are too clumsy and utterly meaningless. Their tools are dead—are death itself and one does not comprehend life in death. Their instruments are negation itself."[28] On another occasion he wrote: "I'm not interested in illustrating my time. . . . I have no brief for signs or symbols or literary allusions in painting. They are just crutches for illustrators . . . . The sublime [is] a paramount consideration in my studies and work from my earliest student days. In essence it is most elusive of capture or definition."[29] So direct was the expression of the symbol, and so far removed from depiction, that Still, along with many of his colleagues, felt constrained to describe art not as a picture but as an act (though not in the sense that Rosenberg said), thereby stripping away the distancing and neutralizing effect of translation. "We are now committed to an unqualified act, not illustrating outworn myths or contemporary alibis," he wrote.[30]

Belief in the ineffability of the symbol is both expressed and explained in Robert Motherwell's statements that his symbols do not depict but are metaphors of the things they express. Of his *Spanish Elegies* he said, "The *Spanish Elegies* are not 'political' but my private insistence that a terrible death happened that should not be forgot. . . . The pictures are also general metaphors of the contrast between life and death, and their interrelation."[31] In another interview, with David Sylvester, he explains this further:

Sylvester: So, the painting—the kind of painting you do, though abstract, is in some way a metaphor of an attitude to reality, of a feeling about reality? Motherwell: Mmm, yes, painting is exactly a metaphor for reality. I do think there are references. I think the so-called "abstractness" of modern art is not that it is about abstract things, but that it's an art really in the tradition of French Symbolist poetry, which is to say, an art that refuses to spell everything out.[32]

The idea of visual metaphors of feeling is explained by Motherwell in terms of relational structures of the mind, carrying, perhaps, echoes of Rudolf Arnheim's isomorphic structures of expression.[33] In "Beyond the Aesthetic," Motherwell wrote:

Structures are found in the interaction of the body-mind and the external world; and the body-mind is active and aggressive in finding them. . . .

The passions are a kind of thirst, inexorable and intense, for certain feelings or felt states. To find or invest "objects" (which are, more strictly speaking, relational structures) whose felt quality satisfies the passions—*that* for me is the activity of the artist, an activity which does not cease even in sleep. No wonder the artist is constantly placing and displacing, relating and rupturing relations: his task is to find a complex of qualities whose feeling is just right— veering toward the unknown and chaos, yet ordered and related in order to be apprehended.[34]

Thus are metaphors made, and this idea is taken up by Harold Rosenberg when explaining the function of images in the work of Hans Hofman and other Abstract Expressionists:

With regard to the tensions it is capable of setting up in our bodies, the medium of any art is an extension of the physical world; a stroke of pigment, for example, "works" within us in the same way as a bridge across the Hudson. For the unseen universe that inhabits us, an accidental blot or splash of paint may thus assume an equivalence to the profoundest happening. . . .

If the ultimate subject matter of all art is the artist's psychic state or tension . . . that state (e.g. grief) may be represented through an abstract sign.[35]

Metaphors essentially condense meaning, and the idea that the symbol is a simple, condensed bearer of very complex truths was a strongly held one among the artists. As Motherwell put it: "The function of the aesthetic instead becomes that of a medium, a *means* for getting at the infinite background of feeling in order to condense it into an object of perception."[36] And as Newman said of his own "embodiments of feeling," "Full of restrained passion, their poignancy is revealed in each concentrated image."[37] Robert Goldwater, friend of the Abstract Expressionists, picks out this tendency to condense and simplify, as the single common assumption in forms of primitivism:

This is the assumption that externals, whether those of a social or cultural group, of individual psychology, or of the physical world, are intricate and complicated and *as such not desirable*. It is the assumption that any reaching under the surface, if only it is carried far enough and proceeds according to the proper method, will reveal something "simple" and basic which, because of its very fundamentality and simplicity, will be more emotionally compelling than the superficial variations of the surface; and finally that the qualities of simplicity and basicness are things to be valued in and for themselves: In other words, it is the assumption that the further one goes back—historically, psychologically, or aesthetically—the simpler things become; and that because they are simpler they are more profound, more important, and more valuable.[38]

Certainly, for the Abstract Expressionists, this is true. From primitivism and mystical thinking they took a symbol which was simple and profound, condensing, as it did, all the complexities and significances of human experience. It was powerful not only because of its simplicity, but because it directly expressed, instead of merely depicting (either in abstract or figurative terms) the truths it condensed; and, in directly expressing, the part became the whole—the symbol became activated with the living presence of the thing it expressed. Being simple, profound, direct, and nondepictive (derived from an inner conviction, a "ritualistic will"[39] not from a visual fact), the symbol was, of necessity, abstract.

Thus was born the Abstract Expressionists' theory of the abstract mystic symbol. As a theory it was coherent and explicitly articulated. But as a theory it still required individual insights and acts of creativity to translate it into art. The move from theoria to praxis was now about to be performed.

Part Two

THE THEORY IN PRACTICE

How did this theory manifest itself in practice, and why did it lead to such very different work from one artist to another? In the chapters that follow, we shall look at five of the major artists—Still, Pollock, Newman, Motherwell, and Rothko—each one representative of a different mode of pictorial thinking.

If one were to examine the development of the theory in each artist, then obviously each would warrant a monograph in his own right. If, however, the theory of the abstract mystic symbol is indeed the basis of each artist's work, then one would expect it to be most fully developed and expressed in his mature paintings. For this reason I shall take representative works from the "mature" period of each artist, individually, and examine the pictorial, aesthetic means by which the theory was realized. One of the few uncontentious things about Abstract Expressionism is the fact that there is general agreement about the critical, pictorial analysis of the work of each of the artists; that is to say, there is very little disagreement about what is there and how it works, though there is of course considerable disagreement about the interpretation one places on those descriptions, and on what the *quality* of the work arises from. These are difficult questions which will be addressed in part 3. Differences of opinion about the overriding value of Abstract Expressionism—about whether it arises from aesthetic or socio-political considerations—do not jeopardize the validity of the present investigation. The argument is not about processes but about the significance of what is achieved.

The Abstract Expressionist artists talked about their work in two quite different though associated ways. The first one was the sort of conversation clustered around their belief and expectation that their art should function as an abstract mystic symbol, as has just been discussed. The second way related to the sort of remarks they made about particular works or particular phases of their work. As was seen in the last chapter, one of the inbuilt characteristics of the abstract mystic symbol is that what it expresses is essentially ineffable. This being so, there is a certain difficulty in describing the heart of the work, the symbol, or what it expresses.

It is at this point that metaphor enters critical discussion. Why it works the way it does is something philosophers of language have gone only a minute way toward discovering. But that it can work is unequivocal and is demonstrated in the fact that most criticism makes use of a descriptive or interpretative metaphor. It is also demonstrated in the fact that a great many artists have an urge to translate the intended character or impact of a particular great work into a verbal metaphor, as a title. The Abstract Expressionists employed metaphors of description too, and in the chapters that follow, I shall look at how some of these function as illuminating and accurate descriptions of the work, and at how they are also descriptions of particular abstract mystic symbols.

One thing that emerges from an examination of the five artists is that each artist not only produces work that is different visually but employs a different kind of aesthetic structure. By that I mean not merely the sort of differences that led Pollock, say, to create a complex image of line, and Newman to make measured and sparse geometric images, and Motherwell to prefer large, squashed, and flattened forms on a flat ground. There are much more fundamental differences than these, differences which relate more to the methods of perceptual manipulation employed by the artists, and some of these processes will emerge in the following chapters. What is interesting about these differing methods, however, is that each one demonstrates the way in which the artists realized the abstract mystic symbol in their work.

In the course of the following chapters many important theoretical issues of criticism will be raised, some of which will be dealt with in part 3, "Modes of Critical Discourse"; others, however, are really the subject of another book. In an investigation of the nature of art-talk, it is inevitable that such issues will be raised—indeed, not to do so would limit the scope and depth of the investigation enormously. I do not think, however, that anything I say in these and later chapters is dependent upon the solution of any of these issues. In particular, the truth about a specific critical analysis and the soundness of theoretical points are obviously desirable, but the emphasis will not be on proving them so. My interest is in examining *what* is said and assumed about art, rather that whether or not it *should* be said and assumed. In other words, my subject is the nature of art-talk as it is, rather than what art should be, though obviously what is said about the former will have certain implications for the latter.

Let us turn, then, to the individual artists, to a consideration of how each has described his own work, and of how the work is generally analyzed and described.

Chapter Six

CLYFFORD STILL

Clyfford Still's attitude to his work was quite unequivocal. He described his paintings as having "the power for life—or for death,"[1] and as vindication of his success in achieving such creative force, remarked that his work was responded to with "resentment or fear." Very little art, he felt, did more than serve the interests of the great "Cultural Moloch" and to attempt to do more, to deny the values of "Institutional Culture," was "treason."[2] "By the end of my twenty-fifth year," he wrote,

having seen and studied deeply the works and acts of those men of art presented in museums and books as masters, I was brought to the conclusion that very few of them merited the admiration they received and those few most often achieved true worth after they had defined their means and mores. . . . To me it became an imperative that if this instrument—this extension of one's mind and heart and hand—were to be given its potential, a fresh start must be made. . . .

Neither verbalizings nor aesthetic accretions would suffice. I had to accomplish my purpose, my emancipation and the exhalting responsibility which I trusted would follow, totally and directly through my own life and hands.[3]

His work, he said, liberated the spirit and, because it did, was received with a resentment which often expressed itself in critical banality. "The elements of my paintings, *ineluctably* co-ordinated, confirmed for me the liberation of the spirit. In the hands of unscrupulous and calculating men it was readily apparent that these elements could be segregated and evacuated to intimidate the mind, blast the eyes with hatred, or seduce with insipid deceit. . . . Thus the genesis of a liberating absolute was buried under a blanket of historical inanities." And he dedicated his work "to all who would know the meaning and the responsibilities of freedom, *intrinsic* and absolute."[4]

These are strong words, and one might be inclined to dismiss them for just that reason, especially Still's claims about a "liberating absolute." And yet it is precisely such terms as these which recur in much of the critical writings. Ideas such as "the absolute," forces of growth and cataclysm, are the kind of metaphors commonly employed. Sometimes they are relatively specific metaphors, but, whatever they might be in particular cases, in general terms they all seem related to an overall conception of art as a realization of fundamental life forces.

I cannot of course actually *prove* that Still's work achieves that goal; nor is it important that I do. What is more to the point is the fact that it can be shown that there are certain features of the work that seem to invite that sort of description. To discover these, let us begin with the more descriptive rather than interpretive considerations.

Probably the most common and obvious formal analysis made of Still's work is that which draws attention to the single-planar unity of his images and of their refusal to break up into figure and ground. The image, as so many critics have observed, spreads across the surface as a continuous skin of paint. But lest this should sound simple, here is Walter Darby Bannard's description of its complexity:

Rather than put the stroke to work as outline, in the service of depiction or Cubism, Still let it do what it could do best: cover surface. Still's painting is surface painting; the paint is used for covering with no concession to illusion, and the effect of the paintings is that of the conditions of surface. The edge is manifestly that of a flat thing which leaves a ragged edge when it is torn, shows other surfaces by opening, and covers and spreads, creeping into holes and crevices on the way.[5]

Walter Darby Bannard is a very perceptive observer of how paintings work, but he never attempts to tell us what they "mean" and rarely describes his own response to them. (He declines to do that, for reasons which he gives, though he is firm in his acknowledgment of the interpretive element as a very important part of a painting.)[6] Perhaps it depends on the inclinations of the critic—and most critics are not inclined to resist the move into interpretative metaphor. It is usual, however, for critics to feel that their analysis is incomplete if it stops with formal analysis, though obviously, of course, it depends on the artist with whom they are dealing.

Formal analysis seems incomplete when applied to Clyfford Still's work, and it is certain that he thought so. "I never wanted color to be color. I never wanted texture to be texture, or images to become shapes. I wanted them all to fuse into a living spirit"[7] is just one of the many statements he made to that effect. But perhaps the best way to demonstrate the necessity for an interpretive metaphor is to turn to some of his best works of the late forties and early fifties.

The five works I want to discuss are similar in size (all approximately eighty by sixty-nine inches) and date from 1948 to 1951. They are *1948-E, November 1950, 1949-H, October 1950,* and *Untitled, 1951* (Cooper Square, New York City).[8]

1948-E is a gray-black "monochrome," textured, and with very small areas of color incident—purple on the upper left edge, yellow in the upper left of center, and red on the lower right side. The gray-black becomes a more intense black in an irregularly shaped area right down the picture from top to bottom, to the left of center. The detail of the texturing, the changes in form from gray-black to black, and the size and placing of the color incidents are all such that one is drawn to continually examine the whole image, returning always to the concentration of black down the left half.

When the balance of all these kinds of elements is "right" in a painting, the eye "takes a journey," as it were, drawn by the tensions from one point to another, pausing to engage in the visual aesthetics of each resting point, but always drawn on, and usually back to the starting point. Only perceptual tiredness (apart from outside distractions) halts the process, and this can be alleviated or postponed by the artist through the quantity and variety of the visual resting stops.

Still's picture works in this way, a remarkable achievement in itself, but the more so when one remembers that it is virtually a monochrome image, since the challenge of making an image of single color interesting is considerable. *1948-E* is so successful that the networks of aesthetic "events" across the canvas, so finely balanced one to another as they are, coalesce into an aesthetic pattern, of which one is drawn to use descriptive language.

It is almost an aesthetic truism to say that an image which is not conceived of in some sense as a whole will lack the power to draw the concentration of the viewer. While this is true in general, it is thrust upon one's attention as a critical aesthetic principle in the case of Still's work. In a representational narrative painting, for example, one can be distracted from a lack of aesthetic wholeness by the story depicted in the image. But in a painting such as Still's *1948-E,* the painting is stripped bare and its aesthetic structure displayed in such a way that, should it not succeed, its failure will be immediately apparent. Put in more specific terms, if one does not sense the raison d'être of each incident and its relationship to the next, then the painting will not invite that process of perceptualization which seeks to translate what is seen into a meaningful pattern.

In *1948-E,* the transitions of tone and texture in the gray-black are so subtle and finely balanced that one reads the surface not as a series of static, individual changes, but as *changing,* as if with its own process of growth. That, along with the directional pull toward the channel of black down the left half (and the channel is located in the strongest area of the rectangle, so that tension is reduced and it sits comfortably and secure), invites one to see the gray-black as becoming stronger and purer in the black channel area. The shape of the form intensifies this feeling, since its many branches are not jagged and violent, but spread gently, both in contour and tonal transition (reminiscent, perhaps, of a meandering river bed, though obviously no literal or illustrative reference is intended), so that the black is seen as "emerging" from the bed of gray-black—though not, of course, in a spatial sense, creating an illusion of depth.

Likewise, the three color incidents, minimal and heavily imbued with dark tone as they are, seem to be developing or growing organically through the ground. For this reason, one thinks of them as elemental within the compound of black, breathing through the ground to the light of vision. In the channel form, too, the black seems to softly materialize from the gray-black, as if it has come into focus. But whereas in the other areas it is color or light which emerges from negative dark, here the black seems positive—a concentrated essence of black emerging from a negative light.

Thus one is presented with the complex visual and emotional paradox of negative light and positive dark, on the one hand, and black as elemental and pure, but also as the compound containing many single elemental colors, on the other. Through this interplay of vision and thought, and also because of the soft and delicate tone and textures, the surface of the image seems to breathe with a life which is both gentle and insistent. The power of the black to transform itself, so that it is seen in such radically different moods and activities or roles, is what gives the painting its impact and magic. And given the strength of that impact, the impulse to think about the forces of black, color, light, and dark in the picture, in metaphysical terms, is very strong. Certainly that is what Still intended, and it is also how the images struck him and others.

In another monochrome painting, *November 1950,* Still dispenses with color incidents and works with an allover image of yellow with a grayish tone. The effect of the gray tone seems to be to switch the attention from the *light* in the color (or from the hue) to the matt crustiness of the paint; but an exploration of the surface reveals traces of other colors, and flesh tones in particular, below the surface. These subsurface colors and the crustiness of the matière provide tiny changes of tone and texture which again are so finely balanced against each other that the whole surface of the picture seems to be in a process of quiet organic growth. Since the picture appears to be composed only of color, and of one color, this makes the color seem very elemental, as if we were faced with the fundamentals of painting and experience.

The painting, being six-and-a-half by five-and-a-half feet (approximately), is larger than human size. Thus because of the relationship of the scale of the painting to the pattern and scale of the tonal and textural changes, perceptually one is drawn into the painting, so that the impression of life and growth breathing through the surface is experienced in an immediate and somewhat personal way. That presumably has to do with the process of perception in certain spatial and scale relationships, but the effect of it is to make one articulate one's perception not simply in formal terms, but in terms of feeling, and even metaphysics. Thus it is not fanciful to describe Still's demonstration of the elemental in painting as a depiction or a metaphor (instance or manifestation, he would say) of an absolute state, especially when one bears in mind that the absolute is generally regarded as ineffable. It is certainly a hallmark of these paintings that their character and impact are very inadequately (and indirectly) described in verbal terms.

Painting *1949-H* works in a different way, being composed of several quite definite small areas of color (white, brown, black, orange, blue, and yellow) on a hard and high-gloss red ground. The color of the ground has the hardness of car duco—a rather unattractive, uncompromising effect, but because the gloss finish shows up the detail of surface and of the paint and the angle of the brush strokes, the texture of the surface is very strong and very sensuous. This blend or, rather, juxtaposition of the harsh and ugly with great sensuousness is, needless to say, very hard to achieve, but one which Still consciously sought—in order, he said, to prevent the viewer from simply being seduced by beauty. Benjamin Townsend reports that Still told him that

he "consciously endeavored in his painting to disembarrass color from all conventional, familiar associations and responses; that is, from the pleasant, luminous, and symbolic. Especially in the paintings of the 'forties he avoided the appealing, sensuous colors of, for example the Fauves. . . . Since he wished to use color to depict directly a new, unique subject . . . he has to use it in a new and, for many, displeasing way."[9]

What is astonishing about this picture is that the red does not register as ground, and the color patches are not seen as forms; rather, one's experience of this painting is a strong sense of the individuality of each color. There is no movement in the picture and the color patches do not seem to be emerging from the red, superimposed on it, equally flat with it, adjacent to it—or, for that matter, to be in any kind of spatial relationship to the red at all. One simply thinks of them as co-existing. The scale and the placement of the patches is critical, and is such that, when one tries to focus on the center of the painting (as is natural), the patches are all on the periphery of vision—sufficiently close that their strength of color is very apparent, but too far for the determinateness of their forms to register. Likewise, when the eye moves to focus on a particular patch, the other patches are just sufficiently in reach to function in the same way; and between each point of focus is a vague area and experience of red. The colors are carefully chosen, with an even balance of strength (aided by the considerations mentioned above) so that no one dominates another.

As with all good paintings, when the degree of control over pictorial dynamics such as those described above reaches a certain point, the effect is magic—an effect which we marvel at and which makes us return again and again to the painting. And in this painting, because of the strength and balance of the hues, and because the spatial relations make us unconscious of the edges of the patches, the painting seems to offer an experience of very determinate color but without the physical constraints of form and place—the pure essence of disembodied color. Many artists have striven for this (Kandinsky was one who succeeded), and perhaps it is part of a very common human urge to transcend the physical, an urge central to almost all religions. When one encounters a successful visual illusion or metaphor of this phenomenon in a painting, therefore, it is natural and appropriate to use such language as "absolute state," "pure essence and existence," albeit metaphorically.

One other metaphor which Still embodies in his work is that of cataclysm. Two paintings which illustrate this are *October 1950* and *Untitled, 1951* (Cooper Square, New York City). *October 1950* is quite different from the other paintings discussed, being composed of very jagged, large areas of color in blue, red, orange, and white, with narrow areas of raw canvas between each one. In contrast to *1940-H,* the color areas are sufficiently closely related spatially for the eye to comprehend their form, and also to be aware of one or more in relation to another. The spatial balance between them, plus the balance of their colors, creates a very taut surface of color and form—so taut that one feels that each form is held in place by the others and by the force of the edges of the picture. The edges of the forms are heightened by the breathing space of raw canvas which serves not merely to give distinctness to the edges but, more important (because of the pattern of spatial relations), to discharge tensions across the neutral gap from one form to another.

The end result is a picture in which very strong forms and colors (and even the white seems strong in this context) co-exist, but in a state of nervous tension: where there is, if only one tiny bit were to change (and one senses that possibility), the threat of any one form extending into another, but with such violence that the image would be rent apart. Still has recognized, however, that the discomfort of that awareness can itself destroy a picture, and has exerted a masterful control so that the resolution of the image is never sacrificed: the tensions and threats are felt merely as potential but not probable.

The same thinking can be seen in *Untitled, 1951,* though here the threat is actualized, but the discomfort minimalized. Like *1948-E,* this is an all-black painting, but without any major changes of tone from one area to another, and with just a tiny streak of red in the upper right-hand section of the canvas. The black is very dense, and the texture so sensitively handled that one finds oneself drawn very close, exploring every part of it—as if hoping to emerge from the enveloping blackness. The only relief comes in the vertical streak of red which, because it is a red with a lot of black tone, seems to be emerging through the surface, as if a dense and heavy veil of black is being rent apart to expose and liberate what lies below. If, in *October 1950,* the subject is possible cataclysm, here the cataclysm has suggestively begun to erupt. It is a welcome one, however, because the black, which is the bed through which it erupts, is sufficiently strong and beautifully textured to engage one in the aesthetic pleasure of it. In the end, however, it is its very strength which leads the eye to seek relief, and the cataclysm is seen as one which brings light.

The power of this painting is remarkable, and it is works like these that explain, and perhaps justify, Still's remark that "the elements of my paintings, ineluctably co-ordinated, confirmed for me the liberation of the spirit"[10] and his conviction that "I know [the painting's] extensions are infinite, its exaltation is without bathos or aggression, and that it will give back courage as freedom without arrogance or despair."[11]

Many of Still's paintings are concerned with the renting apart of surfaces and the resultant suggested cataclysm; others more gently insinuate the presence of elemental forces. Sometimes they work through suggestions of seepages and organic growth, and sometimes they are generated through tensions across surfaces. But whatever the behavior of these forces, they are always seen as elemental; and beyond that point of interpretation, Still was not prepared to go.

That they are seen as expressions of the elemental is probably due in part to the abstract, nonreferential nature of the forms (about which we will have more to say in later chapters), a factor which only operates with that effect when the images also have great strength of impact. Paintings combining those two factors are inclined to leave the viewer impressed, but with nothing to say, and of course this is exactly how Still thought an abstract mystic symbol should affect one. In his usual idiosyncratic idiom, he expressed it thus: "I felt it necessary to evolve entirely new concepts [of form and space and painting] and postulate them in an instrument that could continue to shake itself free from dialectical perversions."[12]

Although Still complained bitterly about the art world generally ("that fraudulent arena of poltroon politicians and charlatan hucksters who pretend they love art for the vile sake of exploitation")[13] and critics in particular, nonetheless there was a large body of opinion, even in the early years, which responded to his work in just the way he wished. The following passage, by a New York critic, was itself quoted in 1970 as a typical critical comment on Still's work. As a typical comment it indicates very clearly that the writer had responded to the work precisely as Still would have wished and, indeed, as all the Abstract Expressionists would have hoped for their own work. It reads:

[Still's paintings] transcend the label of abstract expressionism and become epochal, timeless statements of man in raw, basic confrontation with himself.

When a deep brown totemic mass (in one of the paintings) moves mythically out over a black space, it can grip and startle with all the primordial power of a childhood fear.[14]

What more explicit statement of the power of an icon can one get?

Chapter Seven

JACKSON POLLOCK

The urge to embody powerful, generalized feeling in their work is evident among the other Abstract Expressionists, too. Likewise, the necessity to use metaphor to describe this feeling holds for them, just as it does for Still, particularly since the feeling expressed in Abstract Expressionist works is so very generalized.

Jackson Pollock, for all the talk about his reluctance and inability to verbalize (the former was true, but the latter was not), supplied his own account of his work, even to the point of providing a metaphor of interpretation. In his notes of 1951, he jotted down what he regarded as the essentials of his work and of his attitude to art, and among them he included the following phrases:

States of order————organic intensity————energy and motion made visible————memories arrested in space.[1]

Pollock obviously thought these descriptions important, and one of them in particular, "energy and motion made visible," is an especially apt crystallization of the character of so much of his work. This has been noted before, of course, and B. H. Friedman adopted it as the subtitle of his biography of Pollock.[2] That it is important and apt can be seen, in the first instance, simply by looking at the works themselves.

Furthermore, this reading of the paintings is reinforced when we look at Pollock's attitude to his work and to the world around him, and the things he placed particular value in. Whenever he talked about these things, and especially when he talked about his work, Pollock was quite unequivocal. What he had to say, therefore, is not only interesting but significant, and it provides a very useful avenue into understanding how this interpretive metaphor operates, and how his works are embodiments of feeling: of abstract, iconic symbols.

If the idea of energy made visible involves a paradox—a paradox of trying to realize, in physical terms and in illusionary space, a non-material force—there is a further paradox in his attitude to abstraction. Two of the things he insisted on were that he was a painter of abstract pictures but that his work was also representational. One's first inclination might be to explain this by pointing out that Pollock was, at various stages of his career, a figurative painter and an abstract artist. (He used figurative forms up until 1947, then became abstract, reverting to figurative forms again, off and on from 1951 onward.) However, the following remark made to Selden Rodman indicates that the answer is not as simple as that. He said, "I'm very representational some of the time, *and a little all of the time*." [My italics][3]

For an explanation we must go back to Pollock's sources. The sources of his subject matter were twofold: the forces of nature and internal human forces. His interest in nature and landscape, and their strong influence on him, are well documented. Lee Krasner, for instance, has remarked:

You recall he said in a '44 interview that here in the East, only the Atlantic gave him a sense of space that he was accustomed to. He did work with his father, who was a surveyor, in the Grand Canyon, so he really had a sense of physical space. . . .

Certainly his relationship to nature was intense. For example, the moon had a tremendous effect on him, and he liked gardening. Just walking on the beach in the wintertime, with snow on the sand was exciting. He identified very strongly with nature.[4]

Tony Smith, too, was convinced that this bond with nature was an important part of the man and his work. In the group of interviews "Who Was Jackson Pollock?" he said:

One of the things that possessed Jackson, was his feeling for the land. . . . This is as typical as anything I know about him. He identified with the land, and in making this pile he established himself upon it. This was elemental; painting is always, to some extent, cultural. I never heard anyone mention it, but I think that his feeling for the land had something to do with his painting canvases on the floor. . . . I don't think that Jackson painted on the floor just for its hard surface, or for the large area, or the freedom of movement, or so that the drips wouldn't run. There was something else, a strong bond with the elements. The earth was always there.[5]

Smith, Lee Krasner, and Alfonso Ossorio have all separately said that they often sat with Pollock, silently watching nature for hours.[6]

Pollock believed very strongly that modern art, and his own art especially, had to express the inner life of the artist. By "inner life" he did not mean simple emotions such as happiness, anger, fear, or whatever; it was one of his and his friends' criticisms that this was indeed what was so wrong with German Expressionism. Rather he thought of his art as expressing inner forces. In his radio interview with William Wright, he was quite explicit about this. He began the interview by making the point that modern artists work from a different source:

The thing that interests me is that today painters do not have to go to a subject matter outside of themselves. Most modern painters work from a different source. They work from within.

. . . The modern artist, it seems to me, is working and expressing an inner world—in other words—expressing the energy, the motion, and other inner forces.[7]

This, of course, did not have to mean only the inner forces that one normally associates with people, but could also mean the inner forces of other things in the world—the energies of nature and of cities, for example, but *as felt* by people. Pollock had a long interest in the occult (dating from his teens), in theosophy, and in Eastern and American Indian religions.[8] Belief in the connections between forces in nature and forces in society was, therefore, very much a part of Pollock's intellectual and emotional background.

This is particularly evident in his interest in sand painting. When the Southwest Indians made sand paintings, they did so in order to transfer, from the images to a sick person, the abstractions of the sacred powers that keep the forces of nature in harmony. (The patient actually sat on the paintings to effect the transfer.) These Indians were especially concerned with what Bernard Haile (a pioneer of Navaho anthropology) has described as the inner forces and harmonies of natural phenomena.[9] Pollock had read a great deal about the Southwest Indians; he had actually witnessed the sand-painting ceremony and was very interested in it.[10] In many respects, their attitudes toward life and nature struck deep chords in his own being. Like them, he saw himself as adapting to nature and harmonizing with its rhythms, rather than trying to shape it to his own needs.

Betty Parsons, in her interview "Who Was Jackson Pollock?" confirms this important element in Pollock's thinking:

He was a questioning man. He would ask endless questions. He wanted to know what I thought about the world, about life. . . . He was also extremely intrigued with the inner world—what is it all about? He had a sense of mystery. His religiousness was in those terms—a sense of the rhythm of the universe, of the big order—like the Oriental philosophies. He sensed rhythm rather than order, like the Orientals rather than the Westerners. He had Indian friends, a dancer and his wife, with whom he talked at length and who influenced him greatly. . . .

He had that kind of overall feeling about nature—about the cosmic—the power of it all—how scary it is.[11]

We know, too, that one of Pollock's most prized books was D'Arcy Thompson's *On the Growth of Form,*[12] a book poetic in its approach to the natural world and that describes form in terms of growth through energies; throughout the book the forces of growth are seen almost religiously, as part of a general, universal life force.

That Pollock himself saw and felt the energies of the world around him as part of his own inner energies, and vice versa, is evident in the response he made to a question about why he preferred to live in New York, rather than the West:

Living is keener, more demanding, more intense and expansive in New York than in the West; the stimulating influences are more numerous and rewarding. At the same time, I have a definite feeling for the West: the vast horizontality of the land, for instance; here only the Atlantic Ocean gives you that.[13]

Tony Smith, in talking about the separate, analytical way in which Pollock would consider things, described his physical relationship to the land as almost a mode of perception: "He had a distinct posture for looking at the ground, another for looking at the horizon and a third for looking at the sky. You might say that that's just the way it is, but for him these seemed to be totally different modes of perception."[14]

On another occasion, Pollock expressed his closeness to nature in a dramatic and very explicit way. Lee Krasner, in talking about his introduction to Hans Hofmann and of what Hofmann had to say about Pollock's work, described it this way:

Well, when he came up to Pollock's place his response was, you are very talented, you should join my class, you work by heart, this is no good, you will repeat yourself, you should work from nature.
[Interviewer]: How did Pollock react?
Pollock said, "I am nature. You see, Hofmann separates himself from nature, he puts nature out there, and he is the observer."[15]

Being finely attuned to the world around him, be it city or country, Pollock felt its rhythms and absorbed them. They became, in turn, his own energies and rhythms, triggered by internal reflections, by physical awareness, or by responsiveness to events around him. It was these energies and feelings that he sought to express directly in his work.

When we turn to his work and to individual paintings, we find there is a strong compulsion to speak of them metaphorically, in terms of the forces of nature. In writing about Pollock's "vast and quite magnificent new canvases," James Fitzsimmons, for example, said:

In No. 10 arabesques of bright orange and patches of watery blue, yellow and green are suspended in a capillary network of sinewy black lines. The use here of flux, of marbleized effects . . . is something new in Pollock. There is a feeling of landscape in No. 11. . . . In No. 12 he abandons sumptuous tapestried textures. A tremendously exciting painting, it suggests the *fluids* of life, intermingling, expanding and undergoing gradual chemical change. . . .

For this reviewer the exciting thing about Pollock's new paintings . . . is the glimpse they afford into the metaphysical and psychological structure of things. For the powerful rhythmic alternations on which they are based are perhaps those of the life process itself. And, what is rare in abstract art, the complexity of their formal-technical characteristics corresponds to, and is justified by, that of their conceptual roots.[16]

In a different style, Will Grohmann writes:

Here is reality, not of yesterday but of tomorrow . . . an exuberance of the continent, the ocean and the forests, the conceiving of an undiscovered world comparable to the time 300 years ago when the pioneers came to his country. And what refinement of pictorial conception: with what differentiation the single layers of consciousness are graded so that in the end the entire "reality" is there, called forth, not merely represented. For nothing is rendered as it is; everything is invented in the spirit of a natural and universal occurrence.[17]

Denys Sutton said that "above all one feels that his painting was influenced by his environment and his vast swirling compositions . . . express something of the energy and size of the U.S.,"[18] while John Russell referred to the "great pounding rhythms which battle their way across the eighteen-foot canvases [and which] never for a moment get out of control."[19]

Blue Poles is certainly not a picture of anything in the physical world, but the massive (though controlled) undulations of power that slowly roll across the canvas are suggestive of the movements of deep and powerful water. In this very densely constructed picture, the layers of drips and line are tightly held spatially, so that they appear to build up from a solid, though penetrable, base of matter. This density and spatial tightness also have the effect of concentrating the energies of the lines down through layers rather than dispersing them along the rhythms of the lines themselves, with a resultant pumping movement, further articulated by variations of surface depth from one area to another. There is very little clotting together of layers, so that where lines do spatially conjoin, they do so by touching and cleanly penetrating, in such a way that their own paths of energy are continued rather than melded, with a change of character and a redirection of energy, into a more anchored, grid-like structure. This tight but un-fixed character of the surface allows the swells a freedom and potentiality that one can only associate with something as vast and powerful as the ocean. The poles, too, far from being a final attempt to "save" the picture, rest in the tangled mass of line, defining planes of concentrated rhythms, and suggesting the buoyancy of power beneath.

At the same time, there is no temptation to read the picture as a *depiction* of the ocean surface: the colors (black-blue, orange, silver, and white) deliberately point one away from that, and the emphasis is, finally, not on texture of surface (as it would be with such a depiction) but on the energies that charge the surfaces and space. Such energies are, of course, necessarily invisible, and imagined or felt, and while they remain the real subject matter of any picture, can never *themselves* be subject to depiction. Pollock, as he so often said, never painted *things,* but energies and feelings. "Energy and motion made visible," not oceans and horizons, was the paradox and metaphor that Pollock employed.

Full-Fathom-Five is another painting in which the forces of the ocean, or forces analogous to them, are expressed. It is a curious picture, for despite its being nonillustrative, it has embedded in it objects such as coins, buttons, thumb tacks, nails, paint-tube lids, cigarettes, matches, and keys;—objects which, on the face of it, might seem to have de-pictive or referential associations, especially in a picture entitled *Full-Fathom-Five.* A heavily impasto picture made up of sea-green and silver, with touches of orange, pink, mustard, and crimson, black drips, and a few fine white skeins, its depth is built up primarily from thicker patches of advancing and receding color, rather than from the skeins, though it should be said that the skeins define the surface, sitting lightly as they do, just as the paint-encrusted objects establish a terrain below. (The fact that the objects are paint-encrusted and are used physically rather than illustratively suggests that they are not incorporated into the meaning of the picture *as* nails, coins, and so on, but rather in the manner of the submerged unconscious imagery of Pollock's earlier work.)

The vertical edges are tight, and the tensions force the eye back toward the central areas and into the depth of the image. And it is in the depth of the image that the force of the picture lies—despite the fact that, in formal terms, the space is in fact shallow, and of Cubist origin. Nonetheless, one feels the energy between planes from surface to base (and like many Analytical Cubist pictures, one has the impression of looking down vertically upon the image), an energy transmitted across volume rather than along lines. Again, this is analogous to the mass and power of very deep water, and it was presumably in recognition of this analogy of feeling that Pollock called it *Full-Fathom-Five*.

In other works (and a good many of them) one does not readily find analogies of feeling in the natural world as such, and this is presumably because Pollock preferred to express energies or feelings incapable of further articulation or specification. In these, one can see the application of the concept "energy and motion made visible"— energy and motion not of particular places and things but *in themselves*. In *One, 1950*, for example, the skeins exist so crisply and individually that they trace their paths with the intensity of an electrical charge. The network is so beautifully controlled that the lines not only flex and tense with their internal force but disseminate energies across the vibrating spaces.

Matisse (whose considerable influence is evident in much of Pollock's work) said of his own drawing: "My line drawing is the purest and most direct translation of my emotion. . . . [The lines] generate light. . . . Once my emotive line has modeled the light of my white paper without destroying its precious whiteness, I can neither add nor take anything away."[20] In the same way, Pollock, too, charged *his* lines so that line and space each become pure energy, in an art close to being pure abstract, not dependent upon analogues of objects known in the physical world. The pure energy and motion of Pollock's pictures—a metaphysical energy almost—are examples of, as Pollock put it in another metaphor, "memories arrested in space."

In describing or articulating the impact and appearances of Pollock's work, it seems appropriate and indeed necessary to talk about them in terms of these metaphors. What then can be said of the formal structure which might reinforce that reading? Greenberg, for example, said of some of the works that they are "high classical art: not only *the identification of form and feeling,* but the acceptance and exploitation of the very circumstances of the medium of painting that limit such identification."[21] [My italics] The identification of form and feeling can only be discovered and established by showing how the structural form is manipulated to give rise to the feeling which one has articulated by the means of a metaphor. Furthermore, as Greenberg so rightly comments, given the nature of two-dimensional image-making, the very elements that make such identification of form and feeling *difficult* must be accepted and exploited in order to make it *possible.* Such is the nature of painting.

As is often remarked, Pollock's space is one which, generally speaking, builds up from the ground of the canvas or support, and projects out toward the viewer. It is not, therefore, a retreating space but a more positive, advancing one. William Rubin refers to this as "non-illusionistic space,"[22] presumably because it gets rid of the illusionistic contradiction of a recession back into the canvas. Of course, Pollock's forward space is also an illusion, since the space implied between planes and lines rarely corresponds with the actual physical space. On the other hand, *some* of the space actually exists, since it is physically plausible to build out, layer by layer, and a good many of Pollock's works, including *Blue Poles* and *Full-Fathom-Five* do this.

Whereas the illusion of traditional receding space is generated through a *contradiction* of physical fact, Pollock's illusion is created simply through an *exaggeration* of physical fact. The illusion is thus dependent upon the viewer's consciousness of layer upon layer of paint—a consciousness of the *reality* of paint as paint, as physical material, but in a way which does not require a shifting back and forth between two different and opposite perceptual languages. In traditional receding space, a suspension of disbelief is necessary in order that one might succumb to the illusion. One has to give oneself over to the fiction of what the patches of paint "stand for" or depict, and to the logic of diagonals and implied relations between objects in a space, all of which begin to operate as soon as that fiction is accepted. But as soon as one allows the eye to abandon the representational meaning and concentrate instead on the paint simply as patches of paint, then the picture becomes immediately what it actually is—a two-dimensional, painted surface. Put simply, the two modes of perception are mutually exclusive.

In Pollock's kind of forward space, however, this sort of perceptual switch is not necessary. The physical buildup of space (and it can be up to half an inch in some pictures) is simply exaggerated by the eye, mainly through the use of colors which we see as sitting on different planes. Our awareness of the depth begins with our awareness of the buildup of pigment. The reality of the space and energy, therefore, is reinforced by our awareness of the reality of the paint as material— and this is a very *modern* phenomenon in art.[23]

At the same time, we recognize the tenuousness of the space built up in front of the canvas: awareness of the paint as paint brings with it an awareness of potential for the lines to lose their energy, elasticity, and structuring force and become *merely* paint; and because Pollock is a *successful* painter, the effect of space and energy is paradoxically strengthened in the knowledge of that potentiality.

Connected with this is an element of transience which Pollock's works tend to have: the suggestion always of energy in flux. This is generated, at least in major part, by the Impressionistic use of scintillation. As Rubin has very accurately described, Pollock's pictures are built up from contrasts of value, so that charges jump across from darks to lights (intensified by the bouncy effect of silver paint) creating energies which are always difficult to "fix," albeit always controlled.[24]

So the volatility and transience within the image (not *of* the image) intensify the impression of invisible energy, while at the same time asserting its reality. The paradox of Pollock's work, therefore, is not simply the traditional one of using a visual medium to express nonvisual entities, but that, within the visual medium, he makes these things in a sense visible by stressing, even utilizing, their invisibility. We do not see the energies passing from line to space and line because we cannot: rather, we feel their effects, and that is precisely the reality of any sort of energy in the physical world as well. Painting is physical and composed of paint, and in discharging and expressing its energies it behaves as does anything else in the physical world. In other words, Pollock takes the reality of how energy is transmitted in the physical world and uses this as part of the pictorial language of his painting.

Thus Pollock brings the physical character of the medium and the language of pictorial and perceptual dynamics closer together than had been previously known. It is this, presumably, that Greenberg had in mind when he talked about "the acceptance and exploitation of the very circumstances of the medium of painting that limit [the identification of feeling and form]." That it should limit the identification of form and feeling is an obvious danger, since it could so easily fall into banality, but it is a danger rarely evident in Pollock's work. This can only be explained by the skill of the artist, but in specific terms it must be accounted for by his determination that what he wanted to do was realize the felt forces of nature in his work.

John Graham, who was always a powerful force in Pollock's thinking, gave an account of the necessity for the abstract in art, in terms very sympathetic with that determination. In an explanation of the character of abstract art, he said:

Abstract art in general (in its best examples) is an art based on profound knowledge of reality, knowledge of anatomy of space and bodies of plastic destination as well as origin of forms. Abstract art uses this knowledge as a *point of departure*. It reevaluates the spaces and forms observed into new terms. It is *evocative*. It is materialistic—it operates directly in the medium itself— paint, stone, etc., with full understanding of their *sensuous qualities* and potentialities instead of relying on make-believe representations. Pure abstract art is a superior kind of art because the artist has a double task before him: a) to take stock of reality and b) to make departure from reality, at the same time. One cannot make departure from reality unless one knows and understands this reality. . . .

Abstract art departs from reality and nature only to draw far-reaching conclusions about this reality. A legitimate abstract work of art can be produced only on the basis of profound knowledge of nature. The artists who stay always within the limits of naturalistic art are those who can see only superficial aspects of nature, because to see manifestations and laws of nature profoundly, requires profound gifts and profound gifts impose great responsibilities.[25]

Pollock knew Graham well, read him and talked with him a great deal, and often discussed him with others. In Graham he found someone who articulated all that he felt and thought about art, just at the time when he was articulating it all to himself. Graham's view of the purpose of art was very much Pollock's as well, and was expressed by Graham thus:

The purpose of art in *general* is to reveal the truth and to reveal the given object or event; to establish a link between humanity and the unknown; to create new values; to put humanity face to face with a new event, a new marvel. . . .

The origin of art lies in human longing for *enigma,* for the miraculous, for expansion, for social communication . . . for continuity and consequently— life eternal. This longing for perpetuity engenders an artist's desire to arrest the eternal motion.[26]

"Energy and motion made visible" was the enigma which Pollock chose to realize; not merely an illustration or representation of energy and motion in the world, but its "direct expression"—an image which he hoped would indeed bring the viewer "face to face with a new event, a new marvel": an abstract, mystic symbol.

Chapter Eight

BARNETT NEWMAN

The abstract mystic symbol that Newman sought to realize in his work was that of "total space." At first glance this might sound more like a formalist, pictorial concept than a metaphysical one, but that Newman thought of it as something transcending mere pictorial mechanics is indicated in another phrase (redolent of religious, mystical connotations) he used—"the fullness thereof." In a television interview, he elaborated further: "I don't really think that my paintings divide. I feel that I do not make divisions. I feel that the exact opposite is what I'm trying to do. And I feel that what I'm involved in is the declaration of the whole area as a single, total area and I'm not manipulating space: I'm not arranging areas; I'm just declaring them."[1]

On other occasions he talked of scale overcoming size, of shape transcending format, and of geometric space, or the space of volumes, being subsumed into overall or total space, as if for each of these physical things there was a metaphysical or "felt" manifestation. Of his triangular paintings *Chartres* and *Jerico,* for instance, he said:

I knew that I must assert its shape, but in doing so I must make the shape invisible or shapeless. I realized that after all it is nothing more than a slice of space, a "space vehicle," which the painter gets into and then has to get out of. It was this drama, my involvement in the existence of the triangle as an object and my need to destroy it as an object that made it possible for me to begin painting them. After all, format as format can be a trap.

I called one painting *Chartres* because of the strong assertion of my inner structure in contrast with the outside format and because of the even light in the painting which has for me the evenness of Northern Light—a light without shadows. The title *Jerico* explains itself.[2]

True space, he says, is a *felt* thing.[3]

Given Newman's preoccupation with the importance of serious subject matter in painting, one might well wonder how this idea of "total space" satisfies that necessity. The answer is that, in Newman's view, the successful rendering, or "declaring," of total space enables individuals, when they apprehend it, to become aware of their relation to the Absolute. "If I succeed in doing that," says Newman, "I feel that I have moved in relation to the true feeling of what it is to be alive."[4] In more specific terms, he said: "Anyone standing in front of my paintings must feel the vertical dome-like vaults encompass him to awaken an awareness of his being alive in the sensation of complete space."[5] And his own need to do this is, as he puts it, a result of the individual's "natural desire in the arts to express his relation to the Absolute."[6]

The means by which this is to be achieved is scale, and it is interesting that Newman speaks of it as both physical and metaphysical. We shall presently talk in detail about what he meant by "total space" and "scale," and we shall examine closely just how scale works in mechanical terms to achieve the ends he claims of it, but for the moment a more pressing thought arises. It is one which persists throughout any discussion of Newman and his writings, and one which articulates an unease that one often feels when engaging with Newman's art discourse. It is the problem of whether or not Newman intends such concepts as "total space" and "scale" (in their metaphysical sense) as metaphors—or whether in fact he is referring to something which, in some sense, physically exists. As soon as we embark on a discussion of what he means by scale, the point of asking this question, and the uncertainty which underlies it, will become apparent.

The first and most obvious point to be made about scale is that it is not equated with size. A large painting is not necessarily of large scale (or, as Newman preferred to put it, does not necessarily "have" scale), and a small painting may indeed have scale. When asked, "By scale, you don't mean size?" Newman replied, "It is beyond the problem of size. It looks big," and he added later, of Veronese's *Wedding Feast at Cana* (a physically enormous painting), "It is really a small painting, that's the trouble."[7]

We are all familiar with the notion that objects may appear to be bigger or smaller than they really are, and the mechanics of this process is much exploited by fashion designers and interior decorators. However, the fact that Newman means this, but also something more, is indicated by the kind of language he uses to describe it. "Scale is a *felt* thing and one has to overcome the size,"[8] he said [my italics], and he frequently talked about the *sensation* of scale and space.

What he is pointing to here is the difference between a picture's looking big and feeling big; and although the pictorial elements which give rise to these phenomena may well be of the same kind but perhaps different in their particulars, the result is a difference in impact. In the first case, one is referring to a physical expansiveness of the image, which, in its simplest form, can be illustrated by the optical largeness of a white square compared with a black one of identical size. In the second case, one is referring to the "emotional" effect that the "largeness" of the image induces—however that might be. Presumably, the difference is also a difference of quality; it is the difference between any old black cube and Tony Smith's six-foot cube *Die,* or the difference between Brancusi's *Endless Column* and its many derivatives.[9]

Newman himself articulates this difference in several ways. When describing his own space and scale, he said:

For me space is where I can feel all four horizons, not just the horizon in front of me and in back of me because then the experience of space exists only as volume. In architecture the concern with volume is valid. Unfortunately, painting is still involved in the notion of space as architectural volumes—intricate small volumes, or pulsating total volumes. I am glad that by 1945 I got out of it. . . .

Anyone standing in front of my paintings must feel the vertical dome-like vaults encompass him to awaken an awareness of his being alive in the sensation of complete space. This is the opposite of creating an environment. A painter friend, Kamrowski, said it well; he said my paintings are hostile to the environment. The room space is empty and chaotic but the sense of space created by my painting should make one feel, I hope, full and alive in a spatial-dome of 180 degrees going in all four directions. This is the only real sensation of space. At the same time I want to make it clear that I never set out to paint space-domes *per se.*[10]

Clearly the kind of expansive power of the image that he envisages here is not one in which the image appears to expand—he is not painting "space-domes," or, as Don Judd puts it, form which runs off the edges to imply a continuum.[11] Rather it is the power of the image to produce a feeling of expansiveness in the viewer—which is a different thing. How this happens is not obvious (though one might make some suggestions), but at least it can be said that Newman is articulating something which seems to make sense and which accords with one's experience of some art.

In speaking of Géricault's *The Raft of the "Medusa,"* 1819, Newman said: "Fantastic! The scale is marvelous. You feel the immensity of the event rather than the size of the canvas. Great! Wild painting! The space does engulf one."[12] Feeling "the immensity of the event" instead of the size of the canvas is another way of putting it, but one which is more readily understandable because, in the case of a representational painting, one is able to cash "the immensity of the event" in terms of the narrative-emotional content. Newman, of course, contended that all good representational art has emotional content; it is true, nonetheless, that with a representational work, and especially with *The Raft of the "Medusa,"* one can better articulate the emotional content, or at least more readily label it, in terms of the structures and events imposed by the narrative. In an abstract work, obviously, articulation of the emotional content must be more generalized.

What does Newman mean, then, when he says that one feels "the immensity of the event" rather than the size of the canvas? Newman has a number of things to say about the phenomenon, but what they add up to is a description of the psychology of the experience rather than an account of its mechanics. Nonetheless, his words provide us with information about his views and of his expectations of his own art.

Obviously, when he talks about *The Raft of the "Medusa,"* part of what he means when he refers to "the immensity of the event" is the significance of the moment, or the narrative, depicted in the work: certainly one is impressed by the desperation of the ship-wrecked people and the power and extensiveness of the sea. Newman thought it was possible, however, to achieve the same immensity of "event" in abstract painting—indeed, it was what he himself strove for, and believed that he sometimes achieved.

To speak of "scale" in relation to abstract work in some ways makes the issues clearer, for as soon as one talks about a painting (per se) as "event," then it is obvious that one has slipped into talking about the object in a special sort of existential way: one is no longer simply talking about the work as a painted picture-on-canvas (as a physical object), but rather as an image (an illusion) which is generated by the marks on the canvas, but which is a consequent, nonphysical thing, dependent upon the conjunction of physical stimuli and our perceptions, and which exists, certainly, but not in the material, touchable way that the picture-on-canvas does.

In that case, it is perhaps easier to see how one might (legitimately) be led to say that the image transcends the canvas or the size. What this usually means is not so much that the image looks bigger than it really is, though it may sometimes do that, but that one is not conscious of the size as such, or of the picture (as opposed to the image) as being contained within the edges. The edges, as an indication of the size of the physical object, cease to demand one's attention.

That, of course, is a very common phenomenon in art, but it is not sufficient to give a picture what Newman regards as "scale." The clue lies, I think, in Newman's use of the word "immensity" of the event, which suggests not simply importance but also largeness—though of course a *feeling* of largeness rather than actual physical size. To put it another way: a picture may feel like a big picture because one's attention is stretched right across the canvas.

There are two ways in which this might happen, one of them more obvious in the context of twentieth-century art. The concept of "all-over" art is normally associated, in its sources, with Analytical Cubist painting, but one could just as well point to early Matisse (*La Danse,* for example).[13] In any case, it is an art in which the subject of the picture is no longer located in the central area of the painting but is distributed, more or less evenly, right across the canvas. In such pictures, one is conscious of seeing the picture, and the image, right to the edges of the painting. In this straightforward physical sense, then, it could be said that one's attention is stretched across the canvas.

However, there are a great many "all-over" pictures which do not have that greatness Newman associates with scale, for there are a great many second-rate Cubist paintings (by Gleizes, for example, and even the occasional Picasso and Braque), as well as countless color field paintings of the fifties and sixties. Moreover, the word "stretched" implies an *intensity* of attention which goes beyond mere observation of edge-to-edge distribution of the image.

Scale, in Newman's terms, is reserved for the works in which the whole canvas is not merely used but enlivened to support and create the image. (Sometimes, of course, that will involve leaving part of the canvas bare, as in some of Clyfford Still's successful works.) In the case of "all-over" art, the technique usually involved some device of visual strength at the edges—whether directly presented as such or not.

For example, in Newman's *Who's Afraid of Red, Yellow and Blue III,* 1966–67, a vast expanse of red is stretched right across a canvas eight feet high and almost eighteen feet long, and pinned at the edges by a narrow strip of blue on the left and yellow, on the right. In *Vir Heroicus Sublimis,* on the other hand, the red—and one's attention—is pushed across the canvas, through the zips (rather than under them), right to the edges of the canvas. Although there is, in fact, a zip close to the right-hand edge, it is the red beyond it which has the strength rather than the zip itself, because, throughout the picture, the red always has the power to roll through (though never obliterate) the vertical zips. In this case, strength at the edges is implied and, indeed, realized, simply by the demonstrated strength of the red itself throughout the whole picture.

The point at which works such as these cease to be merely canvases divided into certain areas of color and become pictures with "scale" is delicate and probably indefinable. However, something can be said about the differences between them. In the case of *Who's Afraid of Red, Yellow and Blue III,* it is interesting that the appropriate phrase seems to be "stretched across the canvas," for one does very much have the sensation of tautness—of the image stretched to its limits, though stable.

Presumably the perceptual explanation for this phenomenon is that the overall combination of relations between height to size, and to area, color to color and to texture is such that the attention is more or less evenly divided between focusing on the center of the picture and scanning both edges equally and simultaneously. That makes an interesting point of comparison with an unsuccessful color field painting of the same "style"; for with such a work one simply tends to read from left to right, observing one element or incident at a time, without really holding anything in relation to something further on in the picture; it is, simply, a collection of color areas. Once made, of course, *Who's Afraid of Red, Yellow and Blue III* can be readily duplicated by anyone prepared to measure exactly and match color, for the picture has no distinctive "handwriting," as it were. But as Newman himself said, in an interview on television with Frank O'Hara, somebody had to get it right in the first place: it took an artist to achieve the scale.[14]

With *Vir Heroicus Sublimis* the line between banality and "scale" is similarly fine, and is perhaps most readily appreciated if one considers the character and functions of the zips. Again, the picture is a very elongated one, being a little under eight by eighteen feet. The red has enormous intensity, and anyone standing close to it is bathed in reflected light (though Newman contends that it was of greater intensity before it was cleaned after acquisition by the Museum of Modern Art).[15] Contrary to all one's expectations of stripes, and especially vertical stripes, the zips in this painting do not divide the painting into segments, nor do they read as being in front of the red. This is presumably because the differences in their color and value establish minute variations in depth so that their placement in relation to the picture plane becomes indefinite—as indeed does the picture plane itself. Because the zips are as far apart as they are—and here the interaction of determinants such as the hue, intensity, and value, as well as the width, is very complex—one is not *conscious* of these variations as changes in depth, and so also reads the image as a continuous surface.

At the same time, the expansiveness of the red assures the unity of the image, while the vertical flow of the zips is just sufficient to make them hold, equal in strength (or interest) to the red. The net effect of these factors is to suspend one's perceptual attention between the felt tensions of overall vertical and horizontal extension, but also of extension across spaces from one zip to the next. These competing tensions must be very finely controlled, of course, or the picture (and the viewer) will collapse into perceptual confusion. This is the other danger that such minimal pictures can easily fall into, when they do not fail through simple innertness.

Newman's own account of his paintings is interesting and reinforces this reading. In an unpublished document of around 1955 to 1956 he wrote:

It was Rothko who when showing his first large work done in his 53rd Street studio, sheepishly tried to explain to Annalee [Newman's wife] that his work differed from mine because my lines acted as dividers in the picture. We then explained to him that he was talking of his own work. Even a cursory examination showed that I had never divided a canvas, that the obvious point in my work was its wholeness, that I did not use lines, that I used only the entire area, that the impact of my canvases was in their singleness. But that he was the manipulator of divided area and color patches, rectangle against rectangle, off-color against off-color. . . . That he had reduced the fire of my image to a table line or horizon line in the old fashioned perspective pictures of a divided scene.[16]

In the best of Newman's works, where one's attention *is* stretched right across the canvas and where the resultant impact of the work is of the wholeness of the image and its feeling of largeness (whatever the size), it does not seem fanciful to say that what one feels is "the immensity of the event." But to test this interpretation of Newman's theory of scale further, we should turn to a pre–twentieth-century work in which the image is not of the all-over kind. In doing so, I shall return to *The Raft of the "Medusa,"* since this is a painting to which Newman attributed "scale."

In all-over paintings there is no central image and no one part of the image seems more important than any other; if anything, strength is concentrated at the edges, because the edges are used to stretch the image out from the center. In conventional painting, however, the edges exert their strength (and it is a considerable one) inward, to fix the image somewhere near the center of the canvas. In that case, the image (or at least that part of it located roughly in the center) is usually a determinate form which can be thought of in terms of figure and ground. In a good painting, of course, the ground is just as important as the figure in terms of its dynamics, though the "meaning" of the image is usually expressed through the figure—be it abstract or representational. To give an example, the spaces between forms in an early Kandinsky are tremendously important in establishing the dynamics which enable us to read the color and line of the forms as detaching themselves and becoming ethereal and disembodied: but because this vision of the world as ether and matter is (in one sense) the subject of the pictures, the significance of the picture and the event is located in the forms.[17]

Nonetheless, in pictures which are centrally focused and which therefore necessarily organize themselves into figure and ground, there is a danger area between the image and the edges, which can so easily become inert and meaningless; in such cases, it would make little difference if the edges were moved in or out a little. Any good picture must avoid that weakness, but not every good picture, according to Newman, has "scale." Scale, he says, is what makes it a great painting.

In Géricault's *The Raft of the "Medusa,"* scale is achieved by relating the image to the edges very tautly and dynamically, and it is through the "ground" that these charges are propelled. As in Newman's own work, the image is pulled out to the edges, and it is this that gives the picture its feeling of extensiveness. This effect is achieved mainly through the tilting of planes in the top half of the picture back toward the picture plane so that those parts of the image are not weakened by recession into distance as they otherwise might be. The top curve of the sail on the left, for example, and the figures above the horizon across the center top to the right, relate very tautly to the edges; and the complexity of planes which structure the central image abut onto one another and discharge tensions across the ground to the edges. (This network of planes is, in fact, surprisingly shallow and, with hindsight, not so very different structurally from the hinged and faceted planes of Analytical Cubism. Picasso was very familiar with the contents of the Louvre, of course.)

As Newman himself pointed out, a great many paintings of the past with traditional perspective are, in fact, "flat" paintings (he gave as example Uccello's *Battle of San Romano*).[18] It is simply that we tend not to notice the "flatness" because we are so involved in reading the image as a representation of objects and events in the physical world. Through these mechanisms the image achieves an extensiveness which makes the edges seem visually irrelevant despite their strong structuring force. The event—both narrative and artistic—dominates one's attention so that one no longer thinks of it as an image contained within a frame; one ceases to think of it as being of a particular size in relation to the space around it and, indeed, ceases to think of it in relation to its environment at all. In this sense it seems to transcend space and size, and it is this that gives a picture "scale."

Newman had other points to make about scale and total space. One of these concerns the role of drawing in the creating of scale, and the second has to do with the manner in which scale is apprehended. Drawing, Newman thought, is the most important element in the creating of scale and heroic art, and it was the most important thing, in his opinion, about his own work:

Drawing is central to my whole concept. I don't mean making *drawings,* although I have always done a lot of them. I mean the drawing that exists in my painting. Yet no writer on art has ever confronted that issue. I am always referred to in relation to my color. Yet I know that if I have made a contribution, it is primarily in my drawing.[19]

Since there are no forms in Newman's work (or at least in the works which he considered to express what he wanted to say—the work from *Onement I,* 1948, onward), he is obviously referring to something other than the delineation of forms. In fact, his criticism of Ingres was that he made the mistake of thinking that drawing is a matter of contouring and failed to understand the importance of relation. He said: "Drawing isn't a question of contouring, of anatomy. Ingres just had no sense of scale. He couldn't relate. But he didn't know it."[20]

This point is obvious enough, since a picture in which all the forms are correctly contoured, whether to produce a realistic form or to otherwise depict what the artist intended, will fail if the forms are not related to one another, and to the edges, in an appropriate way. A picture in which the forms do not relate is only a collection of well-wrought images to be scrutinized, one after another—as Newman claimed one had to do with Ingres. Such a picture may also "succeed" in a minimal way—that is, be of interest—not only because of the accuracy of the delineation of individual forms but also because of the quality of paintwork, whether it be tonal and color balances, texture, or whatever. But to Newman's mind, such qualities were no more than props if scale, or relational drawing, was lacking. Needless to say, these qualities make the work a better picture than it would be if they were lacking, and they might be so finely executed as to arouse admiration and invite scrutiny. But without overall relational drawing, a painting cannot be great.

The necessity for relational drawing in a great painting is obvious when put in those terms and might not appear to be a very interesting claim. But considered in relation to Newman's own work, it is interesting, for, as he himself said, people usually think of his works in terms of color, not drawing. After all, where is the drawing? Well, as Newman clearly knew, drawing is not just a matter of tracing an outline around a form, of dividing an area off from another, of "manipulating divided areas and color patches," but of thinking across space from the spot where one marks the canvas or paper to another definitive point.

In that case, one could draw a zip in *Vir Heroicus Sublimis* only by thinking across, imaginatively, to the next one, and, indeed, across the whole painting; one has to, in a sense, imaginatively hold the whole painting (or potential painting) in mind, in order to make the line. A line must always be thought of in relation to the whole, even where the whole is as yet unrealized, perhaps even in imagination: it must be at least vaguely "felt" as one proceeds, and this is one of the well-known trials and frustrations of creativity.

Thought of in this way, the line becomes not just the edge between one form and another, but a thing in its own right, existing, in itself, in relation to other lines in the space (as Pollock obviously thought of it). Newman put it quite explicitly when he said of Delacroix's *Women of Algiers:*

Beautiful! It could have been done by the Impressionists. *This* man could draw. (Pointing to one woman's naked foot, he adds:) Drawing here doesn't only break up space, it exists as a line, as a thing.[21]

Of course Newman did not want his line to break up space, because, as he said, he wanted to present space whole[22]—total space, in which nothing, whether line or color, divided the whole up into parts. He clearly thought of space in a different way from those for whom it is an emptiness or a void, into which one might put things, or in the case of a painting, colors, lines, and forms. For him, space existed as a positive element, and he believed that an awareness of space in this way would make one aware of one's own being.

This is not as fanciful as it might sound at first, for, when we think about it, we realize that space is a crucial medium in which our bodies and persons exist. It would not be surprising if the way we relate to that space affects our sense of self, whether it be in terms of expansiveness and well-being, or of isolation and dissonance. People who are physically fit often report a feeling of enjoying the space around them. Whatever the actual cause of this feeling, many people do experience space in that way.

It is for this reason that Newman talked about "the fullness of space"—not a space full of *things,* such as architectural volumes ("intricate small volumes, medium volumes, or pulsating total volumes"),[23] but a space full of itself and its own presence. Before he began to understand (in the mid-forties) that one might hope to paint space in that positive way, Newman's subject matter was frequently the undesirability of the void. As he put it:

I have always hated the void and in certain of my work of the Forties I always made it clear. In my work of that time, I notice, I had a section of the painting as a kind of void from which and around which life emanated—as in the original Creation—for example, *Gea,* done in 1945 and *Pagan Void,* 1946.

When I started moving into my present concern or attitude in the mid-Forties, I discovered that one does not destroy the void by building patterns or manipulating space or creating new organisms. A canvas full of rhetorical strokes may be full but the fullness may be just hollow energy, just as a scintillating wall of colors may be full of colors but have no *color*. My canvases are full not because they are full of colors but because color makes the fullness. The *fullness thereof* is what I am involved in. It is interesting to me to notice how difficult it is for people to take the intense heat and blaze of my color. If my paintings were empty they could take them with ease. . . .

I don't manipulate or play with space. I declare it. It is by my declaration that my paintings become full. All of my paintings have a top and a bottom. They are never divided; nor are they confined or constricted; nor do they jump out of their size.[24]

So Newman did not want to paint objects, shapes, or colors that fill space, but the feeling of the space itself and its sense of wholeness. The totality of the image and the totality of the space are what he was aiming for. As long as one is painting things (forms) in space rather than the space itself, then one is in danger of forsaking wholeness for the character of the individual parts. Such an image, Newman said, is scrutinized, bit by bit, in an episodic way, and is not apprehended all in one instant. Looking at it from another point of view, we can say that if one wants to achieve a wholeness of image, then it is better to avoid painting things, or forms, which are themselves fragments in space, and to paint the only whole and continuous thing that exists—space. The problem is, of course, how to do that and make it interesting as an image.

This point about apprehending the wholeness of the image in one act of perception is one which recurs in Newman's writing and is true of his best painting. It is also intimately tied to his concept of true space. In his television interview *USA: Atists: Barnett Newman,* he put it this way:

My work has nothing to do with nature—nature meaning landscape.

I would say that the issue is that it's a special kind of space. In the first place it moves away from natural space, and not involving the actual depiction of space in nature. Neither is it, however, on the other side of the coin, a manipulation of the spaces of an area in painting like a relational painting where you manipulate the space. I feel that the thing that interests me is the declaration of space so that you don't have to stand and scrutinize how the canvas moves in and out and so on. And I have described the sensation ["sensation," note] as being true space. Anyway I hope that my painting gives someone who looks at it a sense of place so that he sees and feels himself.

It seems to me that my work denies the relation to landscape nature. I also think it denies the notion of a specific time. I think that what I am trying to do . . . is that at one instant one gets the whole painting and the painting should be unforgettable, and at the same time there's nothing to really examine. The feeling is instantaneous, complete and you can't ever sort of wipe it out of your mind. If I succeed in doing that, I feel that I have moved in relation to the true feeling of what it is to be alive.[25]

The point here about instantaneousness is that if there *is* anything to examine, then one is automatically involved in the discovery of the characteristics of things within the image rather than feeling the impact of the image itself. One sort of painting involves the viewer in metaphorically standing back and taking in the wholeness of the image, while the other involves close-up examination of pieces—or examining, as Newman put it, "the sense of wool," "the sense of silk" in two of Ingres' portraits.[26] Of Uccello's *Battle of San Romano,* he said: "Fantastic. Absolutely totality. One image. I suppose this is so because the light is even from corner to corner. No spotlight—like Courbet. . . . Physically, it is a modern painting, a flat painting. You grasp the thing at once. What fantastic scale!"[27] And of Courbet: "This is the nearest thing to Uccello. There is nothing to scrutinize. You get it or you don't."[28]

As a specific instance of this general phenomenon of parts disappearing into the whole when a work has scale, Newman points to color. Again, of Uccello's *Battle of San Romano* he says:

It is a strictly symmetrical picture. Hence its totality. It is like the symmetry of man. It has no color: it is beyond color. It is not black, nor red. The color is pure light—night light, perhaps, but light. What bothers me is color as color, as material, as local. In Poussin, a pink is a pink.[29]

It is symmetry which enables the color to disappear as "chromo," but he clearly does not mean geometric symmetry, since he complains of Veronese's *Wedding Feast at Cana* that it does not work because of its symmetry—"It is so symmetrical that the symmetry overshadows everything."[30] And of Ingres' *Apotheosis of Homer,* Newman said: "It makes that big Veronese look like a good painting. It is pure mirror symmetry. Ridiculous. He had to find a guy with a mustache for the right side of the picture because the other guy, on the left side, had one."[31]

What he has in mind is not "mirror," or geometric, symmetry but a human symmetry in which the balance of the picture is not literal but felt. In terms of his own paintings, it is a symmetry which comes when the "parts"—the size, color, tones, zips, relations—are organized so that attention is evenly and instantly distributed across the whole picture. In that case, colors do not speak individually as color— pink as pink, as material, as texture, as "chromo." Rather it is the *effect* of color that one is aware of—color as light, color as enlivening space and revealing it. Of his own involvement with color, he said:

To test myself as part of my own education, to test myself to see if I was just being beguiled by these big expanses of color, I did a painting eight feet high and one and a half inches wide, to see if I could make that painting . . . contain the sense of scale I was involved in and also have the feeling that my big paintings have. . . .

I had been working a lot with color and I felt that perhaps I was being intoxicated and beguiled by what happens with color for me, and the challenge for me was to see whether I could do it without any color at all. And so the limits I put on myself were to work with black, only with black, and to handle the raw canvas in such a way that the raw canvas would become color and have a sense of light. This was, I suppose, the only technical thing that went into my mind to try. And I was pleased that with this limitation I was able to get the raw canvas to act as a kind of color (I don't like to use the word "field" of color); but I think I activated the whole area with a feeling of life, and I also found that I was able to get some of the white of the canvas to look like white paint, and some of it to look sort of neutral.

. . . And it was then, at the end of doing the fourth one, that it came to me suddenly that in a sense the kind of tension and intensity that I thought I was getting was for me the beginning of a series which I then realized would be the Stations.[32]

The absence of hue in the *Stations of the Cross,* then, was intended to establish (in his own mind) that one could create a sense of color simply with black and white, and this can only mean that he was interested in the quality of *light*—the general feeling—that is generated by an area of color, be it black, white, or any hue in the spectrum.

That is what Newman meant by scale and total space: the capacity of an image to transcend mere physical size; to fix the attention of the viewer in an intense, concentrated gaze; to impress the observer with the impact of its wholeness; and to enable the viewer to feel the totality of space—of space extending in all four directions and upward.

This is also, of course, a description of a particular abstract mystic symbol, and if we return to that notion now, a further interesting and important point about Newman's work will emerge. One of the crucial elements in the abstract mystic symbol is that its image and forms are nondepictive. Newman constantly deplored "illustrative" art as limited and shallow, and for this reason he insisted that in painting "total space," he was in no sense depicting it—"I never set out to paint space-domes *per se.*" He preferred to say he "declared" the space, and in terms of the pictorial dynamics we have just analyzed, what this must mean is that he set out to create the *feeling* of total space. In fact, he himself talked about wanting to paint the "sensation" of true space, and he said this in the context of not actually depicting "space-domes."[33]

Until the time of the Abstract Expressionists, it had been generally assumed by artists that if one wanted to convey the feeling of a particular event or experience, it was necessary to depict that event in some way and "clad" it, as it were, with its attendant feeling. There were some isolated artists before Abstract Expressionism who believed—or hoped—otherwise; Kandinsky was one, for example, but the German Expressionists generally preferred depiction, and created an art which was, in the view of their later American Expressionist colleagues, illustrative and embarrassingly autobiographical.

Given that there are many different ways in which a particular feeling can be evoked, it would not be surprising to find that one could do so in a painting by some other means than depiction. After all, what better example of the truth of this could one have than music, which certainly has expressive power, but which (except in an eccentric way) lacks the capacity for representational imagery? The Abstract Expressionists, and especially Newman, were not unsophisticated about music; they numbered several composers among their friends, and their tastes ranged from John Cage, Morton Feldman, through the classics, to jazz.[34]

Newman certainly believed that, as with music, which is abstract, so with painting—that one might evoke or express a feeling by means other than illustration. The means he adopted involved manipulation of the perceptions in such a way that a feeling is induced which is *analogous* to the experiencing of space in a certain way. By what perceptual and psychological processes this occurs, next to nothing is known. It is tempting to think that it might be physiological, and certainly some scientists have believed so,[35] but this can only be speculation at this stage. What is important is that it happens often in the abstract arts, and that Newman was successful in finding an analogue for the particular feeling he wanted to express.

Although in Newman's case the analogue of feeling is induced by "physical" means—the manipulation of perception, rather than by emotive association of ideas, the analogue of feeling is, nonetheless, an analogue—or as Motherwell preferred to put it, a metaphor of feeling.[36]

This fact provides us with the answer to the problem raised early in this chapter—namely, of whether Newman was talking about his work in physical or metaphysical terms. In offering his account of the dynamics of scale and in seeking a realization of "total," or "true," space in his work, Newman appears to be offering a literal, physical account of the pictorial structure of his paintings. But of course it is bound to appear that way given the physical, rather than emotional, associative way he chose to create his analogue of feeling. The means is literal and physical, but the end product is a metaphor of feeling; and since what he was interested in describing when he talked about his work was the final result achieved, rather than the technique of realizing it, it is clear that when he talked about "scale" and "total," or "true," space, these terms were used as interpretive metaphors: they described his particular abstract, mystic symbol.

It is perhaps appropriate to close this chapter with a quotation which encapsulates these points very nicely. It is not a remark by Newman, but a quotation from, perhaps not surprisingly, Mallarmé. Robert Motherwell is the one who quotes it, and he prefaces it with his own remark: "What better definition of modern art is there than Mallarmé's . . . the expression of the mysterious meaning of aspects of existence, through human language brought back to its essential rhythm." He then adds the further passage from Mallarmé, and it is one which describes the aspiration and achievement of the Abstract Expressionists in general, but is particularly appropriate in the case of Newman. It reads: ". . . for I am inventing a language that must necessarily spring from a very new poetics: *to paint, not the thing, but the effect that it produces.*"[37]

Chapter Nine

ROBERT MOTHERWELL

If, with the other artists we have examined so far, we have concentrated on the identification of their particular abstract mystic symbols, Motherwell's work demands a different approach. This is partly because the feelings his works express are both various and difficult to describe, since they are a compound of many different elements. But perhaps more important, there is something in the aesthetic structure of his works which resists the approach adopted with the other artists.

Motherwell's art is very complex, not so much in its physical, pictorial structure, which is no more and no less complex than in any other kind of art, but certainly in its theoretical, aesthetic structure. And from it we can learn a great deal, not just about Motherwell's work itself, but about how certain Abstract Expressionist principles were theoretically structured, and of how they might be realized in practice.

We can, for example, learn something about *how* feeling can be imported into paintings, and there is the opportunity to discover how the principles of "direct expression," as against "illustration," might work. At the very least, it should enable us to learn more about what the Abstract Expressionists meant by these concepts, even if it cannot be conclusively demonstrated that the artists effected, or achieved, them.

Motherwell has written and said a great deal about his own art and Abstract Expressionism generally. Much of it we have already sampled in the chapters concerned with the development of the abstract mystic symbol. There is another part of his writing, however, which is concerned with the specific nature of his painting; it has quite a different character from the rest of his art-talk, and deals with quite different elements of painting.

It is also true that the critics have tended to use a different approach to Motherwell's work from the one they have taken to the other Abstract Expressionists. By this I simply mean that they, like Motherwell, have tended to focus on quite different aspects of its structure. This may be partly because they have been influenced by the way Motherwell has talked about it, but it is more likely to be so because the work invites a different kind of consideration.

One of the questions which constantly arises, in a way which it does not with the other artists, is that of meaning. Being one of the few artists who uses determinate forms, and probably also because of the kinds of titles he uses, some people, presumably frustrated by not being able to deal with the other artists in traditional ways, have gone to great lengths to attribute iconographical meaning to Motherwell's forms. The paintings do not seem to bear this out, and certainly none of the well-known critics has ever taken this view, but it has provoked some discussion about how meaning is generated.[1] Much of the following discussion, therefore, will concern itself with meaning in Motherwell's works, with how it operates in theoretical, aesthetic terms, and with the problem of reference in particular.

If the emphasis with Newman's work was on the perceptual processes involved, with Motherwell it is the epistemological processes which need to be elaborated—and this is not to say that his work is cerebral and nonsensuous and nonemotional. Rather, it is through the epistemological process that one will discover how Motherwell made his abstract mystic symbols, and it will involve an analysis of such ideas as collage and poetic evocation. It also involves consideration of the appearance of spontaneous generation in his works, and dissection of the mechanics of this process. All in all, the discussion is geared toward finding out how it all happens, rather than with describing what is there.

Let us turn first to the question of subject matter. When Samuel Kootz arranged an exhibition of Abstract Expressionist works, called *The Intrasubjectives,* he wrote in the preface to the catalogue: "Intrasubjectivism is a point of view in painting, rather than an identifiable painting style."[2] One could perhaps go further and say that not only were the Abstract Expressionists united in their attitudes to art and creativity, but that they were even concerned with the same subject matter. Motherwell's explanation of the "gesture" in painting—"The 'gesture' was, so to speak, that of an artist standing alone before the Absolute"[3]—was remarkably similar to Newman's description of "man's natural desire in the arts to express his relation to the Absolute,"[4] and there are numerous other statements by the artists which echo this desire to engage with the profound feelings of human experience. Motherwell's later description of Abstract Expressionism and of his own work is particularly apt and expressive. "What I am trying to do," he said, "is what I think abstract expressionism in part was always trying to do, to make a work, huge as it is, as a spontaneous gesture of the spirit, that one did in a single moment of passion, so to speak."[5]

What is interesting, though, apart from the important fact that the artists succeeded in realizing those objectives, is that they are realized in different ways. Motherwell's work looks very different from Newman's and Pollock's, and their work from that of each other; that this is so, is very important. It is perhaps inevitable that the works look different, since they are expressions of "felt thought," always an individual endeavor. Motherwell put it thus: "I happen to think primarily in paint—just as musicians think in music. And nothing can be more concrete to a man than his own felt thought, his own thought feeling."[6] And the different expressions of "felt thought" are embodied in the work and evoked in the viewer by quite different kinds of perceptual, emotional, and intellectual "manipulation" from artist to artist. It is these differing methods of aesthetic manipulation that I refer to, in what follows, as "theoretical aesthetic structure."

If one were to characterize the aesthetic structure of Motherwell's work, it would be in terms of poetic evocation through association of feeling. Motherwell himself has often mentioned "metaphors of feeling" in relation to his work, and the idea of poetry in painting has been an important one to him. As well as asserting the direct and indirect influences of the arts on one another (and he quotes that beautiful line of Baudelaire's "The arts aspire, if not to complement one another, at least to lend one another new energies),[7] he believes that good painting in some way incorporates the essence of poetry. In the preface to Marcel Raymond's book *From Baudelaire to Surrealism,* he writes:

True painters disdain "literature" in painting. It is an error to disdain literature itself. Plainly, painting's structure is sufficiently expressive of feelings, of feelings far more subtle and "true" to our being than those representing or reinforcing anecdotes: but true poetry is no more anecdotal than painting. Both have sought in modern times to recover the primitive, magical and bold force of their mediums and to bring it into relation to the complexities of modern felt attitudes and knowledge; no modernist painter can read in this marvelous book of some of the ideas of French poets without a sharp sense of recognition.

Perhaps the "plasticity" that we painters so admire is no less than the poetry of visual relations.[8]

That phrase "the poetry of visual relations" is an interesting one because it is obvious that Motherwell means something more specific than simply the "magic" of visual relations (which is how the term is most commonly used). There are two distinct though connected concepts which might be meant by "poetry" here, and they are two aspects of aesthetic structure in poetry. The first one is particularly important and requires some explication.

One of the principles of philosophy and poetry is that words are not only the bearers of their explicit meaning but also have connotations through association of ideas. Thus "black" not only refers to the color but also has connotations of darkness, evil, hopelessness, a racial group, intensity, unacceptability, and so on. In poetry, it is common to assemble words and phrases so that the direct meaning of a word is underplayed or suppressed, and its connotations are permitted to come into play.

Motherwell argues (and indeed, the point is hardly contentious) that colors and forms can be manipulated in painting in an analogous way.

In his article "Beyond the Aesthetic," he argues that there is an inevitability about this process, and that, without it, colors and forms would cease to function as aesthetic elements:

The "pure" red of which certain abstractionists speak does not exist, no matter how one shifts its physical contexts. Any red is rooted in blood, glass, wine, hunters' caps, and a thousand other concrete phenomena. Otherwise we should have no feeling toward red or its relations and it would be useless as an artistic element.[9]

How this is operative in his painting becomes clearer when we turn to the "meaning" of his images. Motherwell has always resisted the attempts of some critics to attach specific meaning to the forms in his works. Of the *Spanish Elegy* paintings he says that they are "not Historical paintings of the Civil War—but [more] like a memorial to it, like a tomb";[10] and of the question of iconography in general, he says:

To me this raises a profound question: . . . [are these colors and shapes] an iconography or a tone of voice. I'd argue that the subject matter of all of the Elegies—of all abstract expressionism—is a tone of voice.[11]

This is quite different from what Motherwell has in mind when he talks about literary, or anecdotal, painting—that is to say, painting in which the forms are used to refer to specific events or objects in the world. Naturally, the explicitness with which the references occur varies, but in Abstract Expressionism generally, and in Motherwell's work in particular, the forms do not function as references but are used to evoke feelings—or at least it might be more accurate to say that the various evocations of the forms and colors as they jostle one another, side by side, together generate the impressions or experience (call it what you will) of a feeling or "tone of voice." These evocations or connotations ("reverberations" is how they are often described) almost always operate at a nonexplicit level, so that when Motherwell says that red is "rooted in blood, glass, wine, hunters' caps," this does not mean that one can therefore turn to a patch of red in one of his paintings and specify which of these or other items is evoked.

The point is that one is not made to *think* of blood, wine, hunters' caps, and so on, but that the feelings associated with these phenomena are evoked—and that is obviously a very different process. This is presumably what Frank O'Hara had in mind when he wrote:

The possibility of the schema's [that is, of the *Spanish Elegies'*] arousing such a broad range of associations, depending on the emotional vocabulary of the viewer, is a sign of its power to communicate human passion in a truly abstract way, while never losing its specific identity as a pictorial statement. The exposure is one of sensibility, rather than of literal imagistic intent, and therefore *engages* the viewer in its meaning rather than *declaring* it.[12] [My italics]

Since this is a subtle and nonexplicit process in the viewer, for the artist too it is correspondingly difficult: a process of discovery for which instructions cannot be given. Like the French Symbolist poets, Motherwell believed that the best way to suppress the particular reference of a word or form and to release the experience and feelings unconsciously associated with its connotations, is to disorient the reason by disrupting the normal pattern of living. Once we have gotten rid of *actual* reference to objects and events, the elements in a poem or a painting can be manipulated, along with their attendant feelings, so that one builds up a work or "relational structure" which communicates a particular state or feeling:

The passions are a kind of thirst, inexorable and intense, for certain feelings and felt states. To find or invent "objects" (which are, more strictly speaking, relational structures) whose felt quality satisfies the passions—*that* for me is the activity of the artist. . . . No wonder the artist is constantly placing and displacing, relating and rupturing relations: his task is to find a complex of qualities whose feeling is just right—veering toward the unknown and chaos, yet ordered and related in order to be apprehended.[13]

For Motherwell, the technical means of disrupting reference and building a "relational structure" of feeling was the principle of collage. Of the practice of collage, he wrote:

The sensation of physically operating on the world is very strong in the medium of the *papier collé* or *collage,* in which various kinds of paper are pasted to the canvas. One cuts and chooses and shifts and pastes, and sometimes tears off and begins again. In any case, shaping and arranging such a relational structure obliterates the need, and often the awareness, of representation. Without reference to likeness, it possesses feeling because all the decisions in regard to it are ultimately made on the grounds of feeling.[14]

The principle of collage, of course, is an important method in poetry. In one sense, all poetry is collage, since, like Motherwell's paintings, it sets out to build up a structure of ideas and impressions which together express a certain feeling or experience. It may do so through discursive language (as most pre–twentieth-century Western poetry does), or it may do so through a succession of juxtaposed images or ideas, such as in Japanese Haiku or T. S. Eliot. Thus:

> Dead my old fine hopes
> And dry my dreaming
> But still . . .
> Iris, blue each Spring
>
>   —Shushiki[15]

and

> His soul stretched tight across the skies
> That fade behind a city block,
> Or trampled by insistent feet
> At four and five and six o'clock;
> And short square fingers stuffing pipes,
> And evening newspapers, and eyes
> Assured of certain certainties,
> The conscience of a blackened street
> Impatient to assume the world.
> I am moved by fancies that are curled
> Around these images, and cling:
> The notion of some infinitely gentle
> Infinitely suffering thing.
>
>   —T. S. Eliot[16]

But whether it be through discursive or nondiscursive language, it is still a process in which the literal meaning of a word is supressed (though not necessarily entirely), and the subterranean associations and reverberations are explored and exploited through encountering them in unexpected ways (which is, after all, the basis or method of metaphor). Thus in Shakespeare's Sonnet 73 we have:

> That time of year thou mayst in me behold
> When yellow leaves, or none, or few, do hang
> Upon those boughs which shake against the cold,
> Bare ruined choirs where late the sweet birds sang.
> In me thou see'st the twilight of such day
> As after sunset fadeth in the west,
> Which by and by black night doth take away,
> Death's second self, that seals up all in rest.
> In me thou see'st the glowing of such fire,
> That on the ashes of his youth doth lie
> As the deathbed whereon it must expire,
> Consumed with that which it was nourished by.
>> This thou perceivest, which makes thy love more strong,
>> To love that well which thou must leave ere long.

Obviously, this principle of poetic structure can be applied to painting as well. It is, however, a very difficult one to deal with critically, since the associations from which the feelings arise are not recognized—only their effect is felt. In that case, all one can say of a patch of red, say, in one of the *Elegies,* is that it has a certain zing and exhilaration (if one subconsciously thinks of hunters' caps), or sensuousness (if one thinks of wine), or drama, danger, or tragedy (if one thinks of blood). Which of these responses are triggered and which are suppressed will depend on a complex network of other factors, but especially on the spatial relationships and tensions and on the manner in which the paint is used.

Spatial relationships and application of color are relatively easy to talk about in the sense that one can point to the dynamic effects that spatial arrangements give rise to. Why they should be associated with certain feelings or metaphysical ideas is not so easy to explain, though there have been attempts made by Gestalt phychologists and by Rudolf Arnheim with his theory of isomorphic structures.[17] So, with Barnett Newman's work, for instance, one can describe the pictorial dynamics in some detail, and can describe their effect in pulling one's attention expansively up and across the picture; and one can explain this process in physiological, perceptual terms. But how one explains that at a certain stage of this perceptual expansion, there occurs a point—if the size, color, and spatial relations are of a certain kind—at which the physiological experience of one's perceptual attention being extended becomes an actual feeling of expansiveness in the viewer, is not so clear. Nor is it easy to explain why a work which has this effect can insistently hold one's attention, and can give the viewer the impression that he or she is in front of an object with a special quality or "power." But that is a problem about all good paintings.

Motherwell's work, though, presents a special problem, in that while the formal, structural dynamics are not merely necessary but very important, the evocation of feeling seems to be much less physiologically based than in Newman's and other painters', and without the same singleness of focus. In Motherwell's paintings, evocation of feeling is more rooted in emotional association than in physiological effect, and his works are more "pluralist" in effect. That is to say, the overall effect of a Motherwell is a very complex blend of feelings, a fact which is probably accounted for by the very strong feelings of nostalgia or, perhaps more accurately, regret for what is lost, which they most often have.

Although it is difficult to offer a precise analysis of this aspect of Motherwell's work, there seems to be general agreement that this is the way they are. What critics do disagree about is the degree of *literal* interpretation that is appropriate. The *Elegies* are the most beleaguered of his work in this respect, and critics occasionally try to interpret them iconographically. Such interpretations do not hold water but, more importantly, are simply not necessary. Motherwell himself has given this sort of approach—especially the sexual and "use of name" interpretations—short shrift.[18] There are, however, some comments which can be made about the structure of his works, and which are more amenable to analytic examination. One of these concerns his use of the principle of collage.

Motherwell has used collage since 1943, and the technique is still an important part of his work; but what strikes one about his paintings is that in some respects they, too, have the feeling (though not the literal look) of collage. The other and connected point is that the appearance of his paintings, and especially of the *Spanish Elegies,* is quite unlike that of any other Abstract Expressionist. On the face of it, this might seem like a very obvious point and not something by which to single him out. However, the force of the point becomes a little clearer when one compares his work with that of Franz Kline, the painter whose work Motherwell's most resembles, at least on the superficial level of style and forms.

Without taking away from the quality of the best of Kline's work, and without denying the individuality of form and structure in his images, it is nonetheless true that Kline's pictures resemble those of several other painters, among them de Kooning, Friedel Dzubas, Al Leslie (in the fifties), Michael Goldberg, and, to some extent, though with a notably different palette, Hans Hofmann. The point of similarity—and it is one which marks these artists off more obviously as "gesture" painters—is that their paintings come out of a similar attitude toward forms, an attitude which emphasizes the beginning and end of an element or form as one stroke of the brush. One can, as it were, trace the history of the forms through the evidence of the brush strokes: that is to say, one is invited to do so, and, in Kline's work in particular, the work is often presented as an enacted passage of time.

This is not so with Motherwell's forms, which have a completely different feel about them. Apart from their monumentality (which Kline and other artists sometimes share), they manage to look as if they came into existence ready-made and completed. This of course contributes to their monumentality and gives them a kind of timeless quality. As Motherwell himself put it when comparing his work with Kline's:

There *is* something about the *Elegy* pictures, as there was to be in Kline, that is very different. Kline at his best is a superb painter, way beyond beautifully using black and white. An explosive energy, cropping and compactness, some kind of directness that is "beyond" painting, or to put it another way, is something that painting can do, and very rarely does. My *Elegies,* though equally direct, are silent, monumental, more architectonic, a massing of black against white, those two sublime colors, *when used as color.*[19]

This impression of instantaneous existence comes in part from the method of facture that Motherwell employs, at least as much as from the shape of the forms and their relations to one another. They are always large, and have a singleness of identity and substance that one does not get in forms which are visibly built up from component parts (as are de Kooning's, Kline's, and Hofmann's, for example). Whereas most of the "gesture" painters use paint to indicate the presence of brush strokes, Motherwell uses it to give a unity and continuity of surface, albeit a textured one. This enables us to comprehend the form as a homogeneous whole but, more important, eliminates any awareness of which parts of the form preceded others in the making.

There is evidence of brushwork, of course, but it is used to build up an edge or to change the direction of the texture; primarily, brushwork is used to create a surface. It is a surface in which no one part asserts any temporal primacy, and yet it is a surface (and a form) which is quite evidently *made*. The net result of these factors is to suggest a form which was made, but all in a single moment of time; and where this occurs in a great painting, as in many of the *Elegies* (especially Number 34), the dual elements of instantaneous creation and permanence (which the lack of "time marks" suggests) not only bring to mind, but serve as a symbol or analogue of, the Divine Act of creation. It is, as it were, man's heroic attempt to emulate the act of creation, or, in Motherwell's phrase, "a spontaneous gesture of the spirit."[20]

This is not simply hyperbole, though I do not wish to suggest that one looks at Motherwell's forms and thinks of the Divine Act, or sees them as an analogue of creation. But whether one actually thinks of that or not, there is the quite tangible fact of form which proclaims that it is made, and yet which is all of a piece and betrays no sign of where the artist began and finished. Because the forms are not only large but monumental in their effect, the mind resolves the tension between these two facts by thinking of the forms, in imagination, as having been brought into existence complete. That feeling seems to me to be inescapable in the best of Motherwell's work; the images are awesome, and stare back at the viewer. They are also moving, and this stems at least in part from the fact that one senses the struggle and achievement of their making.

The size of the forms is important in several ways. In the first place, they are always large in relation to their space and they tend to sit tensely beside their neighbors, often with a jammed, but not quite bursting, look. The forms are also very flat, and being conceptually self-contained as they are, they have an appearance of being not so much forms made through brushstrokes (though one remains very aware of the medium), as pieces which have been brought together in one place. It is this, along with their flatness, that gives the feeling of collage.

The flatness within the forms comes about because the inflections are small and uniform and because, over a large area, depth within small elements tends perceptually to flatten out. (This is one of the inherited consequences of small-piece all-over cubism, handled in various ways by the Abstract Expressionists and acutely analyzed by Walter Darby Bannard.)[21] Consequently the forms are flat like paper or thin metal, and of course this intensifies their appearance as "things." This independence of being in no way isolates them from the ground, however, and the forms are neither superimposed nor imprisoned "behind"; in fact, the depth of space (which is not at all consciously visible) is so finely controlled that the forms, though distinct, blend into the ground as if they are all of the same substance.

This thinness and flatness of the picture plane is intensified by the fact that all the perceptible movement in the pictures is lateral and never forward and back. In fact, in the *Elegies,* although there are horizontal pressures in the fullness and tension of some of the forms, the pulse of the paintings is always vertical (like the vertical strokes of calligraphy), despite their horizontal format. The sense of the forms' being calligraphic is an odd one, for there is no sense in which they *resemble* handwriting; on the other hand, one has a strong feeling of their having been made, as if by some giant brush. But whereas Kline and others might incorporate or simulate brush trails at the beginning and end of a form or element, Motherwell's effect is achieved through the continuity of small strokes which serve as evidence of facture, but without the impression of a composition built up from small parts. The forms, then, are evidently made, and in one piece, and since they resemble nothing at all (that is to say, they look like nothing but themselves), one tends to think of them in the only way possible—as marks by a person, of some calligraphic sort, but, of course, on a giant scale. Critics have sometimes described them in terms of punctuation marks, a thought which presumably comes from the same source or impression.[22]

This impression of strange calligraphic marks made on a giant scale carries with it an air of mystery, since one is uncertain of how the marks came to be. This effect is compounded by the fact that one shifts from thinking of them in a number of different ways at once—as calligraphic marks; as thin, assembled "things"; and as having the monumentality of architecture. The tensions implied between these phenomena and the ambiguities they generate intensify one's feeling of being confronted with something new and strange. The genesis of the forms is suggestively mysterious, a characteristic very important to Motherwell's having conceived of them emotionally as "a spontaneous gesture of the spirit . . . [done] in a single moment of passion."

One of the interesting critical points, though, is the way in which Motherwell succeeds in manipulating the concept of collage so that this effect is achieved. And, on the face of it, this is surprising, since one does not normally associate collage with passion. What he takes from collage, from the technical point of view, is its flatness and the idea of its elements being prefabricated and brought together and "placed." "There is an analogy to collage," says Motherwell, "where I am working with ready made elements. In the Elegies the ovals and the vertical panels are *a priori* elements in my mind."[23]

In the emotional dimension, what Motherwell borrows from collage and develops is its nondiscursiveness and emotional condensation—the feeling that the normal "connecting" pieces have been eliminated and that only the raw centers of thought and feeling have been brought together and rudely juxtaposed. In much of Motherwell's work there is the sense of brevity, but also of things deleted and discarded, and this is due partly (especially in the *Elegies*) to the monumentality of the image, of the scale of the forms in relation to the space, and to the impression they give of having been wrenched from a larger whole: they are closed-up fragments from a lost whole, with a sense of loss, though complete in themselves as images.

Much of this is, when one thinks about it, the visual application of the principle of collage as the French Symbolist poets conceived of it—that disruption of patterns and discursiveness, the dislocation of the image so that it is presented as a powerful, "pure" symbol in a void. This is not how one usually thinks of collage in the visual arts, however, and that is because, like so many fertile ideas, it wears a very different face according to which of its dimensions is emphasized. And because most of our experience of it comes from Cubism, we are used to encountering it in a very different manifestation.

Collage has developed mostly within the Cubist tradition of art, and even when it is used to generate relationships of feeling (as in Schwitters, for example), it is still employed within a context of Cubist assumptions about how pictures are made and how they must look. Like Cubist art generally, collage has traditionally been used in an all-over pattern of shallow space, where edges push back and forth to visibly define the pictorial structure and to declare the picture as having certain kinds of deliberate structural interests.

What Motherwell had to avoid was any association with the collage of Cubism, since this would run counter to the impression, so important to his work, of spontaneous generation. What he had to avoid, especially, was any feeling that the elements have a strong structural function—that they are an armature through which one manipulates the appearances of entities and space. Of course the elements in a Motherwell painting are used structurally (for a painting without structure falls apart), but they are not used *as if* this is their primary purpose, and they do not draw attention to the structure in a conscious, deliberate way.

So we find that Motherwell's forms do not create movement and space back and forth; all the tensions are lateral, and movement as such is eliminated in favor of monumental immovability. Although the "ground" is always dynamic, Motherwell avoids spreading the forms across the surface in an all-over way, so that one is not tempted to think of them as basically illusion—a structuring of space. Rather, they are items, icons, definite "things," specifically located, and with certain emotional and mystical powers. For this reason, too, the impression of overlap, so common in Cubist collage, is avoided; where it occurs physically in the actual collages, its space-structuring potential is deem-phasized and its emotional reverberations drawn out.

Yet in both cases he retains the feeling of abrupt juxtaposition and elimination characteristic of collage—in the paintings by "cramping" forms which individually retain their separateness and strength. This latter element ensures that the tensions across a space between forms are not one-way, thus avoiding the problem of a dominant form emotionally overlapping another. The point about overlapping is that it would not only visually emphasize the structural function of the forms but would also introduce the idea of the work's being *assembled,* one piece at a time. This would obviously run counter to the impression of spontaneous generation in the images, and specifically to the impression that the painting is primarily the product of "the passion and spirit of man."

These then are some of the ways in which Motherwell uses the principle of collage to realize poetic evocation in his work. By its very nature it is difficult to talk about its appearance in particular works, since the emotive associations raised are no longer connected with particular things, at a conscious level: all that is recognized is the feeling. It is the collage principle that is used to eliminate or suppress those connections from rising to the surface, and, again, its actual operation is not really accessible to examination.

At a more physical level, however, one can say that the look, or feeling, of collage is achieved by making the forms seem flat and thin, by cramping them together, and by giving them the appearance of having been made in a previous existence, prior to their presence in the painting. The mystery of their genesis is intensified by their size and by the impression they give of having belonged to a larger whole. These are important elements in helping Motherwell achieve his desired aim, but there are still further ways of considering his ends and their means, to which we must address ourselves.

To return, then, to the problem of meaning, there are one or two questions which arise that require clarification and which throw further light on the impulses of Motherwell's work and of Abstract Expressionism generally. Motherwell's insistence (and he is like the other artists in this) is that the content of his works is feeling, but without reference to anything specific; especially, the meaning is not dependent upon the use of symbols which *stand for,* or evoke, certain objects or events. In other words, his forms are not used to *refer.* This is somewhat problematic from a theoretical point of view, since there are occasions in Motherwell's work where it might seem approriate to point to certain apparently relevant references, and somewhat unnatural to deny them. For example, in *Spanish Prison (Window),* 1943–44, there is the suggestion of a figure (the same sort of figure as that portrayed in *Pancho Villa, Dead and Alive,* 1943) caught behind bars; and in *Personage,* 1943, and *Pancho Villa* it is said that there is a coffin superimposed over the space where the figure is seen or is implied.

It is not possible to deny the presence of a figure in *Spanish Prison* and *Pancho Villa,* and difficult to argue against the coffin in *Personage* (whether it was consciously intended or not), and especially difficult when one bears in mind the fact that the subject matter of all those paintings is, in some of its aspects, death. In that case, it might seem perverse to deny the references of some of the forms. Of course it must be remembered that these are early works (though not the lesser for that), done before Motherwell had abandoned figuration completely.

However, I do not think Motherwell would regard these paintings as being any different from his later works in their deep aesthetic structure. He would not deny that the forms have these particular references, but would think that this has very little and perhaps nothing to do with the fact that they work the way they do—that is, succeed in expressing a feeling about a death.

This point emerges when one looks at what Motherwell has to say about the affinities his *Elegy* forms have with architecture. On one occasion he remarked:

I think it's [the meaning of the *Elegies*] deeper than what's obvious and I think it has something to do with the human but I also think it has something to do with architecture. I know a psychoanalyst who I play poker with, who collects German Expressionist paintings. He is originally a German and he sent me from Greece one summer a photograph of some Greek columns, three Greek columns with the—what is it—the pediment across the top that has been taken at twilight so that the columns and the bar across the top appear black against a kind of twilight whiteness and it looked very much like my pictures.[24]

Motherwell has also thought of his work in terms of Stonehenge, Lascaux, and Altamira.[25]

The interesting point is that although certain entities, (such as a figure, a prison, a coffin) are represented in the earlier pictures, one would be hard put to say that of the *Elegies,* which are also concerned with a feeling of death; if one were disposed to see them as abstracted images, then one might equally well fix on some other derivation. Yet it seems appropriate to describe the works (as Motherwell himself does) in terms of, for example, architecture. This raises crucial questions about how meaning is generated in general and of why Motherwell is so insistent that his forms do not have figurative or abstracted reference. If paintings like *Spanish Prison, Pancho Villa, Dead and Alive,* and *Personage* are about death, why would the images of prison bars, a man, and a coffin not be part of the central meaning? And if some of the *Elegies* have architectural qualities, why would it not be relevant to say they were images of Stonehenge or similar structures, if such a conclusion seems visually appropriate?

Even if we accept that the paintings are not meant to be visual *descriptions* of specific things, might it not be that, in depicting them visually (however abstractly), one might catch some of their expressive qualities—the "feeling" of them—as one's central subject matter? In that case, it could be said that the particular forms are symbols which refer to Pancho Villa's story, to the Spanish Civil War, and so on; as symbols of these events they are used to express the feeling of those events, without being simply anecdotal.

However, this is precisely where the problem lies, for Motherwell would deny that the forms are symbols and that they refer to those events or to anything else: and yet, that the forms are in the paintings at all—and their titles, as well, testify to that fact—is evidence that they have some relevance. What can be meant when Motherwell says that the *Elegies* are not about political events in Spain but that they commemorate the death of something important there? In his words, as noted earlier, the *Elegies* are "not Historical paintings of the Civil War—but [more] like a memorial to it, like a tomb." "The *Spanish Elegies* are not 'political' but my private insistence that a terrible death happened that should not be forgot."[26] But does that not amount to the same thing? Surely the latter is just a more generalized political point, but a political point nonetheless, and surely it makes the content of the paintings political too?

This is the theoretical question that nags beneath the surface of discussions such as that of E. A. Carmean's in the catalogue essay of *Subjects of the Artist*[27] and lurks behind common Abstract Expressionist talk about "expressing" versus "illustrating." The question that must be asked is whether or not there can be any difference between "expressing" and "describing," or "illustrating," and how a painting can be about something which at its roots is a political event or phenomenon, and yet not be a "political" painting, or "about" politics.

The answer lies, I think, in the nature of Motherwell's subject matter. There is no doubt that his subject matter is feelings, and he has had much to say about this. It is the subject of his article "Beyond the Aesthetic," the central theme of which is his conception of a painting as the concentrated realization of a feeling. He writes:

The function of the aesthetic [the sensuous] instead becomes that of a medium, a *means* for getting at the infinite background of feeling in order to condense it into an object of perception. We feel through the senses, and everyone knows that the content of art is feeling; it is the creation of an object for sensing that is the artist's task; and it is the qualities of this object that constitute its felt content.[28]

Thus the meaning of a painting *is* its feeling, since the painting itself is not a picture *of* anything, but rather a feeling condensed and objectified.

The conception of art which Motherwell (and the other Abstract Expressionists) rejects is that which tells a story, whether it be a description of an event or a description of a feeling. Of course one does not have to be an abstract artist to do this, for, as Motherwell points out, an artist like Cézanne paints so that his subject matter becomes not the items arranged in his still life but the feeling they together generate: "It is Cézanne's feeling that determined the form of his pictorial structure. It is his pictorial structure that gives off his feeling. If all his pictorial structures were to disappear from the world, so would a certain feeling."[29] The point is that the feeling is created for its own sake and not in order to direct us to something else: it is the end rather than the means.

Motherwell constantly attempts to detach the feelings he has created in his works from particular things and events. He is most insistent that they are not paintings (or feelings) *about* things, and that what is important is that they simply be felt, rather than associated with other things. When speaking of the *Spanish Elegies,* he is always careful to point out that they are elegies to feelings, not events. However, as these feelings are a very specific and complicated blend of emotion and experience (as well as being *sui generis*), there is a problem of how to refer to them in discussion.

Motherwell not unnaturally likens them to (but does not equate them with) both his various experiences which have fed into the painting emotionally, and the events and experiences in the public domain which have a similar feeling. For example, he says: "I've always been spellbound by drumrolls, the contrast between the clear rolling sound and the period of silence. The Elegies—in the pattern of the black forms against the white—have a similar feeling."[30] The point to be remembered is that the paintings are elegies, but elegies of a particular *feeling,* not an event; and since people feel a need to talk about the paintings, Motherwell thinks it appropriate to offer something as an *analogy* to feeling. In his television interview with Bryan Robertson, he said:

I suppose [the Spanish Civil War] was the first public event which I felt deeply emotionally involved in as did many artists and intellectuals of my generation. . . . It seemed to me something beautiful and marvelous died, at least temporarily, in that conflict, and if I were going to elegize something, since it is against my principles to elegize autobiographically, I preferred then to connect it with something that seemed to me of great consequence.[31]

In other words, as an aid to articulation, Motherwell offers the experience of the death of something in Spain as a similar feeling to that in his paintings. It is a visual equivalent of that experience—a metaphor, as it were. "They are absolutely metaphors, not descriptions." He is not describing those events in any sense in the paintings, but uses the titles to remind us of something provoking a similar reaction:

As a metaphor, some people think that, in that particular image, I hit (in the Jungian sense of the word) an archetypal image. There are quite a few people not liking abstract art who are moved by that particular image. Therefore the image by definition has something that is beyond or outside art; exactly what it is, I don't know. . . . The image is akin in feeling—a visual equivalent—to the feeling in Garcia Lorca's *Lament for Ignacio Sanchez Mejias,* and was meant to be. The force of Lorca's poem and its resonance are far beyond the death of a matador, but perhaps not beyond the death of Spain. I *meant* the world "elegy" in the title.[32]

The other point is that as elegies, the paintings have to be dedicated to something—something important, and public, and something having a similar feeling. The dedication does not mean that the paintings are *about* the thing referred to in the dedication, any more than the dedication of soufflé to a ballerina means that soufflé is about the ballerina. It is, simply, an appropriate dedication. When speaking of the development of the first *Elegies,* Motherwell makes this point clear:

When I painted the larger version—*At Five in the Afternoon*—it was as if I discovered it [the image] was a temple. . . . And when I recognized this, I looked around for who represented what the temple should be consecrated to, and that that was represented in the work of Lorca. . . . To be more concise the "temple" was consecrated to a Spanish sense of death, which I got most of from Lorca, but from other sources as well—my Mexican wife, bullfights, travel in Mexico, documentary photographs of the Mexican revolution, Goya, Santos, dark Hispanic interiors.[33]

If we put this in theoretical terms, Motherwell's paintings can be said not to *refer* to things (whether events or feelings) but to *express.* Reference is always one step removed from the real thing, since, in semiological terms, it is a sign, or symbol, or image, which itself is only a mark or substitute that points to the existence of the real thing. What the Abstract Expressionists, including Motherwell, strove for was direct expression through the actual embodiment of the feeling itself in the work; their images, therefore, are not referential and do not rely on reference for their meaning: instead, they express or present actual feelings.

But is this literally true, or is it simply a convenient figure of speech which aptly expresses an important difference of approach to the making of art and articulates, perhaps, a difference of emphasis? To answer this, we must go back to our earlier discussion of reference versus poetic association. There we saw that meaning can be generated in several different ways, and that a sign can have several levels of meaning. For instance, a sign can be used straightforwardly to refer to its usual, what we call "central," meaning; thus the sign quite simply denotes, or refers to, a boy or man.

However, a visual symbol might be used in a certain way in a particular context, so that certain associated ideas or feelings—what we usually call the "connotations"—are evoked predominately over the central meaning. Thus, for instance, the vase with a lily in the Master of Flémalle's *Annunciation,* c. 1425, is so painted and arranged that its symbolic use as Purity overwhelms its material function as a decorative flower in a vase. (It is not simply because we know the symbolic use of the lily, it should be noted, but because the arrangement and handling of painting makes it a highly concentrated and isolated form, that the association of ideas is exploited.)

The suppression of central meaning and manipulation of connotations is a very common phenomenon in art. In the case of the lily just cited, the central meaning of "flower" is suppressed in favor of the connotation or associated idea "purity." Furthermore, an image can be manipulated so that associated ideas, or the feelings associated with those ideas, are evoked. Most often both are evoked and one or other emphasized. As we saw with Motherwell, it is possible to do this so that the associated idea is suppressed entirely and all that is triggered is the feeling that is part of it. In fact, most often we do not even identify the smaller component feelings from which the general feeling of the work is built up: all we register is the overall feeling or "tone of voice."

The suppression of associated ideas in favor of their related feelings is perhaps easier to achieve if one avoids figurative images and works with abstract forms. In that case, because abstract forms are not images *of* something else, and thus are not used to recall something else not present, the artist is forced to use them in another way. What is required is a concentration on the forms' relational properties and an exploitation of the feelings or "felt qualities" (as Motherwell puts it) that they generate, so that a satisfactory whole is created. Thus the felt qualities are not arrived at by means of recognition of something which is associated with that feeling (through recognition of a swan which is associated with grace, for example). If that were so, one's mind would be engaged with images and ideas which are essentially only the technical means by which the point of the work is achieved, and with bad nonabstract painting—of which there is a great deal— the images all too often get in the way of their feeling.

Preferring to avoid this danger, Motherwell manipulated the relational structures so that all that is present to consciousness is a concentration of feeling: the unnecessaries are removed, so to speak. As he put it in 1951:

In modern times the problem has been to project an experience, rich, deeply felt, and pure, without using the objects and paraphernalia, the anecdotes and propaganda of a discredited social world. The means left for the painter are those inherent in his medium, its structure, rhythm, color and spatial interval.

With these few means, abstracted from the complex of relations that constitute the external world, modern painters have succeeded in their task, to create a painting that is rich, felt and pure.[34]

More recently, he has elaborated on this, making the point that all good painting, whether figurative or abstract, is dependent upon its "felt" relational structures, so that, once this is recognized, the necessity for figuration evaporates:

I have continuously been aware that in painting I am always dealing with, and never not, a relational structure. Which in turn makes permission "to be abstract" no problem at all. All paintings are essentially relational structures whether figuration is present or not is not the real issue. So that I could apprehend, for example, at first sight, my first abstract art. For painters with either literary or art school backgrounds, at least in my time, to make a transition from figuration to abstraction was a threatening problem. . . . I understood too that "meaning" was the product of the relations among elements, so that I never had the then common anxiety as to whether an abstract painting had a given "meaning."[35]

In fact, that Motherwell's paintings are not dependent upon reference for their meaning is strikingly pointed up by his account of the development of the *Elegy* paintings:

There are quite a few people not liking abstract art who are moved by that particular image. Therefore the image by definition has something that is beyond or outside art; exactly what it is I don't know. Some people think it's sexual, but I don't think so. Once I deliberately made one more overtly phallic, and it didn't change the felt response at all. Its specific feeling is not mainly dependent on sexuality—that I am sure of.[36]

The real content of a work, therefore, is not the things that might be referred to by the forms—the absent things, as it were—but the feeling which is present in the relational structures. Abstraction is simply the process of emphasizing or isolating that. As Motherwell says: "The real content of a painting is the rhythms and the proportions on the canvas, just as a person is his own inner rhythms and proportions, not what he happens to say when you meet him on the corner. This inner life is a mysterious and elusive thing. Still it is there, but not on the surface, which is why modernist artists do not paint the surface of the world."[37]

It cannot be easy to abandon reference and depend entirely upon sensing and developing the feeling and reverberations of relations between forms. With referential forms, one works from the known, but with Motherwell's kind of abstraction, one starts with the unknown and seeks to uncover something which one then recognizes. This demands a finely honed sensitivity to the medium. Motherwell's comments on the medium are illuminating because they not only express this sensitivity but they place very clearly his attitudes to the role of the medium. "But the most common error, among the whole-hearted abstractionists nowadays," he writes, "is to mistake the medium for an end in itself, instead of a means."

On the other hand, the surrealists erred in supposing that one can do without a medium, that in attacking the medium one does not destroy just one's means for getting into the unknown. Color and space relations constitute such a means because from them can be made structures which exhibit the various patterns of reality.

Like the cubists before them, the abstractionists felt a beautiful thing in perceiving how the medium can, of its own accord, carry one into the unknown, that is, to the discovery of new structures. What an inspiration the medium is! Colors on the palette or mixed in jars on the floor, assorted papers, or a canvas of a certain concrete space—no matter what, the painting mind is put into motion, probing, finding, completing. The internal relations of the medium lead to so many possibilities that it is hard to see how anyone intelligent and persistent enough can fail to find his own style.[38]

The question we return to now is whether or not the distinction between reference or description and direct expression is a viable one and a fundamental difference of kind. Is there literally a phenomenon such as direct expression, or is it just another form of reference—but to feelings, rather than things? Perhaps a precise answer cannot be given to this, but at least some points can be clarified.

A good deal depends on what the epistemological process of this phenomenon is. If the experience of direct expression in a painting is generated through remembered feelings and experiences, then these sensations are evoked, remembered, from past experience in much the same way that ideas and things are evoked, remembered, from past experience too. From this point of view, neither ideas nor feelings are actually *in* the work, but are evoked in the viewer by symbols in the painting and different processes of reference. If that is so, then the reference/direct expression dichotomy is actually a continuum—though this does not necessarilly diminish the felt differences between them.

It may be, of course, that direct expression contains no element of reference at all. It may be, for example, that Rudolf Arnheim's theory is correct, that certain forms, colors, and so on (relational structures) express certain feelings because their structural patterns parallel certain psychoneurological ones which then trigger particular affective responses. Or it may be that a work is expressive when it contains something like a Jungian archetype, the unconscious recognition of which evokes certain feelings.

But whatever the epistemological process, de facto the difference between description and expression is very real and results in works of very different character. Works built up in the way that Motherwell's are, seem more intense than more "literary" paintings because there isn't any conscious reference to sap the energies of concentration. Motherwell's work is very much a single-focus experience, where success or failure is very conspicuous: all one has is the feeling—the isolated, pure symbol of French Symbolism.

This heightening of experience is obviously one reason why Motherwell would wish to detach his images from any form of conscious reference. Another reason and, like the first, one which was shared by the rest of the Abstract Expressionists, was that there was nothing in the political and material world which could be trusted sufficiently to make it the home of such profound feelings and experiences. Apart from being notoriously treacherous, in the domain of art, political ideas and events will necessarily limit and confine the experience attached to them. Better to trust feelings and let them speak for themselves. (This, of course, would be unthinkable to the political illustrator.)

The third reason Motherwell had for wanting to detach the feeling from specific events and things is the most important. By breaking the connection between the feeling and specific events, he isolated the feeling and enshrouded the symbol in a veil of mystery, since we no longer have any knowledge of its origins. By being presented *in vacuo* in all its intensity, isolated from anything which might "explain" it and make it emotionally more manageable, it takes on a separate existence more fundamental and awesome than its particulr manifestations in particular events would be: if it looked like something within the human domain before (albeit not always controllable), now, as a pure symbol, it is certainly beyond it.

This effect is reinforced by the point noted earlier that in Motherwell's paintings, the image—which is the bearer of feeling—looks as if it came into being in some mysterious way. In other words, the evidence of its facture is such that one both knows it is made and yet cannot imagine it as having been made over a period of time: it looks made, yet made all of a piece. From the visual point of view, then, too, the origins of the image are mysterious.

When one asks why Motherwell (and the other Abstract Expressionists) should want to present the symbol and feeling in this way, the answer again lies in his beliefs about subject matter. Like his fellow artists, he wanted his art to be about the most fundamental elements of human existence, and with them he shared the very natural human conviction that the great events and experiences of human life are in major part mysterious. This is presumably because what is fully known is to some extent overcome. Fear, apprehension, and awe are a fundamental part of man's primitive being, and it is very natural to project this onto religious symbols. And, in the broad sense, that is what Motherwell's paintings are—religious symbols, abstract icons: a conception of art quite foreign to the succeeding generation of artists.

Chapter Ten

MARK ROTHKO

Each of the artists so far discussed has provided us with a different insight into how the theory of the abstract, mystic symbol was realized in practice. More needs to be said, however, about how the image might function iconically—about how it can be made to exert a hold on the viewer. Rothko's work is particularly interesting in this respect, and it should be possible to discover some of the ways in which this might happen. The extraordinary thing about Rothko's work is that for all the difficulty in describing it and specifying what it is "about," there is a remarkable unanimity of response among the critics; and it is through this avenue, initially, that we will approach the artist.

In turning to a consideration of Rothko's work, we note that one characteristic attributed to it recurs in all the critical writing. It is associated with the fact that Rothko chose to represent the same kind of image through all his work from 1949 onward. This is not to say that all the pictures are the same, of course, for each one has its own distinctive quality and experience. Nor is the format always precisely the same, for there are minor variations of form from time to time, and a more perceptible one in the black and gray pictures of the last year of his life. Nonetheless, it could fairly be said that despite their individual dynamics, all the work of Rothko's mature years has the same appearance: he used the same image continuously.

Related to this point is the curious characteristic the works have of fixing the gaze of the viewer and holding one in an almost mesmeric relationship. Many critics have commented on this in their own particular ways. Robert Goldwater, for instance, has referred to "the visual hold of these canvases, . . . their immediacy, and . . . their enigmatic, gripping presence."[1] In a more analytic passage, Eric Newton, critic of the *Manchester Guardian,* said of Rothko's canvases:

Simplicity could not be carried further and their immense size makes their simplicity their central characteristic. Described thus, one would expect them to be, at best, pleasingly decorative, at worst pretentiously empty. Yet in their physical presence one begins to succumb to a spell that emanates, goodness knows how or why, from their calm but insistent surfaces.

Decorative is certainly not among the first adjectives that occur to one, and empty they emphatically are not.

On the contrary they seem to stare at one and past one like sphinxes. Silent, unhurried, impersonal, devoid of movement or sentiment, they leave it to the spectator to guess at the reason that prompted Rothko to paint them. Yet one knows that if one could become as simple in one's reactions to them as they are in their impact on one's eye—or whatever receptive mechanism is capable of receiving their impact—the reason would become clear. A sphinx, despite its silent inscrutability, is always charged with meaning, even though it may be meaning that defies translation into words.[2]

And, finally, as Brian O'Doherty so succinctly puts it:

The frontality of Rothko's art stops and embraces us in a single action. The aspect of frontality, here called the "stare," can be identified with authority, will, and control. How is it modified? How is it that the work is not simply declarative and instantaneous, but hypnotic and sustained in its effect on the viewer?[3]

How much more intensified this stare becomes when one proceeds through Rothko's oeuvre and encounters the same insistent, repeated image! A repeated image is not so very unusual in modern art, and is often used to work out, or perfect, a particular line of thought or expression: after that the artist generally moves on to another format.

In the case of Byzantine art and primitive art images, however, the image is repeated after it has been perfected because it serves the ulterior purpose of being an icon. Icons are believed to capture the actual presence of the object or person they depict, and it is understandable that such a doctrine will encourage conservatism within the art form. Indeed, with Byzantine icons the requirements of the particular image (say, of a certain saint) are often laid down in a manual to safeguard success, and deviation from this appearance is likely to jeopardize the real presence of, or access to, the saint.[4] The artist's repetition of the same image as icon then becomes part of a religious ritual of invocation. As Werner Haftmann has observed of Rothko's icons:

I will say by way of prelude that what attracted me to these paintings, . . . was the singular urgency of Rothko's obsession with repeating the patterns of his picture themes: dark, luminous stripes and rectangles on diffused monochrome backgrounds full of light. Strangely enough, there was nothing dogmatic or fanatic in this constant repetition. . . . This compulsive repetition resulted in a deliberate, determined, but rather gentle litany, as the sing-song of the chants of Eastern monks, or the turning of the prayer-wheel, or the ever-repeated invocations of the Loreto Litany.[5]

Rothko's paintings certainly have a strange effect on their viewers, and many critics have described the curious ability of the pictures to draw the viewer up into them. Peter Selz put it this way:

Seen close up and in penumbra, as these paintings are meant to be seen, they absorb, they envelop the viewer. We no longer look *at* a painting as we did in the nineteenth century; we are meant to enter it, to sink into its atmosphere of mist and light or to draw it around us like a coat—or a skin.[6]

Like Selz, Werner Haftmann notices that the viewer's relation to the pictures is no longer that of the nineteenth century. It is worth quoting this passage at length, as it gives the flavor of how other people have reacted as well:

The obvious connection to "concrete art," originating from the form, was abruptly broken off when, on studying these pictures, one repeatedly became aware of the romantic experience, of a breath-taking space which went beyond the ultimate. However, it was just this romantic spatiality that helped me to reach an unexpected and, as it turned out, useful and helpful association. Absorbed in the study of a very large painting [of Rothko's], C. D.

Friedrich's painting "Monk by the Sea" came to mind. But I was now the monk and was looking into the great breadth of an enormous, breathing space, stirred by the dark light. The person—that monk—had stepped out of the picture, returned to it and contemplated the spaciousness of his numinous background, directly and without any psychological or metaphorical switching. Where C. D. Friedrich had placed the monk—as a helpful, symbolic figure with which the viewer could identify himself—there now stood the painter himself. His picture, replying to the experience of space, became purely a product of contemplation and, as seen by the viewer, an object of meditation.

Rothko's paintings have a suggestive, even hypnotic power in their colorfulness. They lure the viewer slowly towards them, demanding of him a penetrating curiosity, but immediately close up when he wants to interrogate them. Only slow meditative investigation brings forth a slow approach to the painting. Only through a process of deciphering does one reach the point from which the picture's message and content are legible.

After standing in front of the vast pictures in Venice a short while, I suddenly felt, like the "figure in front," that I was being drawn into the space of the picture itself, absorbed into its rhythmic breathing, and I understood that the painter's main concern was not an aesthetic thing called a "picture" but the relationship that was established between him and the space he had created to transform us.[7]

These extracts emphasize the mystic character of Rothko's work, and there are several elements that are mentioned and which recur over and over in all the critics. These are worth isolating, since they may help us to understand the real basis of these reactions and what it is in the works which induces them. There is general agreement that Rothko's images have simplicity; that color is crucially important; and that they are filled with light (even when dark-hued). The repetition of the image is important to their power; they have authority, frontality, and a physical presence. The image is often described as calm, still, and silent, an image which "stares" and which is charged with an untranslatable meaning. The oddness of the viewer–image relationship is usually commented upon, writers often describing it in terms of the displacement of an implied traditional figure in the picture, to an external viewer's position. In conjunction with this, writers usually describe the sensation of being drawn up into the picture, and comment on the odd kind of space within the image.[8]

In an attempt to unravel some of these reactions and to explain the source of the mysticism in the pictures, I want to take four aspects that seem to be key elements in the critical reactions described above. They are the fixedness of the image, the tendency of the image to draw in the viewer, a sense of imminence in the image, and the idea of the image as fragment.

The characteristic of the fixedness of the image is not peculiar to Rothko. All great art, in fact, affects the viewer in this way. Presumably this phenomenon is the result of certain arrangements of form, color, line, and space which are present (whether in a minimal or a complex way) regardless of whether the picture is representational. These structures vary from picture to picture, and from kind of picture to kind of picture, but are similar to those described earlier, in for example, Newman's *Who's Afraid of Red, Yellow and Blue III,* Still's *1948-E,* or Géricault's *The Raft of the "Medusa."*

What it is that makes these structures satisfying, or interesting, or arresting, is not something that can be answered in general, though in particular cases it is sometimes possible to suggest an answer: at least it is usually possible to point to what it is in the structure that seems important to one's response.

Nonetheless, it is the underlying structure that is crucial to the response, though in the case of representational, or at least referential, paintings, the apprehension of that structure is woven into the cognitive and emotional references that the forms have. This means that the perceptual, structural impact of the work is essentially associated with ideas, events, or feelings outside the work.

While this does nothing at all to lessen the impact of the work, it means that such works are very different in their structure, in this respect, from Abstract Expressionism. Since Abstract Expressionism does not generally contain images which refer to external ideas, the impact of the particular pictorial structure is focused back onto that structure in an intensified and somewhat riveting way; the mind will feel the impact of the image and struggle to articulate it in terms of human feeling, but it will not make historical or social excursions of a particular kind. Put crudely—in Newman's *Who's Afraid of Red, Yellow and Blue III* one thinks about the feeling of space, whereas in Géricault's *The Raft of the "Medusa"* one thinks about the drama and distress of the event.

To put the point in another way, reference, especially in representational works, tends to particularize and therefore limit feeling, whereas Abstract Expressionism aims for that state in which the perceptual structures and impact of the work are felt to be too basic and generalized (because nonreferred) to be capable of precise description. And being nonspecifiable and basic, they are also, therefore, to some measure mysterious. This characteristic of Abstract Expressionist paintings focuses attention on the structures of the work itself (along with the desire of the viewer to articulate further the generalized and mysterious expression in the work), and accounts for the fact that the fixedness of the image is more explicit than in the art of earlier artists.

All this is true of Rothko and the fixedness of his images is so explicit that critics have constantly remarked on it. Rothko's pictures work in a very unusual way. In the first place, there is no line, and while this may not be an item for comment in another artist, in Rothko's painting it signals a very different pictorial structure from those in other Abstract Expressionist works. George Dennison observes this and attributes it with a metaphysical dimension:

His complete avoidance of line is important. Line is analogous to the gesture (motion) and to the event, the thing-in-itself which limits the possible. Line is also the highway of ambiguity. Despite its character of definition and clarity, we see that it divides a surface it never touches and creates shapes that do not contain it, all the while registering minutely the decisions and delights of the artist. And it is through line that space becomes involved in a paradox. A great deal is involved, then, when Rothko adjures it. We find the results of this decision in the stability and monumentality of his work, its spaciousness and clarity.[9]

From a formal point of view, however, the absence of line is fundamental to that paradox typical of Rothko's best work—namely, the tension between incorporeality and the fixedness of the image. Rothko's images are usually composed of rectangles on a ground (often of a related hue); they characteristically have a strong impression of light (though not brightness), even, and perhaps especially, when the colors are dark-hued, and they are single-plane images of ethereal rather than solid appearance.

Many factors contribute to the single-plane effect, the most obvious being the absence of line. Rothko's images never read as figure and ground, because he avoided the sort of edge or line in his rectangles that might encourage the eye to read the image as composed of a rectangle *on* a ground. Line tends to define an edge and accentuates any change in depth that may exist there. With the blurring of the edges, any change in depth is minimized, because one does not have ordered points assembled along a straight or curved path to focus the eye on what contrast in depth there exists. In Rothko's images, instead, the eye follows the very wide "edge" of the form, taking in differences in the thinness of paint and consequent slight changes of edge and the variations of texture.

This blurring of the edges is achieved through scumbling over a dry ground, a technique which allows the color beneath to be visible through the surface color and which therefore suggests the transparency of air. Because the scumbling varies in texture across the broad "edge" of the form, it is indeed a moot point exactly where the edge is, or whether there are several edges. All these variations the eye takes in as it contemplates the edge, so that all incipient contrasts (such as planar depth) tend to be broken down and the rectangles seem to merge into the substance of the ground surrounding them. The transparency and aerial effect of the scumbling also dissolves solid form, so that the question of solid and separate planes no longer exists anyway.

This might lead one to expect that Rothko's images are moving, changing, even dissolving entities. Although, as Max Kozloff has put it, the "fragile transitions and faded edges" generate vibrations which break up the planes,[10] this is only perceptible at the edges of the forms, and any incipient movement it might generate is firmly held in check by the proximity of the outer edges of the rectangles to the edge of the canvas. The compressed tension stabilizes the forms and gives them their permanence, while their scumbled edges emphasize their incorporeality. This balance is necessarily a very finely held one which permits permanence and imminence to sit side by side without discomfort. The resultant tension, and one's awareness that it is generated around the outer edges of the forms, leads one to feel the potential expansiveness of the image and to "think around the edges."

Inevitably this raises the question of scale and the characteristic of Rothko's works, noted by critics and insisted upon by the artist, of drawing the viewer into them. Peter Selz has commented that "they have a human scale. Stand up close, and you are drawn into them,"[11] and as Alan Bowness, writing in the *Observer* has also remarked, "as one moves up to stand squarely before a picture, it is not difficult to feel oneself absorbed into the great fields of colour with their suggestion of infinite space."[12] "We are for the large shape," wrote Rothko along with Gottlieb, "because it has the impact of the unequivocal."[13]

Large pictures were not new in the history of art at that point, but it is true that the impact of the large pictures of Rothko and his confrères was different from that of earlier painting. One important difference is that the large pictures of the past were centripetally organized so that the edges exerted tensions on the image, containing it, focusing attention in toward the picture, and, therefore, to that extent, diminishing its apparent size. One thought inward from the edges and discounted the area outside the edges of the painting. With Abstract Expressionism, and Rothko in particular, the energies are centrifugal and the area toward the outer edges of the canvas is activated to become a visibly important part of the painting. And because the tensions in that area tend to push toward the edge, rather than inward, the area immediately around the painting becomes alive in the sense that the image has a resultant incipient expansiveness. In that case, the image tends to look bigger than it really is; more important, though, it feels bigger because one's attention is stretched to concentrate on its outer edges.

The second important difference between the large pictures of the past and those such as Rothko's is that in earlier pictures one's sense of scale was established by objects of the familiar world. Large pictures prior to the twentieth century were almost always history pictures or, occasionally, portraits of a sort, but in any case they were composed of human figures or other items such as trees and animals familiar to us from our visual world. Whether the subjects were over- or under-life size (and in fact they were usually life size or under), the pictures still contained familiar items against which we as viewers could gauge our relative size. Unless an artist was prepared to work larger than life—and that was rarely the case unless a work was intended for a more distant viewing point, a fact which merely corrected the scale to life size—one's relationship to the picture never exceeded a certain scale even though the picture might be very large. In paintings like Couture's *Romans of the Decadence* and Delacroix's *Death of Sardanapalus*, for example, the viewer's attention wanders through the picture, relating to each figure in turn, though always in familiar life-scale terms.[14] One is impressed by the size, of course, but even where there is grandeur to the picture, the immensity of size (and, perhaps, scale) never takes us into the realm of the mysterious and uncertain, because the images themselves are known. The fact that the scale is usually slightly less than life size must also have something to do with the desire to keep everything within the comfortable sphere of the familiar.

In Rothko's work, and in other Abstract Expressionist works as well, the identification with a life-size scale is not possible, since there is nothing familiar in the picture against which one can measure oneself. It is probably true, too, that one's *experience* of the scale can no longer be deflected into cognitive and emotional processes associated with the "story" represented by the forms, and hence the scale is more consciously felt. One is left with the raw image and the raw experience. As with Newman's work, there is, in a sense, nothing in the image but the scale.

Nonetheless, the effect of scale works in different ways from one Abstract Expressionist artist to another. In Newman's work, for instance, there is usually a quite definite and fixed, appropriate viewing point, determined by the need of the viewer—guided by the structural dynamics of the picture—to fix on and hold the outer vertical edges of the image. The solid, even plane of color of such paintings as *Vir*

Heroicus Sublimis and *Who's Afraid of Red, Yellow and Blue III* also serves to keep the viewer back at a certain point because the pictures are impenetrable and do not invite close scrutiny.

Quite the opposite dynamic seems to operate in Rothko's paintings, however, because scrutinize is precisely what one wants to do:

I paint very large pictures. I realize that historically the function of painting large pictures is painting something very grandiose and pompous. The reason I paint them, however—I think it applies to other painters I know—is precisely because I want to be very intimate and human. To paint a small picture is to place yourself outside your experience, to look upon an experience as a stereopticon view or with a reducing glass. However you paint the larger picture, you are in it. It isn't something you command.[15]

Rothko's pictures are more dependent upon the right light conditions than most. If the light is not right, they die, but when seen in favorable conditions, the colored, yet also transparent, rectangles hang in space, almost disembodied. Rothko stained his color deep into the fabric of the canvas and then created diaphanous overveils through scumbling. The image was pulled over the stretcher so that it began on the sides touching the wall, thus eliminating any sense of edge or frame and turning the image into an object that hung on the wall. As Werner Haftmann has observed, "This colored intermediary zone causes the painting to detach itself from the wall and project itself towards the viewer."[16]

The combination of the transparency of the veils and the tendency of the image to float forward has the effect of inviting the viewer to scrutinize more closely, as does the tension between the incorporeality and the fixedness of the image. Rothko's images are elusive because of his use of color, and that elusiveness draws the viewer closer to try to "settle the matter." T. B. Hess has commented on this effect in a different way when writing about the darkness of the Houston pictures.[17] He says:

Colors and shapes develop so delicately and imperceptibly across the great spread of painted surface that one sees them as it were with peripheral vision. If you look dead on, you see almost nothing, but out of the side of your eye, the shapes and colors emerge, like a path on a dark night. Rothko obviously understood the optics of this effect, and by insisting that dim lights are the only proper illumination for his paintings, and by setting them against off-off-white walls, he heightened their magical "floating" quality.

He creates a tension between the colored images stained into the weave of the cotton—facts, all these, there for you to perceive—and the sense of dematerialized aura which he emphasizes in low key nuances and refined transitions. . . .

His use of an intimate architectural scale, so big that it enfolds the spectator and urges him to a participant's—even a communicant's—role, is in a tradition that includes the great Humanist murals of the 16th and 17th centuries.[18]

Another element which contributes to the effect of large scale and intimacy is the appearance the image has of being a fragment of a much larger whole. Here, again, the relation of image to edge is crucial, for one must have the sense of the proximity of the lost whole if the image is to register as fragment. Thus the feeling of the image pressing away the edges of the canvas, or the sensation of the image hovering over the extent of the canvas, are both characteristics that permit the existence, in imagination, of a further, more whole and comprehendible image.

The experience one has with Rothko's work, as with Motherwell's, Newman's, Pollock's, Kline's, and Still's, to name a few, is of slight unease at what is not made explicit; one always has the feeling that the *presence* of more is felt, even though it is not specified. In painting of the late eighteenth and early nineteenth centuries, this same effect was often achieved by the presence of distant mountains shrouded in mist and mystery; in Abstract Expressionism it is generated by the visual implication of an unfinished image. And with a fragment, of course, there is also the suggestion of rupture and loss, a poignancy particularly appropriate to Abstract Expressionist subject matter. Once again, closeness to the image, and especially to an image that is unrecognizable and that contains "nothing," as Rothko's are said to do, heightens this sense of fragment and loss.

Christian icons too have a suggestion of the unknown in them, since they are images through which communication with the "real presence" is effected. So that they do not merely look like portraits of the person on the street, elements of stylization are developed. The eyes become the focal point of attention through enlargement and other means, and especially by the full-frontal stance of the image which invites full and conscious engagement. There is no catching an icon unawares. Similarly, Abstract Expressionist icons have a frontality often commented upon. O'Doherty has described it as "the stare," and "the magnetism of the close-up," inherited, he suggests, both from our experience of movies and of the intimacies of a lover's face.[19] It is perhaps not accidental that Rothko wrote at length about art as a continuing portrait, of artists always seeking to reveal the same character in all their work:

In a sense they have painted one character in all their work. What is indicated here is that the artist's real model is an ideal which embraces all of human drama rather than the appearance of a particular individual.

Today the artist is no longer constrained by the limitation that all of man's experience is expressed by his outward appearance. Freed from the need of describing a particular person, the possibilities are endless. The whole of man's experience becomes his model, and in that sense it can be said that all of art is the portrait of an idea.[20]

Many writers have commented on the need of artists like Rothko to create a new relationship between the painting and the viewer, and it is interesting that it should be in terms of large scale and intimacy, two ideas which, on the face of it, might appear to be incompatible. Intimacy, one might have thought, is more likely achieved through small size, where the viewer feels comfortably within reach of what is depicted; with large size, on the other hand, one expects to feel overwhelmed by the immensity of the objects depicted. The important point about intimacy in Abstract Expressionist works, however, is that it is not intended to be comfortable, since it is an intimacy with the deep and disturbing events of human existence—"only that subject matter . . . which is timeless and tragic." In that case, the overwhelming aspect is very appropriate, for how else can one react to the gravity of human experience?

The intimacy that is talked about, therefore, is not that of an easy and enjoyable relationship, but rather the knowledge that comes from close experience. That sort of intimacy in an overpowering situation is not something to be controlled, and regulated, and made safe; and that is exactly the experience that Rothko sought to convey in his art. "I paint large pictures," he wrote, "because I want to create a state of intimacy. A large picture is an immediate transaction; it takes you into it. . . . . All art deals with intimations of mortality."[21]

This intimacy of relationship is obviously an important element in the iconicity of Rothko's painting, as well as that of the other Abstract Expressionists. Centrifugal pictorial organization, which is featured in so much of their work, inclines one to feel close to the image anyway, and this, combined with the effect almost all the artists achieve, of the image being a fragment of a larger whole, is an important source of the sense of intimacy.

Add to the intimacy between painting and viewer the fact that the image is a large and strong one, and there is the potential for a particularly compelling relationship between painting and viewer. It is, in a mild way, a kind of thrall, and it is not surprising that the artists came to describe it in terms of iconicity. After all, their art, more than most, is concerned with the relationship between viewer and image, and it is one in which the image holds great power—a mystic symbol, presented in strange, abstract form. Rothko's art demonstrates one of the ways in which this can be achieved.

Despite the fact that each of the Abstract Expressionists developed a style that was individual and quite different from the others', each of these styles grew out of a common set of concerns. In articulating their theory of the abstract mystic symbol into an individual, physical idiom, they in fact shared some important elements of theoretical, aesthetic structure.

In attempting to make paintings which were each an abstract mystic symbol, and in particular an abstract icon, they relied heavily on the phenomenon they described as "direct expressionism." As an associated part of this intention, they also aimed to produce works which have that quality referred to as "iconic stare." The means they chose to achieve these ends was the elimination of referential elements in their works, and the generation of raw, generalized feeling, detached from particular objects and events.

In the case of Clyfford Still, his works avoid all representational references and any narrowly sensuous interpretations. They leave one, instead, with an effect and impression which is difficult to articulate except in such general terms as "cataclysm" of what, one knows not, "transcending the physical," and "absolute state." The cracks and rents that appear in the surface of his images are not depictions of anything: yet, being the focus of tensions, they claim a pictorial significance that, when combined with the impact that the best of these images have, forces an interpretation in the only terms remaining available—namely, generalized, primal forces.

Because the possibility of reference to particular entities is deliberately removed, the impact of the work (which arises from the complex interactions of pictorial structure and perception, the very rudiments of which are as yet scarcely understood in explicit terms,[1] is felt as raw feeling, detached from objects or events.

Still was not the only painter to detach feeling from objects or events. Pollock's work, for instance, is not merely nonreferential; it abandons all possibility of reference when it employs line as trajectory rather than as a form-defining device. Since there are no forms at all, there cannot be abstracted forms, and the webs of lines that characterize Pollock's work are used in a straightforward, literal way to discharge energies. The impact that this technique has, however, in a well-resolved image such as *One, 1950* or *Blue Poles* is such as to seek translation or description in highly generalized terms.

In Still's work cataclysm and disruption along an edge are translated from purely visual to metaphysical terms because the sheer power of the image resists a mundane physical interpretation. In Pollock's work, too, the power of the image is such that the observation of particular energies active along paths of line is immediately transcended by consideration of the energies on a grander scale; the network of dynamic charges is felt as raw, powerful energy expressive of, for example, the forces of nature. The quality of the work, as it were, creates the need to generalize the particular into more significant, cosmic terms. Unlike the case of Still, though, the interpretive term or metaphor does not imply human involvement or consequences: it describes the world rather than symbolizing human events.

Newman and Rothko made their art in a similar way, avoiding forms and reference and relying on the force of their images to make the viewer move from physical effect to metaphysical interpretation. Newman's insistence that the zips in his paintings were not to be read as dividers was probably due to the fact that such a reading would tend to suggest that the image was composed of forms—geometric ones in this case—thus opening up the possibility of referential interpretation.

Even in his own account of his images as "total positive space" he pointedly denied that they were "space-domes" or depictions of space, and asserted, instead, that they induced the *feeling* of total space. They are not, in fact, depictions of anything at all. "These paintings are not 'abstractions,' " he wrote, "nor do they depict some 'pure' idea. They are specific, and separate embodiments of feeling, to be experienced, each picture for itself. They contain no depictive allusions."[2]

Rothko, like the other artists discussed, cultivated an image whose pictorial and perceptual dynamics are sufficiently powerful and compelling to be accepted simply as feeling. Again, his pictorial structure is such that he does not need to rely on the generation of feeling by association with events and objects in the world. Motherwell, on the other hand, works differently. His images, too, avoid reference to things, and certainly are not used to symbolize entities or ideas. But he does not deny the role of association and, indeed, considers it to be a very important part of his own pictorial structure.

Although Motherwell uses forms, he uses them for the most part in such a way that they do not invite referential interpretation. In the occasional cases where they do, he has pointed out (rightly, in my opinion) that such interpretations short-circuit the richer possibilities of the painting. These richer possibilities are generated by exploiting the emotive association of idea and experience embedded in form and color at a subconscious level. Thus he uses a particular form, a patch of color, in such a way that it is not associated consciously with any particular object or event; and yet, because we have experienced forms and colors in association with a myriad of objects and events, the form develops an accretion of feeling which is recalled only in general, detached terms. As Motherwell has said, the picture is built up from a number of such "incidents" until the resulting aggregate of feeling is difficult, perhaps impossible, to articulate and is felt *in vacuo,* quite unrelated to any of its sources.

This idea of detaching feeling from specific reference so that it is experienced for its own sake is an important and innovative one in Abstract Expressionism, and it is obviously this concept that the artists had in mind when they talked about "direct expression." It is easy to see why this might have been regarded as more basic and more powerful than conventional modes of expression, especially when one remembers the artists' insistence that representational images are now worn out through thousands of years of exposure.

The other important element of Abstract Expressionism which contributed to the realization of an abstract mystic symbol is the characteristic iconic "stare." This is partly due to the capacity of the image to project forward rather than recede. In Abstract Expressionist works, there is no recession in depth at all. Any space that there is, is built up on a solid, impenetrable ground and projects forward toward the viewer; however, because this space is minimal, sometimes almost imperceptible, the energies built up are projected forward and discharged laterally through the picture plane toward the edges. Because the image is thus activated at its extremities, it tends to fix, so that there is no movement of the image itself. Its energies are felt, however, and a tension develops between energy and immobility.

The consequent effect is one that holds the viewer in a mesmeric relationship, because, like the dynamic structure of the picture, the perceptual processes both charge and fix, mirroring in experience the tensions of the picture. The large size of the pictures and the scale of the images obviously has something to do with this, since it is by this means that the viewer is drawn into an intimate relationship with the image. When the image is a powerful one, this intimate relationship is the means by which this mirroring is made possible.

These are the physical dynamics of the iconic "stare"; but none of it would be possible, or at the least worth noticing, if it were not for that detachment or abstraction of feeling which characterizes the Abstract Expressionists' work. Because the feeling generated within the image is abstracted and not related to any object or event, the cognitive and emotive faculties remain focused on the image—or, to put it another way, one focuses on the image and feeling for its own sake. All that is important to the painting is present in the image, physically embodied and accessible. Because there is no reference, there is no sense in which the real impact of the painting lies in events outside the work and is "commemorated" in the image. The abstraction of feeling, in other words, makes possible the transfer of potency from object and event to image. It is, if you like, another manifestation of the principle of *pars pro toto*.

That is how the process works in theoretical terms, but from a practical point of view, the effect is simply to confine the attention to what is present before one. Thus this impression of the separateness of feeling, and its presence in the image, especially when the painting has a great deal of power, intensifies the stillness and fixedness of the image and gives rise to the impulse to think of the image in terms of an iconic "stare."

These are some of the ways in which the theory of the abstract mystic symbol is realized in practice. To achieve the result, important formal innovations and a new conception of what pictorial dynamics might be used for had to be discovered. These developments grew out of need. As Pollock put it, "Method is . . . a natural growth out of a need, and from a need the modern artist has found new ways of expressing the world about him."[3] Needless to say, most artists do not succeed in doing this, even when they perceive the necessity. To both perceive the necessity and succeed in developing the means is truly an achievement. "The problems of inventing a new language," wrote Motherwell, "are staggering. But what else can one do if one needs to express one's feelings precisely?"[4]

Part Three

MODES OF CRITICAL DISCOURSE

Chapter Eleven

ARTISTS' TALK

In tracing the development of the artists' theory of the abstract mystic symbol and in examining its articulation and expression in individual works of certain of the artists, we have relied heavily on what the artists have had to say themselves. The assumption contained in this approach is, of course, that what the artist has to say is relevant to an understanding of the work. Just how it might be relevant is a complex question requiring unraveling and clarification.

Perhaps not surprisingly, we encounter a great diversity of comment when we examine the sorts of statements the artists make about their work and about art in general. But whereas among critics, diversity in criticism tends to occur from critic to critic, when it comes to the artists, we find that each artist tends to talk in different ways on different occasions. In the concern to be careful historians, we may forget that artists, like everybody else, are ordinary people who need to talk for all sorts of reasons. Not all of the talk is endowed with a solemn significance and fit (or intended) to become authoritative comment on the work—despite the efforts of some historians to make it so. We should remember, too, that art history is a very recent discipline and that systematic art criticism is really a phenomenon of the twentieth century. The habit of appropriating the artist's words is something which has only been developed in the last five or so decades.

In that case it is probably prudent to ask what expectations we have when we look at what an artist has to say about his work. And perhaps the single most prevalent idea is that his talk will "explain" the work or, to put it another way, will present us with a verbal equivalent, or translation, of what is realized in the painting. There is, of course, criticism that sets out to do this; some of Ruskin's criticism of Turner would be a classic example.[1] Significantly, there was much more of this sort of criticism when access to art through any form of reproduction, and especially color reproduction, was limited, and it was probably intended as a substitute for seeing the original work.

In recent times, however, the intention of this type of criticism is more often directed at getting us to "see" what is there. Frank O'Hara's comments, for example, draw attention to the character of line in Pollock's work:

There has never been enough said about Pollock's draftsmanship, that amazing ability to quicken a line by thinning it, to slow it up by flooding, to elaborate that simplest of elements, the line—to change, to reinvigorate, to extend, to build up an embarrassment of riches in the mass by drawing alone.[2]

And in a different tone, though using the same method, Bryan Robertson's description of *Blue Poles* reads:

The pictorial space created by Pollock in *Blue Poles* and other all-over paintings was new as a conception and mysterious as a realization. No other paintings in this century suggest the space contained in these pictures. The adamant frontality and lack of recession shock the eye: the mind is bemused by the crisp, direct equation of space with time which generates a universe; for the measure in space of the marks made in each picture and their duration in time across the surface exactly embody the duration of the gesture made by Pollock and the measure of his scale as a man acting as a physical *deus ex machina*.[3]

Criticism of this sort by artists of their own work is very rare, and I have not found a single example among the writings of the Abstract Expressionists. But if criticism which offers a verbal equivalent is lacking, there is criticism of a related sort, in which the work is "explained," usually in terms of a key metaphor. Much of this talk we looked at in earlier chapters, in which concepts like Still's "cataclysm,"

Pollock's "energy made visible," and Newman's "total space" were discussed. In all the Abstract Expressionist artists, we can find statements, phrases, metaphors, in which they attempt to express in words what is expressed visually in their work in general, or in a section of their work. This involves a form of translation and, like the kind of criticism discussed above, it is used to "accurately" describe, or categorize, the work, or to get someone to "see." It serves, therefore, the same purpose as criticism of this sort, but is usually proferred in a few words rather than in extended passages of criticism.

As to the question of the standing of such statements, we would have to ask whether, in such cases, the artists' statements are to be regarded as authoritative. Certainly we would have to say that there might be times when it is felt that the evidence of the pictures simply did not bear out the interpretation offered, and in that case we would be weighing up the work against the interpretation presented, just as we would with any one else's interpretive remarks. In other words, we would treat the artist's remarks just as we would those of any critic, and judge accordingly. In fact, what emerged in part 2 was that the artists' remarks were indeed appropriate and helpful. This is not surprising, since, in the first place, as good artists they know a considerable amount about art; and, in the second place, they are in an advantageous position of familiarity and privileged access, since they were, as one might put it, "present at the creation."

Perhaps surprisingly, however, such talk forms a very small part of the total art-talk engaged in by the Abstract Expressionists. Like any art movement that is new and mostly unappreciated or misunderstood, they spent a fair bit of their time explaining what they were *not*. The final paragraph of Gottlieb's and Rothko's letter to the *New York Times* gives the flavor of this—"no interior decoration; pictures for the home; pictures for over the mantle; pictures of the American scene; social pictures; purity in art; prize-winning pot-boilers; the National Academy, the Whitney Academy, the Corn Belt Academy; buckeyes; trite tripe, etc." Pollock's insistence that he was not "illustrating" feelings, Newman's denial that his work was formal arrangements of color and planes or that he was painting "space-domes" as such, and Still's rejection of the claim that he was painting abstracted landscapes—these are all examples of what the artists felt they had to dissociate themselves from. Much of this comment is an attempt to close off paths that lead into misunderstanding, and to suggest the expectations appropriate to an understanding of their own art. Sometimes, of course, such response is an exaggerated attempt to minimize the influence of other art on their own and to insist that their work is more different, and more radical, than it really is.

This, however, only accounts for a small part of the talk the Abstract Expressionist artists engaged in. In general terms, it should be noted that whatever different aspects of their art their talk was focused on, its overriding and usually unconscious purpose was to articulate verbally what they were trying to do in their art. Their comment was a way of understanding it, of testing its realization, of standing back and recognizing what they had done by trying various descriptions against it. This is not surprising if we remember that the making of the art object and the formulating of the art-talk are engaged in by the same mind, and it is natural that that mind might want to approach something it is focused upon from several different points of view and through different conceptual mediums. There will, therefore, be a hesitancy about much that is said by the artists—not so much about particular statements, but in terms of direction: a hesitancy that comes from feeling their way toward a visual as well as a verbal articulation of their work and achievement.

These considerations might be the reasons behind their art-talk (or some of the reasons, since the artists' thinking and motivation were no doubt more complex than my account has so far suggested), and it is well to bear this in mind. But since our interest is in establishing the connection between their talk and their work, we need to look not only at why they engaged in the talk but also, and perhaps more important, at what light it sheds on the work—and if, indeed, it can do so at all.

With respect to a very small part of their talk—namely, that in which some of the artists offer interpretive metaphors for their work— we have seen that this sort of discussion can be regarded as a critical comment, and its worth assessed in those terms. Unlike comment by critics, it is never developed at length with supporting evidence in the form of pictorial analysis. It is not that it could not be so supported, but simply that the artists do not set out to be critics. Rather, they prefer simply to offer key ideas which they think "explain" or "open up" the painting, and leave us, as viewers, to do the work.

The bulk of their talk falls into two kinds, both of them interesting and important. If we look at the substance of the three-day Studio 35 talks and at other recorded comments, it will be seen that much of their conversation centers on the subject of creativity and process. On the process of painting a picture, they emphasized not the technical aspects of the task, but the psychological passage of the work. At the center of their practice was the insistence that they did not start with a preconceived idea of how the work might look, but rather that the image was unfolded—to them as well as to the onlooker—as the picture developed. The explanation for this lay in the fact that the image was not something derived from the visible world and therefore essentially depictive, albeit abstracted; rather, the image was sought from within, shaped gradually in the subconscious, and developed out of "chaos." The problem arises, therefore, of "recognizing" it when it emerges: the passage, in other words, of the image into consciousness, and of "seeing" what has been realized.

This is how the artists' images arose, they believed, though they recognized that other artists chose to work differently and had done so in the past. They believed that their attitude toward painting and their experience of making art was both new and important—necessary for them to sustain their own creativity and inventiveness, and certainly important for the development of future art. They were very conscious, therefore, of the consequences which this process of picture-making had for them, and this awareness surfaces in their conversation constantly. The experience, they said, was one of venturing into the unknown, with no specific articulated goal, and without recognizable procedures or techniques to structure the process. Since what they were doing was new, there were no prescriptions they could rely on—size, scale, anything—and they were therefore heavily dependent upon the intuitive processes of unconscious creativity. Not unnaturally, this generated a good deal of anxiety that the inspiration would "dry up," a problem heightened by the fact that, since there were no familiar refuges of illustration, recognizably skilled craftsmanshsip, or decorativeness behind which to hide a lack of inspiration, any failure in the work would be immediately apparent. And added to this was the bitter knowledge that the public could generally be expected to pass their work without giving it a chance to speak. The "risk" of art-making was therefore great and various.

Talk of the creative process in terms of venturing, discovery, and risk has been profoundly influential in the postwar art scene. So influential has it been that it is now common for artists of all persuasions, including those whose styles demand a planned and considered process, to adopt this attitude to creativity as the correct description not only of their own processes, but usually of all artistic creativity. Students in art schools commonly talk that way—even ceramicists, whose practice of sitting down at the wheel with a definite form in mind makes the claim patently absurd. It has become a fashionable and pervasive credo.

In the case of the Abstract Expressionists, however, it was their own formulation of the process they went through in the making of an art that was radically new. The description of the states of mind involved was genuinely that—a description of what was in fact involved for them, rather than a prescription for how they thought artists *ought* to feel. The processes of mind were the outcome of the desire to make a certain kind of art, developing out of natural necessity; and one can sense in those descriptions the same struggle to articulate what it involved for them that one saw in their attempts to articulate what it was they saw their art as being. In later generations it simply became an axiom that was handed down.

If that explains the need to engage in talk of this kind, there is still the question of what it in fact tells us about the work. In one sense, of course, it tells us a great deal about the work, for it is only a certain kind of art which would *necessitate* that method of working. Furthermore, someone who understood the achievement of the art would not be surprised to be told that it necessitated such an artistic process of venturing, discovery, and risk. It may even be possible to speculate, from an intimate knowledge of the paintings, that that would have been the case. This point is problematic, however, since in fact it is not really possible for someone to have an intimate knowledge of the paintings without also knowing something of the art context of which they are part. Even if it is technically possible for someone to carefully consider the paintings and come to understand them without knowing anything about the artists, their background, and so on, it is quite unlikely to happen, given the social dynamics of how we develop an interest in a subject and seek to learn more about it.

Whatever the answers to these questions, however, it is nonetheless clear that while this sort of talk bears indirectly on the character of the works under discussion, it is actually a description of the psychology of making rather than of the object produced. Whether or not we regard such talk as throwing light upon the object depends upon what we think about the closeness of the process of making to the appearance of the object produced. In fact, little is known about this relationship as yet, so we can offer only a speculative opinion about how close they are. Suffice it to point out that the creative process and resultant work are two distinct elements.

A similar situation applies to the second major area of art-talk engaged in by the artists. In earlier chapters we considered the aesthetic theory that forms the base structure of their art—namely, the theory of the abstract mystic symbol. The theory demanded that their art should concern itself first with feeling—the expression of basic truths of human experience—and only secondarily with aesthetic effect.[4] Furthermore, since this feeling should be expressed with force, it needs to be directly expressed, as in primitive art, rather than simply illustrated. And if this sounds like an impossible ideal, the artists would remind us of the well-documented special power art sometimes has seemingly to put us in direct contact with whatever is its central subject matter, so that by a magical act of creativity the feeling referred to, itself becomes embodied in the image—*pars pro toto.* To heighten the impact, this feeling is concentrated into an apparently simple symbol, and it becomes an icon whose power is intensified because all representational associations are removed so that it can be encountered only on its own abstract terms.

Obviously the artists would consider their art a failure if none of this theory was realized in their work, and in fact earlier chapters have shown that the best of their work did achieve that aim. This being so, we could not possibly argue that this area of their talk bore no relation to their work. The question is, however, What does this tell us, and what is the nature of this relationship?

In attempting to answer this question, we need to take into account the often overlooked fact that the art work is not a discrete object available to be understood purely in terms of what is accessible to observation. Because it is an artifact, valued, and made by a complex process of creativity—of interaction of medium and conceptualization—there is always the question of what aspect of this complex phenomenon our attention is focused upon. This is very often not clear even in our own minds, and it can give rise to a great deal of confusion if we accept certain questions as "key" questions, without thinking about what *aspect* of that complex phenomenon they relate to.

The point is that when we are offered a piece of criticism by a critic, writings or comments by the artists, or even biographical and other background information, we need to think about what it relates to, and then ask whether it is informative. It might, for example, be comment related to the sort of personality required in the artist, the effects art might be expected to have, the psychological process of realizing an image, the translation of the achievement of the art into social and cultural terms, the peculiar characteristics of the medium, matters of craft and technique, of what is to be valued in the art, or a host of other issues.

What has not yet been effectively investigated is the relationship between these aspects, and the way what takes place in one, might affect the character of another. We really know next to nothing about how, for example, the psychological process of creativity connects with the actual realization of an image, and with the manipulation of the essential characteristics of the medium. We know that this or that goes on and that something or other is produced as a result; but what goes on in between, when the one is mystifyingly and somewhat magically translated into the other, we know nothing about. And because we do not yet know how to integrate all this information, we tend to focus our interest on particular aspects and concentrate on them. Perhaps we could not reasonably do otherwise, given the complexity of the whole phenomenon.

Because of this state of affairs, though, people sometimes come to believe that the aspect that their interest is focused on is the only worthwhile element to be looked at and even that it is the essence of the art. Whatever one's reasons for taking such a perspective (and the reasons are sometimes ideological and extrinsic to art), it usually generates confusion. When people assess the value of a piece of information or critical comment, they often do so, not seeing that its value should be assessed relative to a particular interest, but assuming, implying, or even proclaiming that their way is the only way it can properly be assessed. All other considerations are eliminated.

Against this background of issues we must return to the question of the art-talk engaged in by the artists. How does the theory of the abstract symbol then fit into the general pattern of the Abstract Expressionists' art-talk? And in what way does this talk relate to their work? Obviously it was a very important idea with them—so important that they talked about it a great deal, not just in the early years of Abstract Expressionism, but in reflecting on the theory in so much of their comment in later years.

Not only did the concept of the abstract symbol convey their view of what art should be, but they also clearly intended it to be a description of their own work. As we have seen, it was indeed reflected in their own paintings, and we could even go so far as to say that we might be able to formulate the essentials of the theory (perhaps without its connections with myth and primitivism) simply by knowing the works well. Certainly we need no background information to feel the power and the expressiveness of the work; nor do we need such information to respond to the almost hypnotic fixedness of the images. The fact that the images are abstract and nonreferential means that the feeling is never identified with a particular event or that its content is never precisely specified. The feeling always remains to some extent generalized and, therefore, it seems, unidentified and mysterious: the more powerful, the more the element of the unknown is heightened.

This detachment of feeling is certainly experienced if the work is responded to it all, though of course it may not be articulated by the viewer in that way. But the effect of experiencing it, along with one's awareness of the power and expressiveness, and the capacity of the image to hold, leads one to respond to these works as icons. This is not an unrealistic expectation of a viewer and is often the way people describe their response to the works.

But if the formulation of the theory of the abstract symbol is an accurate description of the artists' work, it is certainly very different from any of the comment offered by critics. Critics have not disagreed that the artists' sentiments accurately describe their works; rather, the sorts of statements critics have made have been of a very different kind. But then the talk centering on the theory of the abstract symbol is also very different from the other talk the artists engaged in when discussing their individual works. I am referring here to the talk in which they offered various metaphors of interpretation for their work. In some cases (Still, for example, and Newman), the same metaphor does not apply to the whole of the artist's oeuvre, and at different stages of their careers the content and therefore the metaphor of interpretation changed.

The point is that the two different kinds of talk serve quite different functions. When the artists talked in terms of "total space," "cataclysm," "energy made visible," and so on, they were indeed describing their work: specifically, they were describing the *content* of their work. They were at liberty to change that content in later work (and often did so) without shifting their position on the theory of the abstract symbol. In fact, all they were doing in offering descriptive metaphors was to describe the content of a *specific* abstract symbol: and any specific content would be acceptable providing it met the requirements of being serious, and basic to human experience.

The descriptive metaphors are therefore specific aspects of a more general theory of the art work. And that more general theory serves a different purpose. It does not describe the specific content of the works, and to react to it as if it did is bound to land one in confusion. It is, rather, an account of how the art should affect one. In other words, it is an account of the general character of art (or at least what art could be), and its relationship to the viewer.

The Abstract Expressionists believed that all art should be like this, that all good art of the past had been, and any art of the future which failed to be—and there was much around them that did not aspire to that ideal—could not be considered art. They did not believe that the art necessarily had to be abstract, of course. Abstraction was merely a pragmatic approach forced on the modern artist because of the tiredness of representational forms; these forms might possibly be rejuvenated in the future, though the artists could not see how such an event might happen.

Of course, in a better world where there was no bad art and no pseudo-art, the Abstract Expressionists would not have needed to expound this theory, because what they aspired to would have been, in their view, the natural condition of art. What they were describing was what they took to be the proper and natural function of art, and it was only because they lived at a time when art seemed to have lost its sense of purpose and quality that they felt driven to articulate their views. And through the articulation of the theory of the abstract symbol, in describing the potential of art to act as a powerful emotional and social force, they intended to reclaim art for the modern artist.

So the theory is essentially a description of the special relationship and communication that is set up between the art object and the viewer—by implication, a comment on the kind of subject matter involved, but more particularly a theory about the *function* of art in society. And as an example of their art-talk, the theory tells us a great deal about the general character of their work and about their attitudes to art-making. It was not, however, intended as a description of the specific content of their work.

If it seems obvious that remarks made by artists about their work can be separated out in this way—into statements which describe the specific content of a work, statements about the function of art in society, about what makes good art good, about the nature of the creative process; about what is involved in being an artist, and so on—it is obvious only because we have spent some time analyzing their talk and looking at their work.

There still remain, however, a number of questions of a more theoretical nature, which need to be resolved and which will be dealt with in the final chapter.

Chapter Twelve

THE CRITICAL APPROACH

In considering how the Abstract Expressionist artists talked about their work, it is inevitable that we should find ourselves thinking about the critics of the time. Despite the fact that the public was slow to accept and understand the artists' work, there were, nonetheless, a number of prominent writers who championed their cause. Among them were Clement Greenberg, Thomas B. Hess, Harold Rosenberg, and Meyer Schapiro.

Each of these critics wrote very different criticism from the rest, and, indeed, some of them were openly hostile to what they saw as either the decadent or the irrelevant approaches of others. It is not my purpose here to do a survey of the contemporaneous criticism and an investigation of the different styles of criticism, for that would be the subject of a book in itself. What is important, however, is that the way the artists talked about their work be seen against the background of the issues of concern to the critics.

When we look at the relationship between the artists' talk and the issues the critics were involved in, it will be evident that there was a gap. This gap was understood by the artists and tolerated because, as Robert Goodnough has said, they were grateful for the appreciation and attention.[1] The artists' primary concern was that the content of their work should be understood and that there should be no mistake about the real nature and purpose of art. Hence their use of metaphors of description, on the one hand, and talk of the abstract mystic symbol, on the other.

The critics, however, were more concerned with the nature of criticism and how to perform it well. And since our ear is more attuned to the critics' talk than to that of the artists, it is natural for us to carry over some of the concerns of the critics into our consideration of the talk of the artists. The relationship between the two kinds of talk is complex because critics speak, as it were, on behalf of the viewer, whereas the artist speaks as the maker. The critic is interested in considerations relating to the quality of a work—in establishing by argument that the work is, by a particular set of criteria, of a certain level of quality and achievement. Artists, on the other hand, are more concerned with establishing the nature of art and what their own art aspires to.

Obviously these perspectives are connected, but the thrust is different, an important difference being that the artist is in a privileged position, having known what went into the making. The critic or viewer, on the other hand, is focused on the issue of his or her own perceptiveness to the work and the question of how much can legitimately be read into the picture. From these different starting points, therefore, the talk of artist and of critic each has a different perspective and flavor.

Needless to say, when we as viewers or critics come to look at the talk of the artists, we naturally bring with us the mental orientation of the viewer, rather than the artist. For this reason some of the theoretical questions which haunt talk and writing about criticism inevitably affect our response to the artists' talk. We find ourselves needing to place this talk in the context of the conceptual framework of criticism.

For this reason it is important to air some of these issues in order to understand the relationship between the two kinds of thought. In considering how the talk of the Abstract Expressionist painters relates to the work that they actually produced, and in considering in particular the metaphors that some of them used to describe their work, one obvious question arises. If one only had the paintings to go by, would one in fact see the interpretation and supporting theory in the work?

Harold Rosenberg thought it a sufficiently important question to base a whole article on when writing about Newman. He puts the critical issue thus:

Not an inch, however, could be yielded to Newman's posthumous insistence that his paintings have to do with such motifs as the creation of man, the division between night and day, the coalescence of order within chaos, the anguish of man's abandonment: in a word—Newman's word—with the sublime. How could all these grandiloquent dramas be seen in the repeated image of a rectangle with stripes? . . .

Newman left nothing on the canvas that might prevent the spectator from perceiving the marked-off space as the reality indicated by the title. On the other hand, there is nothing to prevent him from considering the painting an organization of colored planes and lines and nothing else.[2]

Indeed, how *could* all these grandiloquent dramas be seen in the repeated image of a rectangle with stripes? Perhaps once we were told what lies behind the painting, we could readily see why the image is the way it is; furthermore, we could make a judgment about whether the painting achieved what the theory required that it achieve and had the specific content that it was claimed to have.

But might it not be possible to ignore the theory and interpretations offered by the artists, and deal with the works in terms of the visual elements alone, on the basis perhaps of "what you see is what you get?" In an age of extreme empiricism, after all, such an attitude has significant appeal. It is also taken by many to be the basis of disagreement between what appear to be fundamentally different critical styles.

The extreme of this view is epitomized in Clive Bell's remark "To appreciate a work of art we need bring with us nothing from life, no knowledge of its ideas and affairs, no familiarity with its emotions."[3] Clement Greenberg too was skeptical about the relevance of much art-talk to an understanding of the works themselves. As he put it so pungently in the following passage:

The difficulty of art criticism is to generate words and stay relevant. The trouble with art criticism, especially of late, is it's too much loaded with culture. It's as though the world's become self-educated instead of educated. So art has to bear the burden not only of being experienced, being judged, but of being interpreted. Sometimes it's phenomenology, sometimes it's Wittgenstein, sometimes it's Structuralism, sometimes it's Walter Benjamin. So art is there in order to be talked about, to be written about, instead of simply being experienced.[4]

But if art is overburdened by interpretations, and if the works can be understood in purely visual terms, then we must ask what the artists, intelligent and informed about art as they were, thought they were doing when they elaborated their theory and offered the interpretations that they did. Surely they could not have been so wrong-headed?

To understand what lies at the heart of this problem, we need to turn to the elements of the critical process. In particular, we must look at what is involved in the process of giving an analysis of a painting in the purely visual terms that Rosenberg described.

Not surprisingly, this itself is a complex phenomenon, and its complexity arises out of the fact that a process of "translation" is involved even at the very basic levels of appreciation and criticism. In the very first stages of apprehension of a work, the phenomenon of translation takes place in terms familiar to gestalt psychology. That is to say, when one perceives the patches of pigment on the support, one does not simply see them as forms of a certain size, shape, and color, but also as having certain dynamic properties. One color is seen as sitting "in front of" another, for example, and a particular form might be "drawn toward" a corner of the picture; or a particular image might be "still" because the "tensions" that hold between forms across spaces and between forms and the edges of the picture are all balanced or held in check so that nothing can "move."[5] Even the terms used in this description reflect the process of translations, since they are, each of them, metaphors.

This is the first requisite to seeing a work as a painting rather than just as paint marks on a piece of canvas. Since the dynamics attributed to the marks are not literal—that is to say, the forms do not really stand in front of one another, or move, and so on—clearly some form of translation, or nonliteral language, is involved. Nonetheless, these nonliteral properties are all of a similar kind at this stage of the critical process: they describe physical phenomena—movement, space, tendencies to appear larger or smaller, and so on.

Even at that level, however, and even in the hands of critics who eschew further levels of interpretation, the language used sometimes takes on a more poetic note. Walter Darby Bannard, for example, has written of Clyfford Still: "Furthermore, the edges which make this contact are ragged and meandering, and push into each other like roots after water, which gives them a great 'combining power.' "[6] And in speaking of the role of color in Hans Hofman, he said:

Light spreads through *Oracle*, . . . radiates like sunlight from the rectangles of *Silent Night*, . . . and like phosphor from the green rectangle of *Golden It Glows into a New Day*. . . . It enlivens the whole ground of *In Sober Ecstacy*, . . . as if an invisible lamp, off to the right, drenches the surface. It glows out of the darkness of *Summer Night's Bliss*, . . . and both comes from behind and highlights the surface of *Cathedral* and *Elysium II*. . . . Color, pigment and surface all conspire to turn the picture on, as if its making was solely in the service of a grand luminescence.[7]

What is interesting about these passages is that they reveal what happens to the critic's language when he is confronted by the quality (the *good* quality, that is) of the work. Had Still's paintings, and in particular the abutting edges of his forms, not had the power and quality that they do, then Bannard would no doubt have been content to use mundane language which simply described their physical properties. But as soon as the work has a magical dynamism, the critical impulse is to describe the physical properties in terms which also metaphorically describe the feeling they generate. In other words, the language is adapted to describe not just the mechanics of pictorial structure but also the *experience* of the work.

The same tendency is to be seen in the following passage on Kenneth Noland, by Michael Fried, an interesting passage, since later paragraphs reveal that he takes himself to be describing something physical and literal. In talking about the bands of color in Noland's horizontal paintings of the late sixties, Fried says:

There is of course a plain sense in which the ochre expanse in *Via Token* just *is* a certain shape, i.e., a particular horizontal rectangle. But my point is that we are made to see that solid rectangle of color as something else: a radically abstract entity whose essence consists, not in its boundedness, and not in the portion of the painting's surface which it covers, but in its unimpeded lateral extension across the plane of that surface. The sense in which the relatively *narrow* bands of color in this and other paintings are not (or are not essentially) shapes is, I think, apparent, at least in front of the paintings themselves: it is as though they essentialize lateral extension as such, as though they are nothing but that lateralness, that extension.[8]

This is a description very close to the dynamics of Newman's ideas of "total space" discussed earlier; it is interesting that it and the earlier passages come from critics who regard themselves as describing strictly "what is there." They represent, therefore, a baseline of criticism, in which is demonstrated an inevitable need to describe the impact or experience of the work.

But in attempting to describe this experience (which many critics, and especially Bannard, regard as essentially ineffable—hence the need for metaphor), it should not be assumed that these critics think this is the *same thing* as accounting for the quality. Bannard, for example, would say that the experience of the work—its impact—is an *indication* of its quality, but that its quality would have to be accounted for in other terms, such as its proportions and relational qualities— characteristics which evidently cannot be specified exactly, since they change from work to work.[9] Whether or not Bannard thinks that that would (theoretically) entirely account for the quality is not clear, but certainly Greenberg believes it would not.[10]

What the passages above illustrate is the fact that there is a certain kind of criticism in which translation or interpretation is confined to metaphor or poetic language used simply to focus attention on a particular physical property of the work. Thus "edges . . . push into each other like roots after water" simply describes the intensity of the penetrating characteristic of the edges. Similarly, "as if an invisible lamp, off to the right, drenches the surface" poetically, as it were, invokes an imaginary other cause in order to intensify a certain effect, at least in the viewer's perception and appreciation. Whatever the dynamics of their poetic effect, these devices are used simply as instruments of intensification and emphasis.

But most interpretation engaged in by critics—and this is especially true of critics of Abstract Expressionism—is of a quite different order. In these cases what is seen is translated, not into terms which heighten our awareness of those phenomena, but into terms and ideas which inhabit another world, as it were. In other words, the physical properties of the work are translated into terms which act as symbols for something else. These properties, whole works, and often whole oeuvres are ascribed with a particular meaning and are "interpreted"—cashed into a different currency. The various interpretations of translations can range, of course, from what most of us would regard as reasonable, to those which are plainly farfetched, an observation which, in itself, hints at many problems.

Many critics regard this rash of interpretive writing about art as a peculiarly twentieth-century phenomena, and indeed it is. Nonetheless it is not quite true to say that the interpretation of art is an entirely twentieth-century phenomenon, for in post-Hellenic Europe, art was traditionally explained as a manifestation of God's goodness. But this belief did not substantially affect the way in which people talked about art since art criticism as an activity or discipline did not get started until the nineteenth century.[11] Indeed, the fact that art was regarded primarily as a "service activity"[12] might have had something to do with the fact that it did not generate a "talk industry." It seems that as soon as art begins to be regarded as having its own distinctive character and value, then the need to talk about it, assess it, and explain it, arises. Being regarded as autonomous and intrinsically valuable, it must bear the burden of elaboration—as being regarded as the signifier of so many other aspects of life. And in the view of at least one writer, this is not always a good thing. Brian O'Doherty, in an article entitled "Criticizing Criticism," put it thus:

A main threat to modern art seems to have gone unrecognized—the people who write about it. For art now has a problem it never had before. It is being overinterpreted, overcriticized, and overdocumented in a strangling undergrowth of verbal redundancies.[13]

Unlike critics such as Walter Darby Bannard, Michael Fried, and Clement Greenberg, who steadfastly refuse to proceed beyond the level of translation described earlier,[14] Harold Rosenberg probably represents the broadest extreme of interpretive writing.[15] His attitude is based on the premise that art is inevitably symptomatic of society—either in simply reflecting the conditions out of which it grows, or in revealing the choices of the artist in reacting to those conditions. Thus the critic's responsibility is a serious one:

The first requirement of art criticism is that it shall be relevant to the art under consideration; how correct are its evaluations of specific art objects is of lesser importance. The accuracy of a critic's judgments cannot be determined by his contemporaries, in any case. But the inflection given by art criticism to the general thinking about art affects not only the responses of appreciators of art but the creative attitudes of artists as well. When this thinking is trivial or beside the point, painting and sculpture become the specialty of feature writers, decorators, dealers, and speculators in masterpieces.

And in order to be relevant and responsible, he says, art criticism

must maintain a continuing sensitivity to major characteristics peculiar to the modern epoch which affect the situation of art, including the outlook, rituals, and objectives of those who create it. A mind blind to the radical material, social and intellectual innovations of the twentieth century, and the influence of these innovations upon contemporary modes of creation can only respond to significant modern works with confusion and/or bitterness.[16]

As it stands, this description might cover, for example, a highly analytical account of the development of Cubist space and antinaturalism (which one could see as a response to photography's usurpation of the traditional role of painting). But this is clearly not what Rosenberg has in mind, as the following passage from "Criticism and Its Premises" shows. In describing the condition of art, he says,

Modern art is saturated with issues and ideologies that reflect the technological, political, social, and cultural revolutions of the past one hundred years. Regardless of the degree to which the individual artist is conscious of these issues, he in fact responds to them in choosing among aesthetic and technical alternatives. By choosing a certain mode of handling line, form, and color he will have affiliated himself with an aesthetic grounded on the obligation of art to communicate judgments of the artist's environment, while a different choice will have identified him with the concept that for art reality is that which comes into being through the act of painting. *Thus, choices having to do with method in art become in practice attitudes regarding the future of man.* Hence, art in our time cannot escape having a political content and moral implications. Criticism that is unaware of this is fatally poverty-stricken.[17]

What this indicates is that Rosenberg believes that every action and choice that is absorbed into the process of making a painting reflects the artist's responses to the complex situation of his or her life and the values consciously and unconsciously held by the artist. It is the critic's job to reveal these facets, and this will sometimes mean revealing them to the artist as well. In some sense, in fact, Rosenberg sees the critic's role as "completing" the work of art—or, as he would prefer to put it, completing the art act. "The art critic," he writes,

is the collaborator of the artist in developing the culture of visual works as a resource of human sensibility. His basic function is to extend the artist's act into the realm of meaningful discourse. Art in our time is itself criticism. Each painting embodies a choice in regard to available styles and works, including the previous work of its creator, and to the possibilities arising from them. Into this dialogue in pigments the critic interjects a vocabulary of words. Having thus put himself into the act (not, he needs to remind himself, at the invitation of the other performers), he assumes the role of responding with a trained rhetoric to the pantomime of the artists.[18]

What this means in practical terms is not so easy to determine, for it is not easy to locate, much less identify and characterize, the complex succession of choices and actions that make up a work of art. However, in speaking of the practicalities of this sort of criticism, Rosenberg had this to say:

Hence all categories of experience, past and present, from fetishism to laboratory discipline, are potentially relevant in making critical evaluations. The critic's primary act of judgment consists of choosing the modes of insight—aesthetic, psychological, social, metaphysical—which he regards as significant in the particular instance. For instance, in writing about the paintings of

Barnett Newman I found it necessary to dwell upon the quality of his taste, his counterstatement to the abstract art from which he derived, the rigor of his logic, his humor, his metaphysics of the sublime.[19]

And in writing about these things (rather than, say, the structure of the painting), Rosenberg clearly intended to present the *sensibility* of the artist or, at least, the relevant parts of his sensibility—all the many factors, whether serious or quirky, which shape his vision and choices, and determine that the work will have the character it does. That the work is an incomplete document of this sensibility, Rosenberg makes absolutely clear when writing about the problem of meaning in Mondrian and Newman. In speaking about Mondrian's asceticism and reductionism, he says:

In the period of its origin, abstract art contained the projected vision of the Marxist revolution in its idealistic, semi-mystical promise of the reconstitution of man and his environment within a totally rational order. Mondrian's de-individualized compositions prefigured in the imagination the communion of the anonymous human units of mass society, the proletariat, reborn through revolution.

He further comments that "social radicalism, though not actually visible in Mondrian's canvases, was reflected in them from the outside, like an image in the blank expanse of a store window," and later goes on to say, in an important and unequivocal passage:

With the passage of time and the fading of the Marxist utopia, Mondrian's paintings have lost their political afterimage. History has diminished them to their bars and rectangles; their social and metaphysical meanings have passed out of the paintings and become data of the biography of the artist. Yet without the dimension of thought affixed to it by the artist or his public, an abstract painting cannot exceed decoration. . . . Today, the paintings of Mondrian are in constant need of being filled out with the thought and will of their creator. Neo-Plastic paintings ought to be seen as "events" that belong to their time. To dissociate them from their intellectual origins on the ground that the spectator must confine himself to what is presented to him on the canvas is shallow aestheticism. . . .

Mondrian was aware that in our epoch a division exists between the artist and his creations. The artist conceives a grand vision, such as the salvation of the human race; his painting expresses itself as an arrangement of lines, shapes, and hues. For its meaning, the painting is dependent on the painter, who writes articles and issues statements and manifestos to explain what he has in mind. Not only Mondrian but abstract artists from Malevich and Kandinsky to Reinhardt and Newman have felt obliged to define in words what they were doing on the canvas. Mondrian was deeply committed to the belief that to achieve wholeness the work of art ought to speak for itself. Yet he knew that the intervention of the artist on behalf of his work is brought about by the diffused character of modern culture, which the individual artist can do nothing to cure. For paintings to convey their full meaning through direct sensation, a new phase in human development would have to be reached.[20]

This view of the incompleteness of the work of art as object is not so very surprising—or disturbing—if one takes the view that the real value and interest of art lies not in the product but in the sensibility, actions and choices of the person making it. If that is so, then one's interest is clearly in a certain kind of history rather than a certain kind of object per se. And this is at least in part a matter of personal preference.

Greenberg, on the other hand, would insist that his object was to address art "as art."

I've found [psychological or psychoanalytical concepts] irrelevant. Depth psychology seems to me to be able to say in some cases a lot, or at least something relevant, about the person of the artists, or writer, or composer, but nothing significant or really relevant about the art itself. . . . Aesthetics is, I think, useful in telling you what you can't say about art, warning you that what you're saying at a certain point is not about the art as *art*, but about the art as something else. I harp on that "art as art," art *qua* art, and then art as something else: as a document, as a revelation, as a sign of the times and so forth.[21]

In making this distinction, however, one is in danger of assuming that the artist's sensibility and history, and the work he creates, are discrete things able to be examined separately. And it is on the basis of that assumption that one postulates the notion of things being either "in" the work or not. The relevance of this point will emerge if we return once more to the question raised earlier and alluded to by Rosenberg: "Would one recognize the theory in the works if one had nothing but the works to go by?"

There is, of course, a sense in which this question is absurd, since it is doubtful that the answer to it could ever be "yes." In what sense can any particular theory be embodied and visible in a painting? Surely what one sees is only forms, lines, and colors and the effects that these generate. Beyond that, one supplements the given data with concepts, emotive connotations, and metaphors of interpretation.

This is not an arbitrary process, of course, because, since the object of the artist is communication, the concepts, emotive connotations, and metaphors of interpretation elicited by the pictorial structure are done so on the basis of a reasonable assumption about shared human perceptual and emotional experience. However, none of this is objectively "in" the work: it is simply that certain physical stimuli in the work act on the perceptions, experience, and attitudes of the viewer and evoke certain responses.

So whatever interpretation is placed on the work, it is essentially a *response,* and external to the work, though legitimized by its physical properties and stimuli. The interpretation, therefore, is never "in" the work, and always external, and imposed on it. In that case, then, the only question is whether or not the physical properties and stimuli of the work justify the particular interpretation offered.

At this stage, and in the light of this information, it might be thought that the question of whether we can recognize the theory in the work is still a reasonable question, if we take the position that the interpretation offered in response to the physical pictorial structure should be one which could reasonably be expected to occur to us without prompting from outside. On the face of it, that looks like a reasonable position, but when we look at what might constitute external promptings, then its plausibility dissolves. The trouble is that, once it becomes clear that what we normally describe as the nature and meaning of the work is in fact a mental construct imposed on the work in response to its physical properties, then it is also clear that there is no obviously hard and fast distinction to be drawn between attitudes, experience, and ways of conceptualizing that can be incorporated into the meaning and those that cannot. What is to count as "outside" information here? Since all such information is essentially outside the work, then surely the only test of acceptability can be whether or not there is general agreement on the part of attentive viewers that the pictorial structure will support that interpretation—that it "makes sense."

To approach the question from a different viewpoint, there is always a problem, whether it be in literature, painting, or any other art medium, as to what counts as internal as opposed to external evidence. The famous article "The Intentional Fallacy," of Wimsatt and Beardsley,[22] and all the subsequent literature, attest to this. The usual criterion for internal versus external is that something was the artist's intention. But as T. S. Eliot has pointed out, "There may be much more in a poem than the author is aware of."[23] The obvious reason why this is so is that the network of ideas, perceptions, and feeling generated by the pictorial structure (or words in the case of poetry)—that Motherwell refers to as "the relational structure"—is so complex and multilayered that it is highly unlikely that any artist is fully aware of it and in control of it, in the making.

The point is that all the ideas, perceptual experiences, and feelings that go to make up the relational structure of a work of art are never isolated elements: they are always, by their very nature, part of an infinite chain of cause and effect of associations. There is no difference in kind between those associations that are "relevant" and those that are not; it is a matter of degree only—of what does not seem "far-fetched," or dissonant with the rest of the meaning. In that case, whether I apprehend a particular feeling or conceptualization in a work, or whether I have to be "told," is only a matter of my own obtuseness; and after I have been "told," the only test of its acceptability is whether or not it "makes sense," or fits with the rest of the evidence of the work.

This point comes into focus more sharply when we remember that all the nonphysical "content" of the work—the relational structure of ideas, perceptions, and feelings—is not "in" the work at all, but is brought to it by the viewer. The question, therefore, of "internal" and "external" cannot arise. Acceptability or relevance is the only pertinent consideration, and that can be decided only in terms of whether or not a particular description or interpretation is supported by the physical facts of the painting. Whether or not the initial thoughts for the interpretation come from my own contemplation of the work or are suggested to me from "outside," is neither here not there. What matters is only whether or not it "fits." And it fits if it is supported by the physical and aesthetic structure of the work.

The artist, of course, is only concerned with whether or not the viewer can see what the artist set out to convey. The question of whether a particular interpretation fits is of no interest, since he already knows what went into the making of the picture and understands its aesthetic structure. Like two arms of a bridge meeting, the artist is interested in whether or not he has communicated successfully, and the viewer wonders whether or not he has read the message correctly.

Put in terms of Abstract Expressionism, we can now return to a question raised at the beginning of the previous chapter—namely, how relevant the artist's talk is to our understanding and appreciation of the work, and in what way. Another way of asking this question is to ask how what the artists have to say bears on what we do when we engage in criticism. That way of putting the question, however, implies that artists' talk is different in kind from criticism. But that is not really the point. It is more helpful to think of the artist and the viewer/ critic as merely approaching the same thing from different standpoints. In a sense the artist conducts a dialogue with the viewer/critic through the medium of the art work and in a special language. It is natural and interesting to check one's response to that process of dialogue against the parallel dialogue in a verbal form.

It may well be that the dialogue conducted through the medium of the artwork needs to be supplemented by the parallel verbal dialogue. Perhaps it is the case that the language of visual art is insufficiently developed to bear the precision and specificity of meaning that is possible in verbal language. Perhaps, on the other hand, it is better equipped to communicate at a different level—namely, through feeling.

But whatever the answer might be, it is evident that we constantly seek to express what we experience in art, in terms of verbal language, and the artist anxiously checks on what we have experienced, in the same way. Perhaps Harold Rosenberg was right when he said that the language of visual art is essentially incomplete. If it is true, as he said, that "for paintings to convey their full meaning through direct sensation, a new phase in human development would have to be reached,"[24] then it may well be that paintings need to be supplemented by other information if their message is to be fully understood.

Whatever the truth of that claim, however, it is undeniable that painting has the power to communicate with force and directness. In the case of Abstract Expressionism, this is particularly true. And when all the talk has been considered and weighed against the evidence of the work, there is ultimately only one thing that matters: to stand in front of the painting and experience it for what it is. In the case of Abstract Expressionist art, it is to experience the painting in all its force, as an abstract mystic symbol.

NOTES

Introduction

1. Serge Guilbaut, *How New York Stole the Idea of Modern Art,* p. 7.
2. Guilbaut, pp. 6–7.
3. Guilbaut, p. 3.
4. Meyer Shapiro, "The Social Bases of Art," p. 103.
5. Schapiro, pp. 108–109, 112.

Preface to Part I

1. "Adolph Gottlieb: An Interview with David Sylvester" (1963), p. 4.
2. Reported in Thomas B. Hess, *Barnett Newman,* p. 27.
3. For a full discussion of this aspect of Abstract Expressionism, see Dore Ashton, *The New York School*; and Serge Guilbaut, *How New York Stole the Idea of Modern Art,* ch. 1.
4. *USA: Artists:* Barrett Newman: (1966).

1. Myth: The Impetus for Art

1. Adolph Gottlieb and Mark Rothko (in collaboration with Barnett Newman), "Letter to the Editor."

2. "Adolph Gottlieb: An Interview with David Sylvester" (1963).

3. Gottlieb and Rothko, "Letter to the Editor."

4. Ibid.

5. The unpublished articles are held by the artist's widow, Mrs. Annalee Newman, and have been included, in excerpts, in T. B. Hess, *Barnett Newman*.

6. *Northwest Coast Indian Painting,* Betty Parsons Gallery, New York, September 30–October 19, 1946; *The Ideographic Picture,* Betty Parsons Gallery, New York, January 20–February 8, 1947; *Pre-Columbian Stone Sculpture,* Wakefield Gallery, New York, May 16–June 5, 1944; *Amlash Sculpture from Iran,* Betty Parsons Gallery, New York, September 23–October 19, 1963.

7. Mark Rothko, introduction, *Clyfford Still* (New York: Art of This Century Gallery), February 12–March 2, 1946.

8. See his writings on the art of his time in Barbara Rose, ed., *Art as Art.*

9. Clement Greenberg, "Art," *The Nation,* December 6, 1947, vol. 165, no. 23.

10. See B. H. Friedman, *Jackson Pollock,* p. 50.

11. Francine du Plessix and Cleve Gray, "Who Was Jackson Pollock?"

12. Letter, quoted in B. H. Friedman, *Jackson Pollock,* p. 91.

13. He meant "West American."

14. Jackson Pollock, "Jackson Pollock," *Arts and Architecture* (1944); published in F. V. O'Connor, *Jackson Pollock.*

15. Ibid.

16. Barnett Newman, *Stamos,* Betty Parsons Gallery, New York, February 10–March 1, 1947.

17. Thomas B. Hess, "William Baziotes 1912–1963," *Location* (Summer 1964), vol. 1, no. 2.

18. Barnett Newman, "The Plasmic Image," in Thomas B. Hess, *Barnett Newman,* p. 38.

19. Ibid., p. 39.

20. Robert Goodnough, ed., "Artists' Sessions at Studio 35" (Introduction); reprinted in Robert Motherwell and Ad Reinhardt, eds., *Modern Artists in America* (New York: Wittenborn Schulz, 1952), p. 9.

21. See Irving Sandler, *The Triumph of American Painting,* pp. 213–214.

22. H. Harvard Arnason, *Robert Motherwell,* note to plate 306.

23. Article and interview with Malcolm Johnson, *New York Sun,* August 22, 1941; quoted in Maurice Tuchman, *New York School,* pp. 57–58.

24. Letter to Gordon Smith, in John P. O'Neill, ed., *Clyfford Still*; quoted in Herschel B. Chipp, ed., *Theories of Modern Art,* pp. 575–576.

25. See the general tone of his comments in *Clyfford Still* (San Francisco: San Francisco Museum of Modern Art, 1976).

26. Mark Rothko, "The Portrait and the Modern Artist" (1943); quoted in Tuchman, *New York School,* p. 139.

27. Narration from film *Jackson Pollock* (1951), by Hans Namuth and Paul Falkenberg; reprinted in Bryan Robertson, *Jackson Pollock,* p. 193.

28. Mark Rothko, "The Romantics Were Prompted," *Possibilities* (Winter 1947–48), p. 84.

29. Rothko, "The Portrait and the Modern Artist," quoted in Tuchman, *New York School,* p. 139.

30. Rothko, "The Romantics Were Prompted."

31. Barnett Newman, "The Ides of Art—6 Opinions of What Is Sublime in Art: The Sublime Is Now" (1948).

32. He meant abstract artists like himself and the Abstract Expressionists.

33. Newman, "The Plasmic Image," in Hess, *Barnett Newman,* pp. 37–38.

34. Gottlieb, "An Interview with David Sylvester," (1963), p. 4.

35. Robert Motherwell, "What Abstract Art Means to Me," *Museum of Modern Art Bulletin* (Spring 1951); quoted in Chipp, *Theories of Modern Art,* p. 563.

36. For a full discussion of this subject, see G. S. Kirk, *Myth: Its Meaning and Functions.*

37. Gottlieb and Rothko, "Letter to the Editor."

38. Newman, "The Plasmic Image," in Hess, *Barnett Newman,* p. 39.

39. Rothko, "The Portrait and the Modern Artist," in Tuchman, *New York School,* p. 139.

40. See Barbara Cavaliere and Robert C. Hobbs, "Against a Newer Laocoon," p. 111; John Fischer, "Mark Rothko: Portrait of the Artist as an Angry Man," p. 22.

41. Preface to Marcel Raymond, *From Baudelaire to Surrealism.*

42. William Baziotes, "Notes on Painting," *It Is* (Autumn 1959); quoted in Tuchman, *New York School,* p. 45.

43. Bronislaw Malinowski, *Myth in Primitive Psychology,* p. 23.

44. Philip Guston, "Statement," in *It Is* (Spring 1958), No. 1; quoted in Tuchman, *New York School,* p. 75.

45. Barnett Newman, interview with Dorothy Seckler, "Frontiers of Space" (Summer 1962), p. 87.

46. Motherwell, "What Abstract Art Means To Me," in Chipp, *Theories of Modern Art,* p. 564.
47. Ibid., p. 563.
48. Mircea Eliade, "Myth," *Encyclopaedia Britannica,* Chicago, 1969.
49. Gottlieb, "The Portrait and the Modern Artist"; quoted in Sandler, *The Triumph of American Painting,* pp. 64, 65.
50. Newman, *Northwest Coast Indian Painting.*
51. Barnett Newman, "The New Sense of Fate," in Hess, *Barnett Newman,* p. 41.
52. Clyde Kluckhohn, "Myths and Rituals: A General Theory," p. 65.
53. Franz Boas, *Primitive Art.*
54. See Friedman, *Jackson Pollock,* p. 40; and Barbara Rose, "An Interview with Lee Krasner," *Partisan Review* (1980), 47(1):87; Barbaralee Diamondstein, "An Interview with Robert Motherwell," *Inside New York's Art World,* p. 244.
55. Carl G. Jung, *Man and His Symbols,* pp. 47–49.
56. Ernst Cassirer, *The Philosophy of Symbolic Forms.*
57. Ernst Cassirer, *Language and Myth.*
58. Biographical information from Susanne K. Langer, *Problems of Art* and *Philosophy in a New Key.*
59. Cassirer, *Philosophy of Symbolic Forms,* vol. 2, p. 69. Kirk quotes this passage and I have used his translation.
60. Gottlieb, "The Portrait and the Modern Artist," quoted in Sandler, *The Triumph of American Painting,* p. 62.
61. Rothko, "The Romantics Were Prompted," p. 84.
62. Ernst Cassirer, *An Essay on Man,* p. 89.
63. Susanne K. Langer, "On Cassirer's Theory of Language and Myth," in Paul A. Schilpp, ed., *The Philosophy of Ernst Cassirer,* pp. 388, 395.
64. Gottlieb and Rothko, "Letter to the Editor."
65. Willem de Kooning, "Content Is a Glimpse . . ."; reprinted in Thomas B. Hess, *Willem de Kooning* (New York: Museum of Modern Art, 1968), p. 148. *USA: Artists: Willem de Kooning* (1966).
66. See Cassirer, *Language and Myth,* ch. 4.
67. Discussed in "Myth," *Encyclopaedia Britannica.*
68. Cassirer, *Language and Myth,* pp. 34–35.
69. Newman, "The First Man Was an Artist," *The Tiger's Eye* (October 1947); reprinted in Chipp, *Theories of Modern Art,* p. 551.

70. Motherwell and Rosenberg, "Editorial," *Possibilities* (Winter 1947–48), p. 1.
71. Andrea Caffi, "On Mythology," *Possibilities* (Winter 1947–48), pp. 87–92.
72. At least one session at the Club was devoted to "the Situation"; see Philip Pavia's notebooks, *Archives of American Art,* microfilm roll D 176.

2. From Myth Into Symbol

1. See, for instance, Barbara Cavaliere, "An Introduction to the Method of William Baziotes."
2. Ibid., p. 125.
3. See Max Kozloff, "An Interview with Robert Motherwell," pp. 36–37.
4. See Cavaliere, "An Introduction to the Method of William Baziotes," p. 125.
5. Dore Ashton, *Yes, but . . . A critical Study of Philip Guston,* p. 90.
6. See H. Harvard Arnason, *Robert Motherwell,* in his note to plate 74. Motherwell says this explicitly.
7. Kozloff, "An Interview with Robert Motherwell," p. 36.
8. This attitude is expressed, on the one hand, in their ruthless elimination of any stylistic elements in their work which were simply inherited and not made over to their own purposes; and, on the other, it is epitomized by their enthusiasm for Surrealist ideas while detesting Surrealist painting in general.
9. For a useful discussion of Symbolist thought, see Raymond, *From Baudelaire to Surrealism.*
10. Paul Valéry, "The Course in Poetics," p. 106.
11. Arthur Symons, *The Symbolist Movement in Literature,* p. 128.
12. Charles Baudelaire, "Théophile Gautier" (March 1859); reprinted in Charles Baudelaire, *Selected Writings on Art and Artists* (Harmondsworth: Penguin, 1972), p. 267.
13. Baziotes, "The Artist and His Mirror," p. 3.
14. Symons, *The Symbolist Movement in Literature,* pp. 131–132.
15. Anna Balakian, *The Symbolist Movement,* p. 82.
16. Quoted by Raymond, in Raymond, *From Baudelaire to Surrealism,* p. 26.

17. Ibid., pp. 26, 27–28.

18. Mark Rothko, excerpts from Pratt lecture, 1958; reprinted in Maurice Tuchman, *New York School,* p. 142.

19. Rothko's obsession with a repeated image is discussed in ch. 10.

20. Raymond, *From Baudelaire to Surrealism,* p. 27.

21. Harold Rosenberg, "Preface" to Raymond, *From Baudelaire to Surrealism,* pp. ix–x.

22. Robert Motherwell, "Preface" to Raymond, *From Baudelaire to Surrealism,* p. viii.

23. Ibid.

24. Goethe's *Theory of Colours* had appeared in 1810, for example, and was widely read. Beethoven is reported to have thought highly of it.

25. Charles Baudelaire, "Richard Wagner and *Tannhauser* in Paris" (April 1861); reprinted in Baudelaire, *Selected Writings,* pp. 330–331.

26. Translation from Raymond, *From Baudelaire to Surrealism,* p. 17.

27. Ibid., footnote.

28. Many scientific hypotheses employ a metaphor as a model; for instance, in psychoanalytic theory a spatial metaphor is used for the notion of consciousness. Theories of interpretation in history usually depend on such models, too; for example, the evolutionary model is a commonly assumed one in current historical writing, and in art history the biological model of the birth, maturity, decline, and eventual death of a particular style is the most usual one encountered.

29. The beginnings of this theory are to be found in the Pythagorean theory of musical correspondences. In Aristotle's *De Coloribus* he associates "simple" colors with the four prime elements. There are traces of it through the Renaissance, and in Newton's *Opticks* he aligns seven elementary colors with the seven notes of the diatonic scale. The "color organ" was first built in the 1730's by a French Jesuit mathematician, R. P. Castel, and it was inspected by Telemann in 1737. From then on, the theory of correspondences, especially between color and sound, was generally in the air.

30. Robert Motherwell, "Beyond the Aesthetic" (1946), p. 15.

31. Barnett Newman, "The Plasmic Image," in Thomas B. Hess, *Barnett Newman,* p. 37.

32. Quoted by Baudelaire, in Baudelaire, *Selected Writings,* p. 339.

33. Ibid., pp. 339–340.

34. Langer, *Philosophy in a New Key,* p. 92.
35. Cassirer, *Language and Myth,* pp. 32–33.
36. Langer, "On Cassirer's Theory of Language and Myth," p. 388.

3. Creating the Symbol

1. See David Hare, "Communication," *Art News* 66(8):10; (December 1967), and Irving Sandler, p. 34.
2. See Maurice Nadeau, *The History of Surrealism,* p. 233.
3. André Breton and Marcel Duchamp, *First Papers of Surrealism,* exhibition at Reid mansion, Madison Avenue, New York, for Coordinating Council of French Relief Societies, October 14–November 7, 1942.
4. See Peggy Guggenheim, *Out of This Century; Confessions of an Art Addict* (New York: Universe Books, 1979), chs. 13 and 17.
5. Ibid., p. 263. Several items from Ernst's collection were included in the *Northwest Coast Indian Painting* exhibition, for which Newman wrote the catalogue essay, for instance.
6. André Breton, "The First Surrealist Manifesto" (1924); reprinted in Lucy R. Lippard, ed., *Surrealists on Art,* pp. 20, 21.
7. Max Ernst, "Beyond Painting," (1937), in Lippard, *Surrealists on Art,* p. 120.
8. Ibid., p. 121.
9. Max Ernst, "What Is Surrealism?" (1934), in Lippard, *Surrealists on Art,* pp. 134–135.
10. André Masson, "Interview with James Johnson Sweeney," *Bulletin of the Museum of Modern Art,* (1946), vol. 13, nos. 4–5; quoted in Lippard, *Surrealists on Art,* pp. 162–163.
11. Max Kozloff, "An Interview with Robert Motherwell," (1965), p. 37.
12. Wolfgang Paalen, "The New Image," *Dyn,* (April–May 1942), no. 1; quoted in Sandler, *Triumph of American Painting,* pp. 37, 40.
13. Max Kozloff, "An Interview with Matta."
14. André Masson, "A Crisis of the Imaginary" (1945); quoted in Lippard, *Surrealists on Art,* p. 164.
15. Sidney Simon, "Concerning the Beginnings of the New York School: 1939–1943., p. 18.

16. See Sandler, *Triumph of American Painting,* p. 37.

17. Kozloff, "An Interview with Robert Motherwell," p. 34.

18. Stanley William Hayter, "Of the Means," *Possibilities* (Winter 1947–48), p. 77.

19. See B. H. Friedman, *Jackson Pollock,* pp. 72–74.

20. Jackson Pollock, "Jackson Pollock," in Francis V. O'Connor, *Jackson Pollock,* p. 32.

21. Ernst, "What Is Surrealism?" in Lippard, *Surrealists on Art,* p. 135.

22. Ernst, "Beyond Painting," in Lippard, *Surrealists on Art,* p. 131.

23. Barbara Cavaliere and Robert C. Hobbs, "Against a Newer Laocoon," p. 111.

24. Ernst, "Beyond Painting," Lippard, *Surrealists on Art,* pp. 126–127.

25. Breton, "The First Surrealist Manifesto," in Lippard, *Surrealists on Art,* p. 130.

26. William Rubin, in *Dada, Surrealism and Their Heritage,* disputes this, but only on the ground that the works are too "designed," but this might only mean that those with such "aesthetic" properties were the ones Arp chose to keep.

27. Masson, "A Crisis of the Imaginary," in Lippard, *Surrealists on Art,* p. 165.

28. Kozloff, "An Interview with Robert Motherwell," (1965), p. 34.

29. Ibid. Also see Masson, "Crisis of the Imaginery."

30. Robert Goldwater has discussed this point in his *Primitivism in Modern Art.*

31. See Marcel Raymond, *From Baudelaire to Surrealism,* p. 27.

4. *The Process of Painting a Picture*

1. Barrett Newman, interview in Dorothy Seckler, "Frontiers of Space" (Summer 1962), p. 87.

2. Gottlieb and Mark Rothko, "Letter to the Editor."

3. From the script of the television film *Art: New York,* 1964.

4. "Unframed Space" (1950), p. 16.

5. Harold Rosenberg, "The American Action Painters."

6. "Artists' Sessions at Studio 35 (1950)," *Modern Artists in America,* p. 12.

7. Ibid.

8. Ibid.

9. For a thorough discussion of this question, see William Rubin, "Jackson

Pollock and the Modern Tradition," *Artforum* (February 1967), vol. 5, no. 6.

10. *USA: Artists: Willem de Kooning* (1966).
11. Harold Rosenberg, "Action Painting: A Decade of Distortion"; reprinted as "Action Painting: Crisis and Distortion," in Rosenberg, *The Anxious Object,* p. 39.
12. Harold Rosenberg, "The Concept of Action in Painting," in Rosenberg, *Artworks and Packages,* pp. 227–228.
13. Rosenberg, *The Tradition of the New,* p. 47.
14. Ibid., p. 40.
15. Harold Rosenberg, "de Kooning," *Vogue*; reprinted as "de Kooning: On the Borders of the Act," in Rosenberg, *The Anxious Object,* p. 127.
16. Rosenberg, *Artworks and Packages,* p. 224.
17. Harold Rosenberg, "Painting Is a Way of Living"; reprinted as "de Kooning: Painting Is A Way," in Rosenberg *The Anxious Object,* pp. 118–119.
18. In discussion with the author, May 9, 1977.
19. In discussion with the author, December 5, 1977.
20. In discussion with the author, June 9, 1977.
21. In discussion with the author, May, 1977.
22. In discussion with the author, December 5, 1977.
23. John Fischer, "Mark Rothko: Portrait of the Artist as an Angry Man."
24. Clyfford Still, exhibition at Institute of Contemporary Art, University of Pennsylvania, October 18–November 29, 1963; and "An Interview with Benjamin Townsend" (Summer 1961); quoted in Tuchman, *New York School,* pp. 153, 148.
25. The article "The American Action Painters" does not even name any of the artists Rosenberg had in mind. Hess reported (conversation with the author, December 5, 1977) that originally Pollock, de Kooning, and one other artist were mentioned but that Rosenberg removed these prior to publication. (Hess was the editor of the magazine.)
26. Recorded in Phillip Pavia's notebooks of Club proceedings, *Archives of American Art,* microfilm roll D. 176.
27. Max Kozloff, "An Interview with Robert Motherwell" (1965), p. 37.
28. Richard Huelsenbeck, "En Avant Dada," *Possibilities* (Winter 1947–48), pp. 42, 43.
29. By the early thirties he was very active in the art world, and was editor of *Art Front,* in 1935.

30. See Barbara Rose's discussion of "action painting" in the second generation artists, in "The Second Generation."
31. Not until the second generation of artists, that is.
32. This was a conference to "wind up" Studio 35. An edited transcript is printed in *Modern Artists in America.*
33. *Modern Artists in America,* p. 11.
34. In conversation with the author, June 9, 1977.
35. *Modern Artists in America,* p. 11.
36. Ibid.
37. Ibid., p. 12.
38. Ibid.
39. These are usually considered to be Pollock, de Kooning, Hofmann, Motherwell, Brooks, Kline, Guston, Tworkov, and Goodnough. The other group, called "color field painters," included Newman, Rothko, and Still.
40. *Modern Artists in America,* p. 11.
41. Jackson Pollock, "My Painting," *Possibilities* (Winter 1947–48), p. 79.
42. B. Friedman, *Jackson Pollock,* p. 140.
43. Jackson Pollock, "Interview with William Wright," taped summer 1950 for Sag Harbor radio station but not broadcast. Published in Francis V. O'Connor, *Jackson Pollock,* p. 81.
44. *Modern Artists in America,* pp. 11–12.
45. Ibid., p. 15.
46. de Kooning did not seem to be influenced by myth and primitivism in the way that the other artists were—at least, he did not talk about such things.
47. See Rosenberg, "de Kooning: Painting Is a Way," in Rosenberg, *The Anxious Object,* p. 119.
48. *Modern Artists in America,* p. 12.
49. Kozloff, "An Interview with Robert Motherwell" (1965), p. 34.
50. Philip Guston, "Statement," *It Is,* (Spring 1958), no. 1; reprinted in Tuchman, *New York School,* pp. 75–76.
51. See Rose, "The Second Generation."
52. *Modern Artists in America,* p. 10.
53. Letter to Gordon Smith, in H. B. Chipp, *Theories of Modern Art,* pp. 575–576.
54. Robert Motherwell, "Painters' Objects," *Partisan Review* (Winter 1944).
55. *Modern Artists in America,* p. 20.

56. Dore Ashton, *The New York School,* ch. 12.

57. Ibid., p. 178.

58. Ibid., p. 177.

59. Ibid.

60. Gladys Kashdin, "An Interview with James Brooks," Sarasota, Florida, March 8, 1965. In *Archives of American Art,* microfilm roll N 69–132, pp. 5–6 of typescript.

61. Wassily Kandinsky, *Concerning the Spiritual in Art* (New York: Wittenborn, 1947). For a discussion of Kandinsky's ideas, see Alwynne Mackie, "Kandinsky and Problems of Abstraction, *Artforum* (November 1978), vol. 17, no. 3.

62. Mark Rothko, "The Romantics Were Prompted," *Possibilities* (Winter 1947–48), p. 84.

63. O'Connor, *Jackson Pollock,* p. 80.

64. Seckler, "Frontiers of Space" (1962), p. 86.

65. Robert Motherwell, *Art: New York* (1964).

66. Barnett Newman, "The Plasmic Image," in Thomas B. Hess, *Barnett Newman,* pp. 37–38.

67. Guston, "Statement," in Tuchman, *New York School* p. 77.

68. *Modern Artists in America,* p. 14.

69. Newman, *The Ideographic Picture* (1947).

70. Narration for film *Jackson Pollock* (1951) by Hans Namuth and Paul Falkenberg; reprinted in Chipp, *Theories of Modern Art,* p. 548.

71. *Modern Artists in America,* p. 12.

72. Ibid., p. 11.

73. Motherwell, *Art: New York* (1964).

74. Robert Motherwell, "Beyond the Aesthetic" (1946), p. 14.

75. Clyfford Still, "An Interview with Benjamin Townsend," in Tuchman, *New York School,* p. 148.

76. Dorothy C. Miller, *Fifteen Americans*; reprinted in Tuchman, *New York School,* p. 147.

77. Barnett Newman, "The New Sense of Fate," in Hess, *Barnett Newman,* pp. 41–42.

78. Newman, "The Plasmic Image," in Hess, *Barnett Newman,* p. 39.

5. *The Abstract Mystic Symbol*

1. Robert Motherwell, "What Abstract Art Means to Me," in H. B. Chipp, *Theories of Modern Art,* pp. 563–564.
2. Ernst Cassirer, *An Essay on Man,* pp. 121–122.
3. Barnett Newman, "The First Man Was An Artist" (1947).
4. Ernst Cassirer, *Language and Myth,* pp. 32–33.
5. Barnett Newman, "Art of the South Seas" (1970), p. 71.
6. Barnett Newman, "The Plasmic Image," in Thomas B. Hess, *Barnett Newman,* p. 38.
7. Barnett Newman, "The New Sense of Fate," in Hess, *Barnett Newman,* p. 43.
8. In "Beyond the Aesthetic" (1946).
9. Clyfford Still, "An Interview with Benjamin Townsend," in Irving Sandler, *The Triumph of American Art,* p. 167.
10. Adolph Gottlieb, statement in "Adolph Gottlieb," *Limited Editions* (December 1945); reprinted in Maurice Tuchman, *New York School,* p. 67.
11. Barnett Newman, statement dated January 1950, on file at Betty Parsons Gallery, New York; copy in Artists' Files, Library of the Museum of Modern Art, New York.
12. Robert Motherwell, *Art: New York* (1964).
13. Adolph Gottlieb and Mark Rothko, "Letter to the Editor."
14. Cassirer, *Language and Myth,* pp. 90–91.
15. Cassirer has a good discussion of this process in his *Language and Myth.*
16. Ibid., pp. 92–93.
17. Newman, *USA: Artists: Barnett Newman* (1966).
18. Barnett Newman, in Frank O'Hara, *Art: New York* (1964).
19. Jackson Pollock, "Interview with William Wright," (1950), in F. V. O'Connor, *Jackson Pollock,* pp. 80–81.
20. Pollock, narration film *Jackson Pollock* (1951) by Hans Namuth and Paul Falkenberg; reprinted in Chipp, *Theories of Modern Art,* p. 548.
21. H. Harvard Arnason, *Philip Guston,* p. 21.
22. Willem de Kooning, *New York Times,* January 21, 1951, Section 6, p. 17; quoted in Sandler, *The Triumph of American Painting,* p. 92.
23. Newman, *The Ideographic Picture* (1947).
24. Newman, statement (1950), Betty Parsons Gallery, New York.

25. Adolph Gottlieb, statement in John I. H. Baur, *The New Decade* pp. 35–36; reprinted in Tuchman, *New York School,* p. 71.
26. Guston, statement in *It Is*; reprinted in Tuchman, *New York School,* p. 77.
27. Bradley Walker Tomlin, statement in *The New American Painting* (New York: Museum of Modern Art, 1959); reprinted in Tuchman, *New York School,* p. 155.
28. Clyfford Still, notes of January 11, 1944; reprinted in *Clyfford Still* (San Francisco, San Francisco Museum of Modern Art, 1976), p. 110.
29. Still, exhibition, University of Pennsylvania; quoted in Tuchman, *New York School,* p. 153.
30. Still, quoted in Dorothy C. Miller, *Fifteen Americans,* p. 147.
31. Robert Motherwell, "A Conversation at Lunch (1962)," Smith College (January 1963); reprinted in Frank O'Hara, *Robert Motherwell,* p. 54.
32. Robert Motherwell, "Painting as Existence" (1962), p. 95.
33. See Rudolph Arnheim, "The Gestalt Theory of Expression," *Psychological Review* (1949), vol. 56; reprinted in Arnheim, *Towards a Psychology of Art* (London: Faber and Faber, 1966), pp. 51–73.
34. Motherwell, "Beyond the Aesthetic" (1946), pp. 14–15.
35. Harold Rosenberg, "Hans Hofmann: Nature into Action"; reprinted in Rosenberg, *The Anxious Object,* pp. 157–158.
36. Motherwell, "Beyond the Aesthetic" (1946), p. 14.
37. Newman, statement (1950), Betty Parsons Gallery.
38. Goldwater, *Primitivism in Modern Art,* p. 251.
39. Newman, *The Ideographic Picture* (1947).

6. Clyfford Still

1. Clyfford Still, letter to Gordon Smith (1959), quoted in H. B. Chipp, *Theories of Modern Art,* p. 576.
2. Clyfford Still, statement, Albright-Knox exhibition catalogue (1960), p. 17.
3. Ibid., p. 16.
4. Ibid., p. 18.
5. Walter Darby Bannard, "Touch and Scale: Cubism, Pollock, Newman and Still," *Artforum* (June 1971), 9(10):64.
6. Walter Darby Bannard, "Cubism, Abstract Expressionism, David Smith," p. 32. See the last paragraph especially.

7. Clyfford Still, statement quoted by Katharine Kuh, without source, in John O'Neill *Clyfford Still* (New York: Metropolitan Museum of Art, 1979), p. 11.

8. *1948-E,* oil on canvas, 6 feet 10 inches × 5 feet 9 inches, Albright-Knox Art Gallery, Buffalo; *November 1950,* oil on canvas, 6 feet 8 inches × 5 feet 8 inches, Albright-Knox Art Gallery; *1949-E,* oil on canvas, 6 feet 8 inches × 5 feet 9 inches, Albright-Knox Art gallery; *October 1950,* oil on canvas, 6 feet 8 inches × 5 feet 8 inches, Albright-Knox Art Gallery; *Untitled, 1951,* painted at Cooper Square Studio, New York, (number 18 in *Clyfford Still,* San Francisco catalogue (1976), oil on canvas, 6 feet 10 inches × 5 feet 8 inches, San Francisco Museum of Modern Art. Unfortunately the four paintings belonging to the Albright-Knox Art Gallery cannot be reproduced, under the terms of the artist's gift.

9. Clyfford Still, "An Interview with Benjamin Townsend," in Irving Sandler, *The Triumph of American Art,* p. 167.

10. Still, statement, Albright-Knox catalogue (1960), p. 17.

11. Clyfford Still, Letter to Edgar Berman, February 19, 1960; reprinted in *Clyfford Still,* San Francisco catalogue (1976), p. 123.

12. Clyfford Still, statement, exhibition at University of Pennsylvania; reprinted in *Clyfford Still,* San Francisco catalogue (1976), p. 124.

13. Jacquin Sanders, "This Man Detests the Art World," *Alaska News,* Anchorage, August 9, 1970; in Artists' File, Library of the Museum of Modern Art, New York.

14. Ibid. The critic is not identified.

7. Jackson Pollock

1. B. H. Friedman, *Jackson Pollock: Energy Made Visible,* p. 178.

2. Ibid.

3. Selden Rodman, *Conversations with Artists,* p. 82.

4. Barbara Rose, "An Interview with Lee Krasner," pp. 85–86.

5. In Francine du Plessix and Cleve Gray, "Who Was Jackson Pollock?", p. 52.

6. Smith, in du Plessix and Gray, "Who Was Jackson Pollock?" p. 54; Krasner, in ibid., p. 51; Ossorio, in ibid., p. 58.

7. Francis V. O'Connor, *Jackson Pollock,* p. 79.

8. This began as early as 1928 in high school. See O'Connor, p. 13.

9. For discussions of these practices, see L. McCombe, E. Z. Vogt, and Clyde Kluckhohn, *Navaho Means People* (Cambridge, Mass.: Harvard University Press, 1951), especially pp. 140–141; and A. H. and D. C. Leighton, *The Navaho Door* (Cambridge, Mass.: Harvard University Press, 1945), especially p. 26.

10. See Friedman, *Jackson Pollock: Energy Made Visible,* p. 91 for evidence of Pollock's reading (footnotes 16 and 18, ch. 2). Lee Krasner, among others, reported Pollock's interest in the sand-painting ceremonies; see Rose, "An Interview with Lee Krasner," p. 85.

11. In du Plessix and Gray, "Who Was Jackson Pollock?" p. 55.

12. Given to him by Tony Smith, and always listed as one of his most favorite books. See Friedman, *Jackson Pollock: Energy Made Visible,* p. 92.

13. Questionnaire, *Arts and Architecture*; Reprinted in F. V. O'Connor, *Jackson Pollock,* p. 32.

14. In du Plessix and Gray, "Who Was Jackson Pollock?" p. 53.

15. Barbaralee Diamondstein, "An Interview with Lee Krasner," series of interviews conducted at the New School for Social Research, New York; reprinted in Diamondstein, *Inside New York's Art World,* p. 202.

16. James Fitzsimmons, review of Pollock exhibition, Sidney Janis Gallery, New York, November 10–29, 1952, in *Art Digest,* November 15, 1952; reprinted in O'Connor, *Jackson Pollock,* p. 66; review of exhibition, Sidney Janis Gallery, New York, February 1–27, 1954, in *Arts and Architecture,* March 1954; reprinted in O'Connor, p. 70.

17. Will Grohmann, review of International Council of the Museum of Modern Art, New York, traveling exhibition, March 1958–February 1959, in *Tagesspiegel,* Berlin, September 7, 1958; reprinted in O'Connor, p. 77.

18. Denys Sutton, ibid., in *Financial Times,* London, November 25, 1958; reprinted in O'Connor, p. 78.

19. John Russell, ibid., in *Sunday Times,* London, November 9, 1958; reprinted in O'Connor, p. 77.

20. Henri Matisse, "Notes of a Painter on His Drawing" (1939); published in Jack D. Flam, ed., *Matisse on Art* (New York: Dutton, 1978), p. 81.

21. Clement Greenberg, "Feeling Is All," review of exhibition; reprinted in O'Connor, *Jackson Pollack,* p. 63.

22. William Rubin, "Jackson Pollock and the Modern Tradition."

23. This does not mean that the other kind of space is *necessarily* inferior aesthetically, though no doubt some would say it is.
24. Rubin, "Jackson Pollock and the Modern Tradition."
25. John Graham, *System and Dialectics of Art* (1937), pp. 116–117.
26. Ibid., pp. 95, 101.

8. *Barnett Newman*

1. Newman, *USA: Artists: Barnett Newman* (1966).
2. Barnett Newman, "Chartres and Jerico" (February 1970), p. 65.
3. *USA: Artists: Barnett Newman* (1966).
4. Ibid.
5. In Dorothy Seckler, "The Frontiers of Space," p. 86.
6. Barnett Newman, "The Ides of Art—6 Opinions of What Is Sublime in Art: The Sublime Is Now" (1948), p. 51.
7. Quoted in Pierre Schneider, ed., *Louvre Dialogues,* pp. 212 and 215.
8. *USA: Artists: Barnett Newman* (1966).
9. Tony Smith, *Die,* 1962, steel, 6 × 6 × 6 feet, Fourcade Droll, Inc., New York; Constantin Brancusi, *Endless Column,* 1937, cast iron, 96 feet 3 inches high, Public Park, Tirgu Jiu, Romania.
10. In Seckler, "The Frontiers of Space," p. 86.
11. Don Judd, "Barnett Newman," p. 68.
12. Quoted in Schneider, *Louvre Dialogues,* p. 223.
13. Henri Matisse, *La Danse,* 1909, oil on canvas, Museum of Modern Art, New York.
14. In Frank O'Hara, *Art: New York:* "The Continuity of Vision" (1964).
15. Conversation between author and Mrs. Annalee Newman, December 16, 1977.
16. In the files of Mrs. Annalee Newman.
17. For further elaboration, see Alwynne Mackie, "Kandinsky and Problems of Abstraction," *Artforum* (November 1978), vol. 17, no. 3.
18. Paolo Uccello, *Battle of San Romano,* 1456, tempera on wood, Louvre Museum, Paris.
19. In Seckler, "The Frontiers of Space," p. 87.
20. Quoted in Schneider, *Louvre Dialogues,* p. 220.
21. Ibid., p. 222.

22. In Seckler, "The Frontiers of Space."

23. Ibid., p. 86.

24. Ibid.

25. *USA: Artists: Barnett Newman* (1966).

26. Quoted in Schneider, *Louvre Dialogues,* p. 221.

27. Ibid., p. 212.

28. Ibid., p. 226.

29. Ibid., p. 212.

30. Ibid., p. 215.

31. Ibid., pp. 216–217.

32. *USA: Artists: Barnett Newman* (1966).

33. In Seckler, "The Frontiers of Space," p. 86.

34. Cage and Feldman were regularly at The Club, and their concerts were supported by many of the artists. There was a general appreciation of classical music, and Pollock, at least, was a great jazz fan. See Barbara Rose, "An Interview with Lee Krasner," *Partisan Review* (1980), vol. 47, no. 1, p. 90.

35. See gestalt theories of expression, Rudolf Arnheim, "The Gestalt Theory of Expression," "*Psychological Review* (1949), vol. 56; reprinted in Arnheim, *Towards a Psychology of Art* (London: Faber and Faber, 1966).

36. Robert Motherwell, *Art: New York* (1964).

37. Robert Motherwell, "Letter to Frank O'Hara," August 18, 1965; reprinted in Frank O'Hara, *Robert Motherwell,* p. 70.

9. Robert Motherwell

1. See the discussion of this in E. A. Carmean and Eliza E. Rathbone, *American Art at Mid-Century: The Subjects of the Artist,* pp. 92–123.

2. *The Intrasubjectives,* Kootz Gallery, New York, September 14–October 3, 1949; quoted in Maurice Tuchman, *New York School,* p. 214.

3. In Max Kozloff, "An Interview with Robert Motherwell" (1965), p. 34.

4. Barnett Newman, "The Ides of Art—6 Opinions of What Is Sublime in Art: The Sublime Is Now" (1948), p. 51.

5. In Barbaralee Diamondstein, "An Interview with Robert Motherwell" (1979), p. 253.

6. Robert Motherwell, statement in John I. H. Baur, *The New Decade,* p. 59.

7. Robert Motherwell, preface to Marcel Raymond, *From Baudelaire to Surrealism.*

8. Ibid., p. viii.

9. Robert Motherwell, "Beyond the Aesthetic" (1946), p. 15.

10. Conversation quoted in Carmean and Rathbone, *The Subjects of the Artist,* p. 101.

11. Ibid., p. 104.

12. Quoted in Frank O'Hara, *Robert Motherwell,* p. 19.

13. Motherwell, "Beyond the Aesthetic" (1946), p. 15.

14. Ibid.

15. Shushiki, in *Japanese Haiku* (Mount Vernon, N.Y.: Peter Pauper Press, 1956), p. 8.

16. T. S. Eliot, "Preludes," in *Collected Poems 1909–1935* (London: Faber and Faber, 1954), p. 22–23.

17. Rudolf Arnheim, "The Gestalt Theory of Expression," *Psychological Review* (1949), vol. 56; reprinted in Arnheim, *Towards a Psychology of Art* (London: Faber and Faber, 1966).

18. See Carmean and Rathbone, *The Subjects of the Artist.*

19. Quoted in Diamondstein, "An Interview with Robert Motherwell" (1979), p. 245.

20. Ibid., p. 253.

21. Walter Darby Bannard, "Cubism, Abstract Expressionism, David Smith."

22. See Carmean and Rathbone, *The Subjects of the Artist,* p. 112.

23. Ibid., p. 104.

24. Ibid., p. 110.

25. Robert Motherwell, note to plate 306, in H. Harvard Arnason, *American Abstract Expressionists and Imagists.*

26. Robert Motherwell, "A Conversation at Lunch" (1962)," Smith College (January 1963); reprinted in O'Hara, *Robert Motherwell,* p. 54.

27. Carmean and Rathbone, *The Subjects of the Artist,* pp. 92–123.

28. Motherwell, "Beyond the Aesthetic" (1946), p. 14.

29. Ibid., p. 15.

30. Conversation quoted in Carmean and Rathbone, *The Subjects of the Artist,* p. 99.

31. Motherwell, *Art: New York* (1964).

32. Quoted in Diamondstein, "An Interview with Robert Motherwell" (1979), p. 244.

33. Conversation quoted in Carmean and Rathbone, *The Subjects of the Artist,* p. 98.
34. Robert Motherwell, "The School of New York," preface to exhibition *Seventeen Modern American Painters* (1951).
35. Quoted in Carmean and Rathbone, *The Subjects of the Artist,* p. 103.
36. In Diamondstein, "An Interview with Robert Motherwell" (1979), p. 244.
37. Robert Motherwell, "The Public and the Modern Painter" (1951), p. 81.
38. Motherwell, "Beyond the Aesthetic" (1946), p. 15.

10. Mark Rothko

1. Robert Goldwater, "Reflections on the Rothko Exhibition," p. 46.
2. Eric Newton, review of exhibition, Whitchapel Gallery, London, October 11–November 8, 1961; in *Manchester Guardian,* October 14, 1961.
3. Brian O'Doherty, *American Masters,* p. 163.
4. For a discussion of this subject, see Leonide Ouspensky and Vladimir Lossky, *The Meaning of Icons* (Boston: Boston Book and Art Shop, 1952); and Gervase Mathew, *Byzantine Aesthetics* (London: Murray, 1963).
5. Werner Haftmann, preface to *Mark Rothko* (Zurich: Kunsthaus), March 21–May 9, 1971, p. vii.
6. Peter Selz, preface to *Mark Rothko* (Basel: Kunsthalle), March 3–April 8, 1962.
7. Haftmann, preface to *Mark Rothko,* p. vii.
8. For a selection of typical critical reviews, see the collection of reviews of the traveling exhibition of 1961–62, organized by the International Council of the Museum of Modern Art, New York. These are collated and available in the Artists' File, Library of the Museum of Modern Art, New York.
9. George Dennison, "The Painting of Mark Rothko," p. 5.
10. Max Kozloff, "Mark Rothko's New Retrospective"; reprinted in Kozloff, *Renderings,* p. 149.
11. Quoted in "Stand Up Close," *Newsweek,* January 23, 1961.
12. Alan Bowness, review of 1961 traveling exhibition, in *The Observer* (Lon-

don), October 15, 1961; available in Artists' File, Library of the Museum of Modern Art, New York.

13. Rothko, "Letter to the Editor" (1943).

14. Thomas Couture, *Romans of the Decadence,* 1847, oil on canvas, 15 feet 8 inches × 25 feet 5 inches, Louvre, Paris; Eugène Delacroix, *The Death of Sardanapalus,* 1827–28, oil on canvas, 13 feet × 16 feet 3 inches, Louvre, Paris.

15. Mark Rothko, statement in symposium "How to Combine Architecture, Painting and Sculpture," Museum of Modern Art, New York; published in *Interiors* (May 1951), vol. 110, no 10; Reprinted in Maurice Tuchman, *New York School,* p. 141.

16. Haftmann, preface to *Mark Rothko,* p. x.

17. Series of panels in the Rothko Chapel, Institute of Religion and Human Development, Rice University, Houston, Texas.

18. T. B. Hess, "Rothko: A Venetian Souvenir," pp. 73–74.

19. O'Doherty, *American Masters,* p. 162.

20. Rothko, Pratt lecture, 1958; reprinted in Tuchman, *New York School,* p. 142.

21. Ibid., pp. 143–142.

Part 2. Summary

1. Though we obviously understand them well at an intuitive level, or art would not exist at all.

2. Barnett Newman, statement (1950), Betty Parsons Gallery, New York.

3. Jackson Pollock, "Interview with William Wright,"; reprinted in O'Connor, *Jackson Pollock,* p. 80.

4. "Letter to Frank O'Hara, August 18, 1965," quoted in Frank O'Hara, *Robert Motherwell,* p. 58.

11. Artists' Talk

1. See any edition of John Ruskin, *Modern Painters.* It is usually available in his collected works. If using the London, 1903, edition, see especially his description of Turner's *The Slave Ship,* in vol. 3, p. 571.

2. Frank O'Hara, *Jackson Pollock,* p. 26.
3. Bryan Robertson, *Jackson Pollock,* p. 53.
4. By "aesthetic" the artists meant something very close to "sensuous," rather than "characteristic or distinctive of art."

12. The Critical Approach

1. In conversation with the author, May 1977.
2. Harold Rosenberg, "Mondrian: Meaning in Abstract Art 1," in Rosenberg, *Art on the Edge,* pp. 51–54.
3. Clive Bell, *Art* (London: Arrow Books, 1961), p. 36.
4. Clement Greenberg, "An Interview," p. 18.
5. For a discussion of the rudiments of this process, see Rudolf Arnheim, *Art and Visual Perception* (London: Faber and Faber, 1954).
6. Walter Darby Bannard, "Touch and Scale: Cubism, Pollock, Newman, and Still," p. 65.
7. Walter Darby Bannard, *Hans Hofmann: A Retrospective Exhibition,* p. 26.
8. Michael Fried, "Recent Work by Kenneth Noland," *Artforum,* (Summer 1969), 7(10):36.
9. See the last paragraphs of Bannard's article "Cubism, Abstract Expressionism, David Smith."
10. Clement Greenberg, "An Interview."
11. Criticism existed before then, of course, but mainly in the form of odd comments. It was not supported by any kind of structure or discipline until the nineteenth century.
12. Mainly, of course, in the service of religion, though it served other social institutions as well.
13. Brian O'Doherty, "Criticizing Criticism."
14. While this is true of Greenberg's art criticism, he does engage in a form of cultural history, which is discussed later in this chapter. When talking about the individual works, however, he describes what one sees, and never what one might feel.
15. Rosenberg's critical writings can be found in *The Tradition of the New, The Anxious Object, Art Works and Packages,* and *Art on the Edge.*
16. Harold Rosenberg, "Criticism and Its Premises," part of a seminar at Pennsylvania State University, entitled *A Seminar in Art Education for Re-*

search and Curriculum Development, no date; reprinted in Rosenberg, *Art on the Edge,* p. 135.

17. Ibid., p. 136.
18. Ibid., p. 142.
19. Ibid., p. 141.
20. Rosenberg, "Mondrian: Meaning in Abstract Art 1," pp. 42–45.
21. Greenberg, "An Interview," p. 18.
22. William K. Wimsatt and Monroe C. Beardsley, "The Intentional Fallacy," *Sewanee Review* (Summer 1946), vol. 54.
23. T. S. Eliot, "The Music of Poetry," *Partisan Review* (November–December 1942), vol. 9, no. 6.
24. Rosenberg, "Mondrian: Meaning in Abstract Art 1," p. 54.

SELECT BIBLIOGRAPHY

General

Alloway, Lawrence. "The New American Painting." *Art International* (March–April 1959), vol. 3, nos. 3–4.

Alloway, Lawrence. "Sign and Surface: Notes on Black and White Painting in New York." *Quadrum* (1960), no. 9.

Alloway, Lawrence. "The American Sublime." *Living Arts* (June 1963), vol. 1, no. 2.

Alloway, Lawrence. "The Biomorphic Forties." *Artforum* (September 1964), vol. 4, no. 1.

Arnason, H. Harvard. *American Abstract Expressionists and Imagists.* New York: Solomon R. Guggenheim Museum, October 13–December 31, 1961. Exhibition catalogue.

Ashton, Dore. *The New York School: A Cultural Reckoning.* New York: Viking, 1973.

Balakian, Anna. *The Symbolist Movement: A Critical Appraisal.* New York: Random House, 1967.

Bannard, Walter Darby. "Cubism, Abstract Expressionism, David Smith." *Artforum* (April 1968), vol. 6, no. 8.

Barr, Alfred H. *Cubism and Abstract Art.* New York: Museum of Modern Art, 1936. Exhibition catalogue.

Barr, Alfred H. *The New American Painting.* New York: Museum of Modern Art, 1959. Exhibition catalogue.

Baur, John I. H. *Nature in Abstraction.* New York: Whitney Museum of American Art, January 14–March 16, 1958. Exhibition catalogue.

Baur, John I. H. *The New Decade: 35 American Painters and Sculptors.* New York: Whitney Museum of American Art, 1955.

Biddle, George. "The Victory and Defeat of Modernism: Art in a New World." *Harper's Magazine,* June 1943 (vol. 187).

Boas, Franz. *Primitive Art.* New York: Dover, 1955.

Brach, Paul. "Postscript: The Fifties." *Artforum* (September 1965), vol. 4, no. 1.

Breton, André and Marcel Duchamp. *First Papers of Surrealism.* New York: Coordinating Council of French Relief Societies, Inc. October 14–November 7, 1942. Exhibition catalogue.

Breton, André and Leon Trotsky. "Manifesto: Toward a Free Revolutionary Art." *Partisan Review* (Fall 1938), vol. 6, no. 4.

Carmean, E. A. and Rathbone, Eliza E. *Subjects of the Artist: American Art at Mid-Century.* Washington, D.C.: National Gallery of Art, 1978. Exhibition catalogue.

Cassirer, Ernst. *Language and Myth.* Translated by Susanne K. Langer. New York: Dover, 1953.

Cassirer, Ernst. *The Philosophy of Symbolic Forms.* Translated by Ralph Manheim. Vols. 1–3. New Haven, Conn.: Yale University Press, 1955.

Cassirer, Ernst. *An Essay on Man.* New York: Bantam Books, 1970.

Cavaliere, Barbara. "Early Abstract Expressionism: The 1940s." *Flash Art* (January–February 1979), nos. 86–87.

Cavaliere, Barbara. "Possibilities 2." *Arts Magazine* (September 1981), vol. 56, no. 1.

Cavaliere, Barbara and Robert C. Hobbs. "Against a Newer Laocoon."*Arts Magazine* (April 1977), vol. 51, no. 8.

Chipp, Herschel B., ed. *Theories of Modern Art.* Berkeley: University of California Press, 1968.

Coates, Robert M. "The Abstract Expressionists and Others." *New Yorker* (December 1951), vol. 27, no. 46.

Cockcroft, Eva. "Abstract Expressionism: Weapon of the Cold War." *Artforum* (June 1974), vol. 12, no. 10.

Cox, Annette. *Art as Politics: The Abstract Expressionist Avant-Garde and Society.* Ann Arbor, Mich.: UMI Research Press, 1982.

Davenport, Russell. "*Life* Round Table on Modern Art." *Life,* October 11, 1948 (vol. 25, no. 5).

de Kooning, Elaine. "Subject: What, How or Who?" *Art News* (April 1955), vol. 54, no. 2.

Diamondstein, Barbaralee. *Inside New York's Art World.* New York: Rizzoli, 1979.

Eliade, Mircea. "Myth." *Encyclopaedia Britannica* (1969), vol. 15. Chicago: Encyclopaedia Britannica.

Ferren, John. "Epitaph for an Avant Garde: The Motivating Ideas of the Abstract Expressionist Movement as Seen by an Artist Active on the New York Scene." *Arts Magazine* (November 1958), vol. 33, no. 2.

Firestone, E. R. "Color in Abstract Expressionism: Sources and Background for Meaning." *Arts Magazine* (March 1981), vol. 55, no. 7.

Firestone, E. R. "James Joyce and the First Generation New York School." *Arts Magazine* (June 1982), vol. 56, no. 10.

Foster, Stephen C. "Clement Greenberg: Formalism in the '40s and '50s." *Art Journal* (Fall 1975), vol. 35, no. 1.

Foster, Stephen C. *The Critics of Abstract Expressionism.* Ann Arbor, Mich.: UMI Research Press, 1980.

Friedman, B. H. " 'Irrascibles': A Split Second in Art History." *Arts Magazine* (September 1978), vol. 53, no. 1.

Fuller, Peter. *Beyond the Crisis in Art.* London: Writers and Readers, 1980.

Geldzahler, Henry. *American Painting in the Twentieth Century.* New York: Metropolitan Museum of Art, 1965.

Geldzahler, Henry. *New York Painting and Sculpture: 1940–1970.* New York: Dutton, 1969. Exhibition catalogue.

Goldwater, Robert. *Primitivism in Modern Art.* New York: Random House, 1938.

Goldwater, Robert. "Everyone Knew What Everyone Else Meant." *It Is* (Autumn 1959), no. 4.

Goldwater, Robert. "Reflections on the New York School." *Quadrum* (1960), no. 8.

Golub, Leon. "A Critique of Abstract Expressionism." *College Art Journal* (Winter 1955), vol. 14, no. 2.

Goodnough, Robert. "Postscript: The Forties." *Artforum* (September 1965), vol. 4, no. 1.

Gottlieb, Adolph and Mark Rothko (in collaboration with Barnett Newman). "Letter to the Editor." *New York Times,* June 13, 1943.

Graham, John. "Primitive Art and Picasso." *Magazine of Art* (April 1937).

Graham, John. *System and Dialectics of Art.* Baltimore: Johns Hopkins University Press, 1971.

Greenberg, Clement. "Toward a New Laocoon." *Partisan Review* (July–August 1940), vol. 7, no. 4.

Greenberg, Clement. "The Present Prospects of American Painting and Sculpture." *Horizon* (October 1947), vol. 16, nos. 93–94.

Greenberg, Clement. "The Situation at the Moment." *Partisan Review* (January 1948), vol. 15, no. 1.

Greenberg, Clement. "Art Chronicle: The Decline of Cubism." *Partisan Review* (March 1948), vol. 15, no. 3.

Greenberg, Clement. "Feeling Is All." *Partisan Review* (January–February 1952), vol. 19, no. 1.

Greenberg, Clement. "Abstract and Representational." *Art Digest* (November 1, 1954), vol. 29, no. 3.

Greenberg, Clement. " 'American-Type' Painting." *Partisan Review* (Spring 1955), vol. 22, no. 2.

Greenberg, Clement. "Modernist Painting." *Arts Magazine Yearbook* (1960), no. 4.

Greenberg, Clement. *Art and Culture: Critical Essays.* Boston: Beacon Press, 1961.

Greenberg, Clement. "After Abstract Expressionism." *Art International* (October 1962), vol. 6, no. 8.

Greenberg, Clement. "Post Painterly Abstraction." *Art International* (Summer 1964), vol. 8, nos. 5–6.

Greenberg, Clement. "The 'Crisis' of Abstract Art." *Arts Magazine Year Book* (1964), no. 7.

Greenberg, Clement. "An Interview." *Artscribe* (1978), no. 10.

Guggenheim, Peggy. *Art of This Century.* New York: Art of This Century Gallery, 1942. Exhibition catalogue.

Guggenheim, Peggy. *Out of This Century: Informal Memoirs of Peggy Guggenheim.* New York: Dial Press, 1946.

Guggenheim, Peggy. *Confessions of an Art Addict.* New York: Macmillan, 1960.

Guilbaut, Serge. *How New York Stole the Idea of Modern Art: Abstract Expressionism, Freedom, and the Cold War.* Translated by Arthur Goldhammer. Chicago: University of Chicago Press, 1983.

Herbert, James D. *The Political Origins of Abstract-Expressionist Art Criticism: The Early Theoretical and Critical Writings of Clement Greenberg and Harold Rosenberg.* Stanford, Calif.: Humanities Honors Program, Stanford University, 1985.

Hess, Thomas B. "Introduction to Abstract Art." *Art News Annual,* Part 2 (November 1950), vol. 49, no. 7.

Hess, Thomas B. *Abstract Painting: Background and American Phase.* New York: Viking Press, 1951.

Higgins, Andrew. "Clement Greenberg and the Idea of the Avant Garde." *Studio International* (October 1971), vol. 183, no. 937.

Hobbs, Robert C. and Gail Levin. *Abstract Expressionism: The Formative Years.* New York: Whitney Museum of American Art, October 5–December 3, 1978. Exhibition catalogue.

Hurlburt, Laurance P. "The Siqueiros Experimental Workshops: New York, 1936." *Art Journal* (Spring 1976), vol. 35, no. 3.

Janis, Sidney. *Abstract and Surrealist Art in America.* New York: Reynal and Hitchcock, 1944.

Jewell, Edward Alden. "Globalism Pops into View." *New York Times,* section 2, page 9, June 13, 1943.

Jung, Carl G. *Man and His Symbols.* London: Allen, 1964.

Kirk, G. S. *Myth. Its Meaning and Functions in Ancient and Other Cultures.* Cambridge: Cambridge University Press, 1970.

Kluckhohn, Clyde. "Myths and Rituals: A General Theory," *Harvard Theological Review* (1942), vol. 35.

Kozloff, Max. "The Dilemma of Expressionism." *Artforum* (November 1964), vol. 3, no. 3.

Kozloff, Max. "An Interview with Friedel Dzubas." *Artforum* (September 1965), vol. 4, no. 1.

Kozloff, Max. "An Interview with Matta." *Artforum* (September 1965), vol. 4, no. 1.

Kozloff, Max. "The Critical Reception of Abstract Expressionism." *Arts Magazine* (December 1965), vol. 40, no. 2.

Kozloff, Max. "The New American Painting." In Richard Kostelanetz, ed., *The New American Arts.* New York: Horizon Press, 1965.

Kozloff, Max. *Renderings: Critical Essays on a Century of Modern Art.* New York: Simon and Schuster, 1968.

Kozloff, Max. "American Painting During the Cold War." *Artforum* (May 1973), vol. 11, no. 9.

Kuh, Katherine. *The Artist's Voice: Talks with Seventeen Artists.* New York and Evanston, Ill.: Harper and Row, 1962.

Kuspit, Donald B. "Two Critics: Thomas B. Hess and Harold Rosenberg." *Artforum* (September 1978), vol. 17, no. 1.

Kuspit, Donald. *Clement Greenberg: Art Critic:* Madison: University of Wisconsin Press, 1979.

Kuspit, Donald B. "Abstract Expressionism: The Social Contract." *Arts Magazine* (March 1980), vol. 54, no. 7.

Langer, Susanne K. "On Cassirer's Theory of Language and Myth." In Paul A. Schilpp, ed., *The Philosophy of Ernst Cassirer*. Evanston, Ill.: Library of Living Philosophers, 1949.

Langer, Susanne K. *Philosophy in a New Key*. New York: Mentor, 1951.

Langer, Susanne K. *Problems of Art*. London: Routledge & Kegan Paul, 1957.

Leider, Philip. "The New York School in Los Angeles." *Artforum* (September 1965), vol. 4, no. 1.

Levine, Edward M. "Abstract Expressionism: The Mystical Experience." *Art Journal* (Fall 1971), vol. 31, no. 1.

Levy, Julian. *Surrealism*. New York: Black Sun Press, 1936.

Lippard, Lucy, ed. *Surrealists on Art*. Englewood Cliffs, N.J.: Prentice-Hall, 1970.

Louchheim, Aline B. "Betty Parsons: Her Gallery, Her Influence." *Vogue,* October 1951 (vol. 118, no. 6).

McNeil, George. "American Abstractionists Venerable at Twenty." *Art News* (May 1956), vol. 55, no. 3.

Malinowski, Bronislaw. *Myth in Primitive Psychology*. London: Kegan Paul, Trench, Trubner, 1926.

Miller, Dorothy C. *Fourteen Americans*. New York: Museum of Modern Art, 1946. Exhibition catalogue.

Miller, Dorothy C. *Fifteen Americans*. New York: Museum of Modern Art, 1952. Exhibition catalogue.

Miller, Dorothy C. *Twelve Americans*. New York: Museum of Modern Art, 1956. Exhibition catalogue.

Morris, George L. K. "On Critics and Greenberg: A Communication." *Partisan Review* (June 1948), vol. 15, no. 6.

Motherwell, Robert, Harold Rosenberg, Pierre Chareau, and John Cage, eds. *Possibilities 1. An Occasional Review* (Winter 1947–48), no. 1.

Motherwell, Robert. *The School of New York*. Beverly Hills, Calif.: Perls Gallery, January 11–February 7, 1951. Exhibition catalogue.

Motherwell, Robert, ed. *The Dada Painters and Poets*. New York: Wittenborn, Schultz, 1951.

Motherwell, Robert and Ad Reinhardt, eds. *Modern Artists in America*. New York: Wittenborn, Schultz, 1952.

Myers, John Bernard. "The Impact of Surrealism on the New York School." *Evergreen Review* (March–April 1960), vol. 4, no. 12.

Nadeau, Maurice. *The History of Surrealism.* Harmondsworth: Penguin, 1978.

Navretta, C. "New Myths for Old: Redefining Abstract Expressionism." *Women Artists News* (Spring 1986), vol. 11.

O'Connor, Francis V. *Federal Art Patronage 1933 to 1943.* College Park: University of Maryland Art Gallery, April 6–May 13, 1966. Exhibition catalogue.

O'Connor, Francis. V. *Art for the Millions: Essays from the 1930s by Artists and Administrators of the WPA Federal Art Project.* New York: New York Graphic Society, 1973.

O'Doherty, Brian. *American Masters: The Voice and the Myth.* New York: Random House, no date.

O'Doherty, Brian. "Criticizing Criticism." *New York Times,* June 1963. Reprinted in Brian O'Doherty, *Object and Idea: An Art Critic's Journal 1961–1967.* New York: Simon and Schuster, 1967.

Paalen, Wolfgang. "The New Image." *Dyn* (1942), no. 1.

Pavia, Phillip. "A Manifesto-in-Progress." *It Is* (Spring 1958) no. 1; (Autumn 1958) no. 2; (Winter–Spring 1959), no. 3; (Autumn 1959), no. 4.

Pavia, Phillip. "Polemics." *It Is* (Spring 1958), no. 1.

Pavia, Phillip. "The Unwanted Title: Abstract Expressionism." *It Is* (Spring 1960), no. 5.

Pavia, P. G. and Irving Sandler, eds. "The Philadelphia Panel." *It Is* (Spring 1960), no. 5.

Raymond, Marcel. *From Baudelaire to Surrealism.* Documents of Modern Art, vol. 10. New York: Wittenborn, Schultz, 1950.

Reise, Barbara M. "Greenberg and the Group: A Retrospective View." *Studio International* (May, June 1968), vol. 175, nos. 900, 901.

Ritchie, Andrew C. *Abstract Painting and Sculpture in America.* New York: Museum of Modern Art, 1951. Exhibition catalogue.

Rodgers, P. "Toward a Theory/Practice of Painting: Abstract Expressionism and the Surrealist Discourse." *Artforum* (March 1980), vol. 18, no. 7.

Rodman, Selden. *Conversations with Artists.* New York: Devin-Adair, 1957.

Rose, Barbara. "The Second Generation: Academy and Breakthrough." *Artforum* (September 1965), vol. 4, no. 1.

Rose, Barbara. *American Art Since 1900: A Critical History.* New York: Praeger, 1967.

Rose, Barbara, ed. *Readings in American Art Since 1900: A Documentary Survey.* New York: Praeger, 1968.

Rosen, Israel. "Toward a Definition of Abstract Expressionism." *Baltimore Museum of Art News* (February 1959), vol. 22, no. 3.

Rosenberg, Harold. "Notes on Fascism and Bohemia." *Partisan Review* (Spring 1944), no. 11, no. 2.

Rosenberg, Harold. "Introduction to Six American Artists." *Possibilities 1* (Winter 1947–48), no. 1.

Rosenberg, Harold. "The American Action Painters." *Art News* (December 1952), vol. 51, no. 8.

Rosenberg, Harold. "Parable for American Painters." *Art News* (January 1954), vol. 52, no. 9.

Rosenberg, Harold. *The Tradition of the New.* New York: Horizon Press, 1959.

Rosenberg, Harold. "Critic Within the Act." *Art News* (October 1960), vol. 59, no. 6.

Rosenberg, Harold. "Art in Orbit." *Art News* (October 1961), vol. 60, no. 6.

Rosenberg, Harold. "Action Painting: A Decade of Distortion." *Art News* (December 1962), vol. 61, no. 8.

Rosenberg, Harold. "After Next, What?" *Art in America* (April 1964), vol. 52, no. 2.

Rosenberg, Harold. *The Anxious Object: Art Today and Its Audience.* New York: Horizon Press, 1966.

Rosenberg, Harold. *Art Works and Packages.* New York: Horizon Press, 1969.

Rosenberg, Harold. *Art on the Edge.* New York: Macmillan, 1975.

Rosenberg, Harold and Samuel M. Kootz. *The Intrasubjectives.* New York: Kootz Gallery, September 14–October 3, 1949. Exhibition catalogue.

Rosenblum, Robert. "The Abstract Sublime." *Art News* (February 1961), vol. 59, no. 10.

Rowell, Margit. *La peinture, le geste, l'action: l'Existentialisme en Peinture.* Paris: Editions Klincksieck, 1985.

Rubin, William. "The New York School: Then and Now." *Art International.* Part 1 (1958), vol. 2, nos. 2–3; part 2, vol. 2, nos. 4–5.

Rubin, William. *Dada, Surrealism, and Their Heritage.* New York: Museum of Modern Art, 1968. Exhibition catalogue.

Sandler, Irving. "The Club." *Artforum* (September 1965), vol. 4, no. 1.

Sandler, Irving. "The Surrealist Emigrés in New York." *Artforum* (May 1968), vol. 6, no. 9.

Sandler, Irving. "John D. Graham." *Artforum* (October 1968), vol. 7, no. 2.

Sandler, Irving. *The Triumph of American Painting: A History of Abstract Expressionism.* New York: Harper & Row, 1970.

Schapiro, Meyer. "The Social Bases of Art." In *First American Artists Congress: Artists Against Fascism*. New Brunswick, N.J.: Rutgers University Press, 1936.

Schapiro, Meyer. "The Nature of Abstract Art. *Marxist Quarterly* (January–March 1937), vol. 1.

Schapiro, Meyer. "Rebellion in Art." In Daniel Aaron, ed. *America in Crisis*. New York: Knopf, 1952.

Schimmel, Paul. *The Interpretive Link: Abstract Surrealism into Abstract Expressionism: Works on Paper, 1938–1964*. Minneapolis: Walker Art Center, 1986. Exhibition catalogue.

Schneider, Pierre, ed. *Louvre Dialogues*. New York: Atheneum, 1971.

Schwartz, Constance. *The Abstract Expressionists and Their Precursors*. Roslyn, N.Y.: Nassau County Museum of Fine Art, 1981. Exhibition catalogue.

Sebeok, Thomas A. *Myth: A Symposium*. Bloomington: Indiana University Press, 1965.

Seitz, William C. *The Art of Assemblage*. New York: Museum of Modern Art, October 2–November 12, 1961. Exhibition Catalogue.

Seitz, William C. *Abstract Expressionist Painting in America*. Cambridge: Harvard University Press, 1983.

Selz, Peter. *New Images of Man*. New York: Museum of Modern Art, 1959. Exhibition catalogue.

Shapiro, David and Cecile Shapiro. "Abstract Expressionism: The Politics of Apolitical Painting." *Prospects* 3, 1977.

Simon, Sidney. "Concerning the Beginnings of the New York School: 1939–43. An interview with Peter Busa and Matta." *Art International* (Summer 1967), vol. 7, no. 6.

Sweeney, James Johnson. "Eleven Europeans in America: An Interview with André Masson." *Bulletin of the Museum of Modern Art (New York)* (September 1946), vol. 13, nos. 4–5.

Sylvester, David, ed. *Modern Art: From Fauvism to Abstract Expression*. New York, Watts, 1965.

Symons, Arthur. *The Symbolist Movement in Literature*. London: Archibald Constable, 1908.

Tagg, John. "American Power and American Painting: The Development of Vanguard Painting in the U.S. Since 1945." *Praxis* (1976), vol. 1, no. 2.

Tillim, Sidney. "The Figure and the Figurative in Abstract Expressionism." *Artforum* (September 1965), vol. 4, no. 1.

Tuchman, Maurice. *New York School: The First Generation*. Greenwich, Conn.: New York Graphic Society, no date.

Valéry, Paul. "The Course in Poetics." *Southern Review* (Winter 1940), vol. 5, no. 3. Reprinted in Brewster Ghiselin, ed. *The Creative Process.* New York: Mentor, 1952.

Westfall, S. "Then and Now: Six of the New York School Look Back." *Art in America* (June 1985), vol. 73.

"What Abstract Art Means to Me." Statements by George L. K. Morris, William de Kooning, Alexander Calder, Fritz Glarner, Robert Motherwell, Stuart Davis. *Bulletin of the Museum of Modern Art* (New York) (Spring 1951), vol. 18, no. 3.

"Wild Ones, The." *Time* (February 20, 1956) vol. 47, no. 8.

Individual Artists

WILLIAM BAZIOTES

STATEMENTS BY BAZIOTES

1944   In Sidney, Janis, *Abstract and Surrealist Art in America.* New York; Reynal and Hitchcock.

1947–48   "I Cannot Evolve Any Concrete Theory." *Possibilities 1* (Winter), vol. 1, no. 1.

1948   In *The Tiger's Eye* (October 20), vol. 1, no. 5.

1949   "The Artist and His Mirror." *Right Angle* (June 1949), vol. 3, no. 2.

1954   "Symposium: The Creative Process." *Art Digest* (January 15), vol. 28, no. 8.

1955   In John I. H. Baur, *The New Decade: 35 American Painters and Sculptors.* New York: Whitney Museum of American Art.

1959   "Notes on Painting." *It Is* (Autumn), no. 4.

ABOUT BAZIOTES

Alloway, Lawrence. *William Baziotes.* New York: Guggenheim Museum, 1965. Exhibition catalogue.

Cavaliere, Barbara. "An Introduction to the Method of William Baziotes." *Arts Magazine* (April 1977), vol. 51, no. 8.

Hare, David and Thomas B. Hess. "William Baziotes 1912–1963." *Location* (Summer 1964), vol. 1, no. 2.

Preble, Michael. *William Baziotes: A Retrospective Exhibition.* Newport Beach, Calif.: Newport Harbor Art Museum, March 24–June 4, 1978. Exhibition catalogue.

Rosenberg, Harold. "The Shapes in a Baziotes Canvas." *Possibilities 1* (Winter 1947–48), no. 1.

Weiss, J. "Science and Primitivism: A Fearful Symmetry in the Early New York School." *Arts Magazine* (March 1983), vol. 57, no. 7.

JAMES BROOKS

STATEMENTS BY BROOKS

1955	In John I. H. Baur, *The New Decade: 35 American Painters and Sculptors.* New York: Whitney Museum of American Art.
1956	In Dorothy C. Miller, *Twelve Americans.* New York, Museum of Modern Art.
1958–59	In Alfred H. Barr, *The New American Painting.* New York, Museum of Modern Art.
1961	James T. Valliere, "Interview with James Brooks." November 9. Archives of American Art.
1965	Gladys Kashdin, "Interview with James Brooks." Sarasota, Fla., March 8. Archives of American Art.
1984	R. Frumkes, "James Brooks: An Interview." *Films in Review* (June–July), vol. 35.

ABOUT BROOKS

Hunter, Sam. *James Brooks.* New York: Whitney Museum of American Art, 1963. Exhibition catalogue.

James Brooks: Paintings and Works on Paper, 1946–1982. Portland: Portland Museum of Art, May 14–September 4, 1983. Exhibition catalogue.

WILLEM de KOONING

STATEMENTS BY DE KOONING

1949   "Letter to the Editor: On Arshile Gorky." *Art News* (January), vol. 48, no. 9.

1951   "The Renaissance and Order." *trans/formation,* vol. 1, no. 2.

1951   "What Abstract Art Means to Me." *Museum of Modern Art (New York) Bulletin* (Spring), vol. 18, no. 3.

1958   "Is Today's Artist With or Against the Past? (Contribution to an inquiry)." *Art News* (Summer), vol. 57, no. 4.

1960   M. C. Sonnabend, *Sketchbook No. 1: Three Americans. Film Script.* Time Inc.

1960   David Sylvester, "Content Is a Glimpse . . ." *Location* (Spring 1963), vol. 1, no. 1. Excerpts from BBC broadcast interview, December 30.

1966   *USA: Artists: Willem de Kooning.* National Educational Television broadcast, July 19. In Film Archive of the Museum of Modern Art, New York.

1967   "An Interview by James T. Valliere." *Partisan Review* (Fall), vol. 34.

1982   "I Am Only Half Way Through." *Art News* (February), vol. 81, no. 2.

1982   *de Kooning on de Kooning.* Film, directed by Charlotte Zwerin. Los Angeles, Calif., Direct Cinema, 1982.

ABOUT de KOONING

Alloway, Lawrence. "Residual Sign Systems in Abstract Expressionism." *Artforum* (November 1973), vol. 12, no. 3.

Ashton, Dore. "New York Commentary: de Kooning's Verve." *Studio International* (June 1962), vol. 168, no. 830.

Bannard, Walter Darby. "Willem de Kooning's Retrospective at the Museum of Modern Art." *Artforum* (April 1969), vol. 7, no. 8.

Beck, J. "Joy of Painting: Willem de Kooning Toward Eighty." *Arts Magazine* (February 1984), vol. 58, no. 6.

Denby, Edwin. "My Friend de Kooning." *Art News Annual* (November 1964), no. 24. Unabridged version in Edwin Denby, *Dancers, Buildings, and People in the Streets.* New York: Horizon Press, 1965.

Fried, Michael. "New York Letter." *Art International* (December 20, 1962), vol. 6, no. 10.

Fuller, Peter. *Beyond the Crisis in Art.* London: Writers and Readers, 1980.

Hennessy, R. "The Man Who Forget How to Paint (a Painter Who Forgot the Rules in Order to Re-invent Them)." *Art in America* (Summer 1984), vol. 72.

Hess, Thomas B. "de Kooning Paints a Picture." *Art News* (March 1953), vol. 52, no. 1.

Hess, Thomas B. *Willem de Kooning.* New York: Braziller, 1959.

Hess, Thomas B. "Willem de Kooning." *Art News* (March 1962), vol. 61, no. 1.

Hess, Thomas B. *Willem de Kooning.* New York: Museum of Modern Art, 1968. Exhibition catalogue.

Kozloff, Max. "New York Letter." *Art International* (May 1962), vol. 6, no. 4.

Liebmann, L. "The Imagination in Sheep's Clothing." *Artforum* (April 1986), vol. 24, no. 8.

O'Doherty, Brian. "Willem de Kooning: Fragmentary Notes Toward a Figure." *Art International* (December 1968), vol. 12, no. 10.

Rosenberg, Harold. "de Kooning." *Vogue* (New York), September 1964.

Rosenberg, Harold. "Painting Is a Way of Living." *New Yorker* (February 16, 1963) vol. 38, no. 52.

ARSHILE GORKY

ABOUT GORKY

Alloway, Lawrence. "Gorky." *Artforum* (March 1963), vol. 1, no. 9.

Breton, André. "The Eye-Spring: Arshile Gorky." *It Is* (Autumn 1959), no. 4.

Davis, Stuart. "Arshile Gorky in the 1930s: A Personal Recollection." *Magazine of Art* (February 1951), vol. 44, no. 9. Reprinted from a catalogue of the Julian Levy Gallery, March 1945.

de Kooning, Elaine. "Gorky: Painter of His Own Legend." *Art News* (January 1951), vol. 49.

Dennison, George. "The Crisis–Art of Arshile Gorky." *Arts Magazine* (February 1963), vol. 57, no. 5.

Fitzgerald, M. "Arshile Gorky's *The Limit.*" *Arts Magazine* (March 1980), vol. 54, no. 7.

Goodrich, LLoyd. "Notes on Eight Works by Arshile Gorky." *Magazine of Art* (February 1951), vol. 44, no. 9.

Greenberg, Clement. "Art." *The Nation* (March 24, 1945) vol. 160; (May 4, 1946) vol. 162; (March 6, 1948) vol. 166.

Greenberg, Clement. "Art Chronicle." *Partisan Review,* (March 1948) vol. 15; (May–June 1950) vol. 17; (Spring 1955) vol. 22.

Lader, M. P. "Arshile Gorky's *The Artist and His Mother:* Further Study of Its Evolution, Sources, and Meaning." *Arts Magazine* (January 1984), vol. 58, no. 5.

Levy, Julien. *Arshile Gorky.* New York: Abrams, 1968.

McConathy. "Gorky's Garden: The Erotics of Paint." *Artscanada* (July–August 1981), vol. 38.

MacMillan, D. "Outsider: Gorky and America." *Art International* (Summer 1979), vol. 23, nos. 4–5.

Mooradian, Karien. *Arshile Gorky Adoian.* Chicago: Gilgamesh Press, 1978.

Poleskie, S. "Art and Flight: Historical Origins to Contemporary Works." *Leonardo* (1985), vol. 18, no. 2.

Rand, H. "Notes and Conversations: Jacob Kainen." *Arts Magazine* (December 1978), vol. 53, no. 4.

Rand, Harry. *Arshile Gorky: The Implications of Symbols.* Montclair, N.J.: Allanheld and Schram, 1981.

Rand, H. "Great Expectations (of Style)." *Arts Magazine* (November 1985), vol. 60, no. 3.

Rosenberg, Harold. *Arshile Gorky: The Man, the Time, the Idea.* New York: Horizon Press, 1962.

Rosenblum, Robert. "Arshile Gorky." *Arts Magazine* (January 1958), vol. 32, no. 4.

Rubin, William S. "Arshile Gorky: Surrealism and the New American Painting." *Art International* (February 1963), vol. 7, no. 2.

Schapiro, Meyer. "Gorky: The Creative Influence." *Art News* (September 1957), vol. 56, no. 5.

Schwabacher, Ethel. *Arshile Gorky: Memorial Exhibition.* New York: Whitney Museum of American Art, January 5–February 18, 1951. Exhibition catalogue.

Schwabacher, Ethel. *Arshile Gorky*. New York: Macmillan, 1957.

Seitz, William C. "Arshile Gorky's *The Plough and the Song*." *Allen Memorial Art Museum Bulletin 1954* (Oberlin College), no. 1.

Seitz, William C. *Arshile Gorky: Painting, Drawings, Studies*. New York: Museum of Modern Art, 1962. Exhibition catalogue.

Vaizey, M. "Muses Flee Hitler (American Art Found Its Own Individuality Through Refugees from Europe)." *Art & Artists* (April 1984), no. 211.

ADOLPH GOTTLIEB

STATEMENTS BY GOTTLIEB

1943	"The Portrait and the Modern Artist." Mimeograph script of WNYC broadcast *Art in New York*, with Mark Rothko. October 13.
1945	"Adolph Gottlieb." *Limited Editions* (December), no. 6.
1943	"Letter to the Editor." With Mark Rothko, assisted by Barnett Newman. *New York Times*, June 13.
1947	"The Ides of Art: The Attitudes of 10 Artists on Their Art and Contemporaneousness." *The Tiger's Eye* (December), vol. 1, no. 2.
1949	In "The Ides of Art: 11 Graphic Artists Write." *The Tiger's Eye* (June), vol. 1, no. 8.
1951	"My Painting." *Arts and Architecture* (September), vol. 68, no. 9.
1955	In John I. H. Baur, *The New Decade: 35 American Painters and Sculptors*. New York: Whitney Museum of American Art, May 11–August 7.
1955	"Integrating the Arts." *Interiors Magazine* (June), vol. 1, no. 114.
1959	In Alfred H. Barr, *The New American Painting*. New York: International Council of The Museum of Modern Art.
1963	David Sylvester, "Adolph Gottlieb: An Interview with David Sylvester." *Living Arts* (June), vol. 1, no. 2; originally broadcast on the BBC Third Program, October 1960.

ABOUT GOTTLIEB

Ashton, Dore. "Adolph Gottlieb at the Guggenheim and Whitney Museums." *Studio International* (April 1968), vol. 175, no. 899.

Berger, M. "Pictograph into Burst: Adolph Gottlieb and the Structure of Myth." *Arts Magazine* (March 1981), vol. 55, no. 7.

Clearwater, B. "Shared Myths: Reconsideration of Rothko's and Gottlieb's Letter to the *New York Times.*" *Archives of American Art Journal* (1984), vol. 24, no. 1.

Doty, Robert and Diane Waldman. *Adolph Gottlieb.* New York: published for the Whitney Museum of American Art and the Solomon B. Guggenheim Museum by Frederick A. Praeger, 1968. Exhibition catalogue.

Greenberg, Clement. "Art." *The Nation* (December 6) vol. 165, no. 23.

Greenberg, Clement. *An Exhibition of Oil Painting by Adolph Gottlieb.* New York: Jewish Museum, November–December 1957. Exhibition catalogue.

Hudson, Andrew. "Adolph Gottlieb's Paintings at the Whitney." *Art International* (April 1968), vol. 12, no. 4.

Kootz, Samuel M. *Adolph Gottlieb.* New York: Kootz Gallery, January 8–26, 1952. Exhibition catalogue.

Newman, Barnett. *Adolph Gottlieb.* New York: Wakefield Gallery, February 7–19, 1944. Exhibition catalogue.

Siegel, Jeanne. "Adolph Gottlieb: Two Views." *Arts Magazine* (February 1968), vol. 42, no. 4.

Waldman, Diane. "Gottlieb: Signs and Suns." *Art News* (February 1968), vol. 66, no. 10.

PHILIP GUSTON

STATEMENTS BY GUSTON

1956	In Dorothy C. Miller, *12 Americans.* New York, Museum of Modern Art.
1957	In John I. H. Baur, *Bradley Walker Tomlin.* New York: Whitney Museum of American Art.
1958	In *It Is* (Spring), no. 1.
1958	In John I. H. Baur, *Nature in Abstraction.* New York: Whitney Museum of American Art.

1958–59   In Alfred H. Barr, *The New American Painting*. New York: Museum of Modern Art.

1965   Bill Berkson, "Dialogue with Philip Guston." *Art and Literature* (Winter), no. 7.

1966   "Philip Guston's Objects: A Dialogue with Harold Rosenberg." *Philip Guston: Recent Paintings and Drawings*. New York: Jewish Museum.

1974   "On Cave Art, Church Art, Ethnic Art, and Art: A Dialogue with Harold Rosenberg." *Art News* (December), vol. 73, no. 10.

ABOUT GUSTON

Alloway, Lawrence. "Notes on Guston." *Art Journal* (Fall 1962), vol. 22, no. 1.

Arnason, H. Harvard. *Philip Guston*. New York: Solomon R. Guggenheim Museum, May 2–July 1, 1962. Exhibition traveled to the Los Angeles Country Museum, May 15–June 23, 1963. Exhibition catalogue.

Ashton, Dore. *Yes, but . . . A Critical Study of Philip Guston*. New York: Viking, 1976.

Ashton, Dore. "Art." *Arts and Architecture* (June 1957), vol. 74, no. 6; (May 1958), vol. 75, no. 5; (March 1960), vol. 77, no. 3.

Ashton, Dore. "Philip Guston, the Painter as Metaphysician." *Studio International* (February 1965), vol. 169, no. 862.

Ashton, D. "Philip Guston: Different Subjects." *Flash Art* (December–January, 1981–82), no. 105.

"Carnegie Winner's Art Is Abstract and Symbolic." *Life* (May 27, 1946) vol. 20, no. 21.

Hunter, Sam. "Philip Guston." *Art International* (May 1962), vol. 6, no. 4.

Hunter, Sam. *Philip Guston: Recent Paintings and Drawings*. New York: Jewish Museum, January 12–February 13, 1966. Exhibition catalogue.

Kozloff, Max. "Art." *The Nation* (May 19, 1962) vol. 194, no. 20.

O'Hara, Frank. "Growth and Guston." *Art News* (May 1962), vol. 61, no. 3.

Raynor, Vivien. "Guston." *Arts Magazine* (September 1962), vol. 36, no. 10.

Sandler, Irving. "New York Letter." *Art International* (April 1961), vol. 5, no. 3.

Schwabsky, B. "The Real Situation: Philip Guston and Mark Rothko at the End of the Sixties." *Arts Magazine* (December 1986), vol. 61, no. 4.

Steinberg, Leo. "Fritz Glarner and Philip Guston Among '12 Americans,' at the Museum of Modern Art." *Arts Magazine* (June 1956), vol. 30, no. 9.

HANS HOFMANN

STATEMENTS BY HOFMANN

1948   *Search for the Real and Other Essays.* Andover, Mass.: Addison Gallery of American Art, Phillips Academy.

1956   "The Color Problem in Pure Painting: Its Creative Origin." In *Hans Hofmann.* New York: Kootz Gallery, November 7–December 3, 1955. Reprinted in *Arts and Architecture,* (February), vol. 73, no. 2.

1959   "Space and Pictorial Life." *It Is* (Autumn), no. 4.

1962   Katherine Kuh, *The Artist's Voice: Talks with Seventeen Artists.* New York and Evanston, Ill.: Harper and Row.

ABOUT HOFMANN

Bannard, Walter Darby. *Hans Hofmann: A Retrospective Exhibition.* Houston: Museum of Fine Arts, February 4–April 3, 1977. Exhibition catalogue.

Bannard, Walter Darby. "Hofmann's Rectangle." *Artforum* (Summer 1969), vol. 7, no. 10.

de Kooning, Elaine. "Hans Hofmann Paints a Picture." *Art News* (February 1950), vol. 48, no. 10.

Fried, Michael. "New York Letter." *Art International* (April 1963), vol. 7, no. 4.

Seitz, William C. *Hans Hofmann.* New York: Museum of Modern Art, 1963. Exhibition catalogue.

Greenberg, Clement. "Most Important Art Teacher of Our Time." *The Nation* (April 21, 1945) vol. 160, no. 4.

Greenberg, Clement. "Hans Hofmann: Grand Old Rebel." *Art News* (January 1959), vol. 57, no. 9.

Hunter, Sam. *Hans Hofmann.* New York: Abrams, 1964.

Kaprow, Allan. "The Effect of Recent Art Upon the Teaching of Art." *Art Journal* (Winter 1963–64), vol. 33, no. 2.

Loran, Erle. "Hans Hofmann and His Work." *Artforum* (May 1964), vol. 2, no. 11.

Rosenberg, Harold. "Hans Hofmann: Nature Into Action." *Art News* (May 1957), vol. 56, no. 3.

Rosenberg, Harold. "Hans Hofmann's 'Life' Class." *Portfolio and Art News Annual* (Autumn 1962), no. 6.

Rosenberg, Harold. "Hans Hofmann and the Stability of the New." *New Yorker* (November 2, 1963) vol. 39, no. 37.

Rosenberg, Harold. "Homage to Hans Hofmann." *Art News* (January 1967), vol. 65, no. 9.

FRANZ KLINE

STATEMENTS BY KLINE

1955   In John I. H. Baur, *The New Decade: 35 American Painters and Sculptors.* New York: Whitney Museum of American Art.

1958   Franz Kline, "Is Today's Artist With or Against the Past?" *Art News* (September), vol. 57, no. 5.

1958   Frank O'Hara, "Franz Kline Talking." *Evergreen Review* (Autumn), vol. 2, no. 6.

1962   Katherine Kuh, *The Artist's Voice: Talks with Seventeen Artists.* New York and Evanston, Ill.: Harper & Row.

1963   David Sylvester, "Franz Kline, 1910–1962: An interview." *Living Arts* (Spring), vol. 1, no. 1.

ABOUT KLINE

Ashton, Dore. "Arts." *Arts and Architecture* (April 1956), vol. 73, no. 4; (July 1958), vol. 75, no. 7; (March 1959), vol. 76, no. 3.

Dawson, Fielding. *An Emotional Memoir of Franz Kline.* New York: Pantheon Books, 1967.

de Kooning, Elaine. "Two Americans in Action: Kline and Rothko." *Art News Annual* (November 1957), vol. 27.

de Kooning, Elaine. "Franz Kline: Painter of His Own Life." *Art News* (November 1962), vol. 61, no. 7.

de Kooning, Elaine. *Franz Kline Memorial Exhibition.* Washington, D.C.; Washington Gallery of Modern Art, October 30–December 27, 1962. Exhibition catalogue.

Franz Kline: A Retrospective Exhibition. Held at the Whitechapel Gallery, London in association with the Museum of Modern Art, New York, May–June 1964. Exhibition catalogue.

Goldwater, Robert. "Franz Kline: Darkness Visible." *Art News* (March 1967), vol. 66, no. 1.

Goodnough, Robert. "Kline Paints a Picture." *Art News* (December 1952), vol. 51, no. 8.

Gordon, John. *Franz Kline: 1910–1962.* New York: Whitney Museum of American Art, October 1–November 24, 1968. Exhibition catalogue.

ROBERT MOTHERWELL

STATEMENTS BY MOTHERWELL

1944	"Painter's Objects." *Partisan Review* (Winter), vol. 11, no. 1.
1944	"The Modern Painter's World." *Dyn* (November), vol. 1, no. 6.
1946	"Beyond the Aesthetic." *Design* (April), vol. 47, no. 8.
1946	In Dorothy C. Miller, *Fourteen Americans.* New York: Museum of Modern Art.
1947–48	In *Possibilities 1* (Winter), no. 1. Editorial preface with Harold Rosenberg.
1948	"A Tour of the Sublime." *The Tiger's Eye* (December 15), vol. 1, no. 6.
1949	In *Robert Motherwell: Collages 1943–1949.* New York: Kootz Gallery.
1951	"The Public and the Modern Artist." *Catholic Art Quarterly* (Easter), vol. 14, no. 2.
1951	"Seventeen Modern American painters." In *The School of New York.* Beverly Hills, Calif.: Frank Perls Gallery, January 11–February 7.
1951	"What Abstract Art Means to Me." *Museum of Modern Art (New York) Bulletin* (Spring), vol. 18, no. 3.
1951	"The Rise and Continuity of Abstract Art." *Arts and Architecture,* (September), vol. 69, no. 9.

1953   "Is the French Avant Garde Overrated?" *Art Digest* (September), vol. 27.

1954   "The Painter and the Audience." *Perspectives USA* (Autumn), no. 9.

1955   In John I. H. Baur, *The New Decade: 35 American Painters and Sculptors.* New York: Whitney Museum of American Art.

1957   In John H. I. Baur, *Bradley Walker Tomlin.* New York: Whitney Museum of American Art.

1959   In *It Is* (Winter–Spring), no. 3.

1959   "The Significance of Miró." *Art News* (May), vol. 58, no. 3.

1961   "What Should a Museum Be?" *Art in America* vol. 49, no. 2.

1962   In David Sylvester, "Painting as Existence: An Interview with Robert Motherwell." BBC radio broadcast, October 23, 1960. Reprinted in *Metro,* vol. 7, no. 7.

1963   "Robert Motherwell: A Conversation at Lunch (1962)." Northampton, Mass.: *Smith College,* January.

1964   *Art: New York.* National Educational Television film, broadcast December 15.

1965   In Max Kozloff, "An Interview with Robert Motherwell." *Artforum* (September), vol. 4, no. 1.

1966   "David Smith: A Major American sculptor." *Studio International* (August), vol. 172, no. 880.

1967   In Sidney Simon, "Concerning the Beginnings of the New York School: An Interview with Robert Motherwell." *Art International* (Summer), vol. 2, no. 6.

1979   In Barbaralee Diamondstein, "An Interview with Robert Motherwell." *Inside New York's Art World.* New York: Rizzoli.

ABOUT MOTHERWELL

Arnason, H. Harvard. "On Robert Motherwell and His Early Work." *Art International* (January 1966), vol. 10, no. 1.

Arnason, H. Harvard. "Robert Motherwell: 1948–1965." *Art International* (April 1966), vol. 10, no. 4.

Arnason, H. Harvard. *Robert Motherwell.* New York: Abrams, 1977.

Ashton, Dore. "Motherwell Loves and Believes." *Studio International* (March 1963), vol. 165, no. 839.

Ashton, Dore. "Robert Motherwell: Passion and Transfiguration." *Studio International* (March 1964), vol. 167, no. 851.

Baro, Gene. "The Ethics of Risk." *Arts Magazine* (January 1966), vol. 40, no. 3.

Collins, B. R. "Fundamental Tragedy of the Elegies to the Spanish Republic, or, Robert Motherwell's Dilemma." *Arts Magazine* (September 1984), vol. 59, no. 1.

Edgar, Natalie. "The Satisfaction of Robert Motherwell." *Art News* (October 1965), vol. 64, no. 6.

Fineberg, J. "Death and Maternal Love: Psychological Speculations on Robert Motherwell's Art." *Artforum* (September 1978), vol. 17, no. 1.

Gardner, P. "When Is a Painting Finished? How Do You Know When a Painting Is Finished?" *Art News* (November 1985), vol. 84, no. 9.

Goosen, Eugene C. "Robert Motherwell and the Seriousness of Subject." *Art International* (January–February 1959), vol. 3, no. 1–2.

Greenberg, Clement. "Art." *The Nation* (November 11, 1944) vol. 159, no. 20; (May 31, 1947) vol. 164, no. 22; (May 29, 1948) vol. 166, no. 22.

Krauss, Rosalind. "Robert Motherwell's New Paintings." *Artforum* (May 1969), vol. 7, no. 9.

Lippard, Lucy R. "New York Letter: Miró and Motherwell." *Art International* (December 1965), vol. 14, nos. 9–10.

Mattison, R. S. "*Emperor of China:* Symbols of Power and Vulnerability in the Art of Robert Motherwell During the 1940s." *Art International* (November–December 1982), vol. 25.

Mattison, R. S. "*A Voyage:* Robert Motherwell's Earliest Works." *Arts Magazine* (February 1985), vol. 59, no. 6.

O'Hara, Frank. "Robert Motherwell." *Art in America* (October–November 1965), vol. 53, no. 5.

O'Hara, Frank. *Robert Motherwell.* New York: Museum of Modern Art, 1965. Exhibition catalogue.

Robertson, Bryan. "From a Notebook on Robert Motherwell." *Studio International* (March 1966), vol. 171, no. 875.

Sandler, Irving. "Robert Motherwell." *Art International* (June–August 1961), vol. 5, nos. 5–6.

Sweeney, James Johnson. *Robert Motherwell.* New York: Art of This Century Gallery, October–November 1944. Exhibition catalogue.

BARNETT NEWMAN

STATEMENTS BY NEWMAN

1943   "Letter to the Editor," from Adolph Gottlieb and Mark Rothko, written by Gottlieb, Rothko, and Newman. *New York Times,* June 13.

1944   *Adolph Gottlieb.* New York: Wakefield Gallery, February 7–19.

1944   *Pre-Columbian Stone Sculpture.* New York: Wakefield Gallery, May 16–June 5.

1946   *Northwest Coast Indian Painting.* New York: Betty Parsons Gallery, September 30–October 19.

1947   *Stamos.* New York: Betty Parsons Gallery, February 10–March 1.

1947   *The Ideographic Picture.* New York: Betty Parsons Gallery, January 20–February 8.

1947   "The First Man Was an Artist." *The Tiger's Eye* (October), vol. 1, no. 1.

1947   "The Ides of Art: The Attitudes of 10 Artists on Their Art and Contemporaneousness." *The Tiger's Eye* (December), vol. 1, no. 2.

1948   "The Ides of Art—6 Opinions of What Is Sublime in Art: The Sublime Is Now." *The Tiger's Eye* (December 15), vol. 1, no. 6.

1962   Dorothy Gees Seckler, "Frontiers of Space: An Interview with Barnett Newman." *Art in America* (Summer), vol. 50, no. 2.

1963   *Amlash Sculpture from Iran.* New York: Betty Parsons Gallery, September 23–October 19.

1964   In Frank O'Hara, *Art: New York:* "The Continuity of Vision: Barnett Newman." Television interview with Frank O'Hara, broadcast on WNDT-TV, December 8.

1965   In Neil A. Levine, "Barnett Newman: The New York School Question. An interview." *Art News* (September), vol. 64, no. 5.

1966	In *The Stations of the Cross.* New York: Solomon R. Guggenheim Museum, April–May 1966.
1966	"The 14 Stations of the Cross." *Art News* (May), vol. 65, no. 3.
1966	*USA: Artists: Barnett Newman.* National Educational Television broadcast, July 12. In Film Archive of the Museum of Modern Art, New York.
	"Artists on Museums: The Museum World." *Arts Magazine Yearbook* (1967), vol. 9.
1969	"Chartres and Jericho." *Art News* (April), vol. 68, no. 2.
1970	"Art of the South Seas." *Studio International* (February), vol. 179.

ABOUT NEWMAN

Alloway, Lawrence. "Barnett Newman." *Artforum* (June 1965), vol. 3, no. 10.

Alloway, Lawrence. *The Stations of the Cross.* New York: Solomon R. Guggenheim Museum, April–May 1966.

Alloway, Lawrence. "Barnett Newman—Some Notes on His Work." *Art International* (Summer 1969), vol. 13, no. 6.

De Deuve, T. "Who's Afraid of Red, Yellow and Blue?" *Artforum* (September 1983), vol. 22, no. 1.

Gibson, A. "Regression and Color in Abstract Expressionism: Barnett Newman, Mark Rothko, and Clyfford Still." *Arts Magazine* (March 1981), vol. 55, no. 7.

Glaser, D. J. "Transcendence in the Vision of Barnett Newman." *Journal of Aesthetics and Art Criticism* (Summer 1982), vol. 40, no. 4.

Judd, Don. "Barnett Newman." *Studio International* (February 1970), vol. 179.

Lyotard, J.-F. "Sublime and the Avant-Garde." *Artforum* (April 1984), vol. 22, no. 8.

Nickas, R. "The Sublime Was Then: Search for Tomorrow." *Arts Magazine,* (March 1986), vol. 60, no. 7.

Rosenberg, Harold. "Barnett Newman: A Man of Controversy and Grandeur." *Vogue,* February 1, 1963.

Rosenberg, Harold. "The Art World: Icon Maker." *New Yorker* (April 19, 1969), vol. 45.

Taaffe, P. "Sublimity, Now and Forever, Amen." *Arts Magazine,* (March 1986), vol. 60, no. 7.

JACKSON POLLOCK

STATEMENTS BY POLLOCK

1944   "Jackson Pollock." *Arts and Architecture* (February), vol. 161, no. 2.

1944   In Sidney Janis, *Abstract and Surrealist Art in America.* New York: Reynal and Hitchcock.

1947–48   "My Painting." *Possibilities 1* (Winter), no. 1.

1950   Excerpts from an interview taped by William Wright, 1950. Reprinted in *Art in America* (1965), vol. 53, no. 4.

1950   "Unframed Space." Interview with Jackson Pollock. *The New Yorker* (August 5), vol. 26.

ABOUT POLLOCK

Alloway, Lawrence. *Jackson Pollock.* London: Marlborough Gallery, 1961. Exhibition catalogue.

Alloway, Lawrence. "Pollock's Black Paintings." *Arts Magazine* (May 1969), vol. 43, no. 7.

Carmean, E. A. "Church Project: Pollock's Passion Themes." *Art in America* (Summer 1982), vol. 70, no. 5.

Davis, W. N. M. *Jackson Pollock.* New York: Art of This Century Gallery, November 9–27, 1943. Exhibition catalogue.

du Plessix, Francine and Cleve Gray. "Who Was Jackson Pollock? Interviews." *Art in America* (May–June 1967), vol. 55, no. 3.

Fried, Michael. "Jackson Pollock." *Artforum* (September 1965), vol. 4, no. 1.

Friedman, B. H. *Jackson Pollock: Energy Made Visible.* New York: McGraw-Hill, 1972.

Glaser, Bruce. "Jackson Pollock: An Interview with Lee Krasner." *Arts Magazine* (April 1967), vol. 41, no. 6.

Goodnough, Robert. "Pollock Paints a Picture." *Art News* (May 1951), vol. 50, no. 3.

Greenberg, Clement. "Art." *The Nation* (November 27, 1943) vol. 157, no. 22; (April 7, 1945) vol. 160, no. 14; (April 13, 1946) vol. 162, no. 15; (December 28, 1946) vol. 163, no. 26; (February 1, 1947) vol. 164, no. 5; (January 24, 1948) vol. 166, no. 4; (February 19, 1949) vol. 168, no. 9).

Greenberg, Clement. "Jackson Pollock's New Style." *Harper's Bazaar* (1952) vol. 85, no. 2883.

Greenberg, Clement and Hans Namuth. "Jackson Pollock." *Evergreen Review* (1956), vol. 2.

Greenberg, Clement. "Jackson Pollock." *Evergreen Review* (1957), vol. 1, no. 3.

Greenberg, Clement. "The Jackson Pollock Market Soars." *New York Times Magazine,* April 16, 1961.

Greenberg, Clement. "Jackson Pollock: 'Inspiration, Vision, Intuitive Decision.'" *Vogue* (April 1967) vol. 149.

Halasz, P. "Abstract Painting in General: Friedel Dzubas in Particular." *Arts Magazine* (September 1983), vol. 58, no. 1.

Halasz, P. "Stanley William Hayter: Pollock's Other Master." *Arts Magazine* (November 1984), vol. 59, no. 3.

Hess, Thomas B. "Jackson Pollock: 1912–1956." *Art News* (September 1956), vol. 55, no. 5.

Hunter, Sam. *Jackson Pollock.* New York: Museum of Modern Art, December 19, 1956–February 3, 1957. Exhibition catalogue.

"Jackson Pollock: An Artists' Symposium, Part 1." *Art News* (April 1967), vol. 66, no. 2. Statements by James Brooks, Adolph Gottlieb, Al Held, Allan Kaprow, Alex Katz, Elaine de Kooning, Robert Motherwell, Barnett Newman, Phillip Pavia, Larry Rivers.

"Jackson Pollock: An Artists' Symposium, Part 2." *Art News* (May 1967), vol. 66, no. 3. Statements by Al Brunelle, Jane Freilicher, David Lee, Joan Mitchell, Kenneth Noland, David Novros, Claes Oldenburg, George Segal.

"Jackson Pollock." Special issue, *Arts Magazine* (March 1979), vol. 53, no. 7.

Jackson Pollock. Exhibition at Centre Georges Pompidou, Museé Nationale d'Art Moderne, Paris, January 21–April 19, 1982. Exhibition catalogue.

Junker, H. "Jackson Pollock/Robert Smithson: The Myth/Mythologist." *Arts Magazine* (May 1978), vol. 52, no. 9.

Kaprow, Allan. "The Legacy of Jackson Pollock." *Art News* (October 1958), vol. 57, no. 6.

Kramer, Hilton. "The Month in Review: Pollock." *Arts Magazine* (February 1957), vol. 31, no. 5.

Mandeles, C. "Jackson Pollock and Jazz: Structural Parallels." *Arts Magazine* (October 1981), vol. 56, no. 2.

Morris, R. "American Quartet (The Author Discovers Four Redoutable Ancestor Figures and Four Key Traditions)." *Art in America* (December 1981), vol. 69.

Motherwell, Robert. "Painters' Objects." *Partisan Review* (Winter 1944), vol. 11, no. 1.

O'Connor, Francis V. "The Genesis of Jackson Pollock: 1912 to 1943." *Artforum* (May 1967), vol. 5, no. 9.

O'Connor, Francis V. *Jackson Pollock*. New York: Museum of Modern Art, 1967. Exhibition catalogue.

O'Connor, F. V. "Hans Namuth's Photographs of Jackson Pollock as Art Historical Documentation." *Art Journal* (Fall 1979), vol. 39, no. 1.

O'Connor, Francis Valentine and Eugene Victor Thaw. *Jackson Pollock: A Catalogue Raisonné of Paintings, Drawings, and Other Works*. New Haven, Conn.: Yale University Press, 1978.

O'Hara, Frank. *Jackson Pollock*. The Great American Artists Series. New York: Braziller, 1959.

Ossorio, Alfonso. *Jackson Pollock*. New York: Betty Parsons Gallery, November 26–December 15, 1951. Exhibition catalogue.

Raynor, Vivien. "Jackson Pollock in Retrospect—'He Broke the Ice.'" *New York Times Magazine*, April 2, 1967.

Robertson, Bryan. *Jackson Pollock*. New York: Abrams, 1960.

Rose, Barbara. "Hans Namuth's Photographs and the Jackson Pollock Myth. Part 1: Media Impact and the Failure of Criticism." *Arts Magazine* (March 1979), vol. 53, no. 7.

Rose, Barbara. "An Interview with Lee Krasner." *Partisan Review* (1980), vol. 47, no. 1.

Rose, Barbara, ed. *Jackson Pollock, 1912–1956: Pollock Painting/Photographs*. With essays by Rosalind Krauss, Francis V. O'Connor, and Barbara Rose. New York: Agrinda, 1980.

Rose, Bernice. *Jackson Pollock: Works on Paper*. New York: Museum of Modern Art, 1970.

Rubin, David S. "A Case for Content: Jackson Pollock's Subject Was the Automatic Gesture." *Arts Magazine* (March 1979), vol. 53, no. 7.

Rubin, William. "Jackson Pollock and the Modern Tradition." *Artforum*. Part

1 (February 1967), vol. 5, no. 6; part 2 (March 1967), vol. 5. no. 7; part 3 (April 1967), vol. 5, no. 8; part 4 (May 1967), vol. 5, no. 9.

Rubin, William. "Pollock as Jungian Illustrator: The Limits of Psychological Criticism." *Art in America* (November 1979), vol. 67.

Selz, Peter. *New Images of Man.* New York: Museum of Modern Art, 1959. Exhibition catalogue.

Solomon, Deborah. *Jackson Pollock: A Biography.* New York: Simon and Schuster, 1987.

Sweeney, James Johnson. *Jackson Pollock.* New York: Art of This Century Gallery, November 9–27, 1943. Exhibition catalogue.

AD REINHARDT

STATEMENTS BY REINHARDT

1953	"The Artist in Search of an Academy." *College Art Journal* (Spring), vol. 12, no. 3.
1954	"Who Are the Artists?" *Art Journal* (Summer), vol. 13, no. 4.
1955	In John I. H. Baur, *The New Decade: 35 American Painters and Sculptors.* New York: Whitney Museum of American Art.
1956	"The Art-Politics Syndrome: A Project in Integration." *Art News* (November), vol. 55, no. 7.
1957	"Twelve Rules of a New Academy." *Art News* (May), vol. 56, no. 3.
1958	"Is Today's Artist With or Against the Past?" *Art News* (Summer), vol. 57, no. 4.
1958	"Panel: All-Over Painting." *It Is* (Autumn), no. 2.
1958	"44 Titles for Articles for Artists Under 45." *It Is* (Spring), no. 1.
1959	"Discussion: Is There a New Academy?" Contribution to a symposium. *Art News* (Summer), vol. 58, no. 4.
1959	"Seven Quotes." *It Is* (Autumn), no. 4.
1962	"Art-as-Art." *Art International* (December), vol. 6, no. 10.
1966	In Bruce Glaser, "Interview with Ad Reinhardt." *Art International* (December), vol. 10, no. 10.
1966	In Bruce Glaser, "Ad Reinhardt: Three Statements." *Artforum* (March), vol. 4, no. 7.

ABOUT REINHARDT

Colt, Priscilla. "Notes on Ad Reinhardt." *Art International* (October 1964), vol. 8, no. 8.

de Kooning, Elaine. "Pure Paints a Picture." *Art News* (Summer 1957), vol. 56, no. 4.

Glaser, Bruce. "Art in Art Is Art as Art." *The Lugano Review* (Summer 1966), vol. 1, nos. 5–6.

Hess, Thomas B. "Reinhardt: The Position and Perils of Purity." *Art News* (December 1963), vol. 62, no. 8.

Kramer, Hilton. "Art." *The Nation* (June 22, 1963) vol. 196, no. 24.

Lippard, Lucy. *Ad Reinhardt Paintings.* New York: Jewish Museum, November 23–January 15, 1967. Exhibition catalogue.

McEvilley, T. "Heads It's Form, Tails It's Not Content (Formalist Critical Tradition of the Postwar Period)." *Artforum* (November 1982), vol. 21, no. 3.

Rose, Barbara. "Reinhardt." *Vogue* (November 1, 1966) vol. 148, no. 8.

Rose, Barbara, ed. *Art as Art: The Selected Writings of Ad Reinhardt.* New York: Viking, 1975.

Sandler, Irving. "Reinhardt: The Purist Blacklash." *Artforum* (December 1966), vol. 5, no. 4.

MARK ROTHKO

STATEMENTS BY ROTHKO

1943   "The Portrait and the Modern Artist." *Art in New York,* broadcast by WNYC, New York, October 13.

1943   "Letter to the Editor." With Adolph Gottlieb, assisted by Barnett Newman. *New York Times,* June 13.

1947   In "Ides of Art." *The Tiger's Eye* (December), vol. 1, no. 2.

1947–48   "The Romantics Were Prompted." *Possibilities 1* (Winter), no. 1.

ABOUT ROTHKO

Alloway, Lawrence. "Notes on Rothko." *Art International* (Summer 1962), vol. 6, nos. 5–6.

Ashton, Dore. "Art: Lecture by Rothko." *New York Times,* October 31, 1958. Includes quotations from lecture at Pratt Institute.

Ashton, Dore. *About Rothko.* New York: Oxford University Press, 1983.

Beaumann, Felix Andreas. *Mark Rothko.* Zurich: Kunsthaus, March 21–May 9, 1971. Exhibition catalogue.

Cavaliere, Barbara. "Horizontal Phantom: Gethsemane." *Arts Magazine* (1981), vol. 56.

Cavaliere, Barbara. "Possibilities 2." *Arts Magazine* (September 1981), vol. 56, no. 1.

Cernuschi, C. R. "Mark Rothko's Mature Paintings: A Question of Content." *Arts Magazine* (May 1986), vol. 60, no. 9.

Clearwater, B. "Shared Myths: Reconsideration of Rothko's and Gottlieb's Letter to the *New York Times.*" *Archives of American Art Journal* (1984), vol. 24, no. 1.

Clearwater, B. "How Rothko Looked at Rothko." *Art News* (November 1985), vol. 84, no. 9.

Crehan, Hubert. "Rothko's Wall of Light: Exhibition at the Art Institute of Chicago." *Art Digest* (November 1, 1954), vol. 29, no. 5.

Dennison, George. "The Painting of Mark Rothko." Unpublished article, Artists' File, Museum of Modern Art Library, New York.

Dunlop, I. "Edvard Munch, Barnett Newman, and Mark Rothko: The Search for the Sublime." *Arts Magazine* (February 1979), vol. 53, no. 6.

Fischer, John. "Mark Rothko: Portrait of the Artist as an Angry Man." *Harper's Magazine,* 1970.

Gibson, A. "Regression and Color in Abstract Expressionism: Barnett Newman, Mark Rothko, and Clyfford Still." *Arts Magazine* (March 1981), vol. 55, no. 7.

Goldwater, Robert. "Reflections on the Rothko Exhibition." *Arts Magazine* (March 1961), vol. 35, no. 6.

Hess, T. B. "Rothko: A Venetian Souvenir." *Art News,* (1970), vol. 69, no. 7.

Kozloff, Max. "Mark Rothko's New Retrospective." *Art Journal* (Spring 1961), vol. 20, no. 3.

Kozloff, Max. "The Problem of Color-Light in Rothko." *Artforum* (September 1965), vol. 4, no. 1.

Liss, J. "Willem de Kooning Remembers Mark Rothko: His House Had Many Mansions." *Art News* (January 1979), vol. 78, no. 9.

MacAgy, Douglas. "Mark Rothko." *Magazine of Art* (January 1949), vol. 42, no. 1.

Polcari, S. "Intellectual Roots of Abstract Expressionism: Mark Rothko." *Arts Magazine* (September 1979), vol. 54, no. 1.

Robertson, Bryan. *Rothko.* London: Whitechapel Gallery, 1961. Exhibition catalogue.

Rosenblum, Robert. *Mark Rothko: Notes on Rothko's Surrealist Years.* New York: Pace Gallery, April 24–May 30, 1982. Exhibition catalogue.

Schjedahl, P. "Rothko and Belief." *Art in America* (March 1979), vol. 67.

Schwabsky, B. "The Real Situation: Philip Guston and Mark Rothko at the End of the Sixties." *Arts Magazine* (December 1986), vol. 61, no. 4.

Seldes, Lee. *The Legacy of Mark Rothko.* New York: Holt, Rinehart and Winston, 1978.

Selz, Peter. *Mark Rothko.* New York: Museum of Modern Art, 1961. Exhibition catalogue.

Waldman, Diane. *Mark Rothko: A Retrospective.* New York: Guggenheim Museum, 1978. Exhibition catalogue.

CLYFFORD STILL

STATEMENTS BY STILL

1950	In typescript, Betty Parsons Gallery, New York.
1959	Letter to Gordon Smith, in *Paintings by Clyfford Still.* Buffalo, N.Y.: Albright-Knox Art Gallery, November 5–December 13.
1960	"Comments." *Gallery Notes.* (Summer), vol. 23, no. 2. Buffalo, N.Y.: Albright-Knox Art Gallery.
1961	In Benjamin J. Townsend, "An Interview with Clyfford Still." *Gallery Notes* (Summer), vol. 24, no. 2. Buffalo, N.Y.: Albright-Knox Art Gallery.
1963	"An Open Letter to an Art Critic." *Artforum* (December), vol. 2, no. 6.
1964	"Letter to the Editor." *Artforum* (February), vol. 2, no. 8.

296 *Select Bibliography*

ABOUT STILL

"Clyfford Still." *Magazine of Art* (March 1948), vol. 41, no. 3.

Clyfford Still. San Francisco: San Francisco Museum of Modern Art, 1976. Exhibition catalogue.

Crehan, Hubert. "Clyfford Still: Black Angel in Buffalo." *Art News* (December 1959), vol. 58, no. 8.

Gibson, A. "Regression and Color in Abstract Expressionism: Barnett Newman, Mark Rothko and Clyfford Still." *Arts Magazine* (March 1981), vol. 55, no. 7.

Goossen, Eugene C. "Painting as Confrontation: Clyfford Still." *Art International* (January 1960), vol. 4, no. 1.

Hess, Thomas B. "The Outsider." *Art News* (December 1969), vol. 68, no. 8.

Kozloff, Max. "Art: Clyfford Still." *The Nation* (January 6, 1964) vol. 198, no. 2.

Kuspit, Donald. "Clyfford Still: The Ethics of Art." *Artforum* (May 1977), vol. 15, no. 9.

O'Neill, John P. *Clyfford Still.* New York: Metropolitan Museum of Art, 1979. Exhibition catalogue.

Paintings of Clyfford Still. Buffalo, N.Y.: Albright-Knox Art Gallery, November 5–December 13, 1959. Exhibition catalogue.

Polcari, S. "Intellectual Roots of Abstract Expressionism: Clyfford Still." *Art International* (May–June 1982), vol. 25, nos. 5–6.

Rothko, Mark. Introduction, *Clyfford Still.* New York: Art of This Century Gallery, February 12–March 2, 1946. Exhibition catalogue.

Sandler, Irving. "Clyfford Still: Emerging from Eclipse." *New York Times,* December 21, 1969.

Topper, D. R. "Historical Perspectives on the Arts, Sciences and Technology." *Leonardo* (1984), vol. 17, no. 3.

INDEX